JOURNAL FOR THE STUDY OF THE OLD TESTAMENT
SUPPLEMENT SERIES
75

Editors
David J A Clines
Philip R Davies

JSOT Press
Sheffield

To Dr. Charles B. Copher

on whose shoulders
the current generation
of African-American biblical
scholars stands

DAVID IN LOVE AND WAR

The Pursuit of Power in 2 Samuel 10-12

Randall C. Bailey

Journal for the Study of the Old Testament
Supplement Series 75

Copyright © 1990 Sheffield Academic Press

Published by JSOT Press
JSOT Press is an imprint of
Sheffield Academic Press Ltd
The University of Sheffield
343 Fulwood Road
Sheffield S10 3BP
England

Printed in Great Britain
by Billing & Sons Ltd
Worcester

British Library Cataloguing in Publication Data

Bailey, Randall C.
    David in love and war
    1. Bible. O.T. David, King of Israel
    I. Title   II. Series
    221.9′24

    ISSN 0309-0787
    ISBN 1-85075-209-5

CONTENTS

ACKNOWLEDGMENTS

This book is a reworking of my dissertation completed at Emory University, Atlanta, Georgia. It began as the brain-child of Professor John H. Hayes, who felt the genealogy of Bathsheba in 2 Sam. 11.3 was a significant piece of data for the historical reconstruction of the reign of David. As I undertook the assignment, my interests in literary critical concerns gave direction and focus to the final product. I am indebted to Professor Hayes for the direction in the original piece and for the freedom to take his idea into other directions.

I am also greatly indebted to Professor David Gunn of Columbia Theological Seminary. His confidence in me and my abilities and his sense of collegiality throughout the process of producing the original work and this current rendition will always be a guide to me for my professional interaction with others. His friendship, critique, and sense of humor are treasures for the days ahead.

This project could not have been completed in such a timely fashion were it not for the Faculty Development Funds granted to me by the Interdenominational Theological Center. Similarly, the assistance of Rev Katheryn Hazel and Ms Janet Snow, students at the ITC, in the preparation of the indexes and in assisting in the proofing of the manuscript, respectively, are greatly appreciated.

The encouragement and prodding of D. Jean Bailey, my partner in life, have helped me hang in, when times got rough. By the same token, the understanding of Omari and Imani Bailey, our children, when quality time got redirected into this project, create a debt I am eager to repay. The pride of Charles and Lorraine Bailey, my parents, makes this milestone a more highly prized accomplishment.

Finally, this book is dedicated to the spirit of all those Bible scholars of African descent who have preceded me—both past and present—those who were able to fulfill their 'calls' and those who were denied the opportunity by institutional oppression. May this work be used as a source of inspiration for those who follow to 'Keep on keepin' on!'

Atlanta, Georgia
November 6, 1989

ABBREVIATIONS

AB	Anchor Bible
AASF	Annales Academiae Scientiarum Fennicae
AJSLL	*American Journal of Semitic Language and Literature*
Ant	*Antiquities of the Jews*
AOAT	Alter Orient und Altes Testament
ASTI	*Annual of Swedish Theological Institute in Jerusalem*
ATD	Das Alte Testament Deutsch
BASOR	*Bulletin of the American Schools of Oriental Research*
BBB	Bonner Biblische Beiträge
BDAT	Die Botschaft des Alten Testaments
BDB	Francis Brown, S.R. Driver, C.A. Briggs, *A Hebrew and English Lexicon of the Old Testament*
Bib	*Biblica*
BLS	Bible and Literature Series
BWANT	Beiträge zur Wissenschaft vom Alten und Neuen Testament
BZAW	Beihefte zur Zeitschrift für die alttestamentliche Wissenschaft
CBC	Cambridge Bible Commentary
CBQ	*Catholic Biblical Quarterly*
ChQR	*Church Quarterly Review*
CJT	*Canadian Journal of Theology*
DH	*The Deuteronomistic History*
FRLANT	Forschungen zur Religion und Literatur des Alten und Neuen Testaments, Göttingen
HKAT	Handkommentar zum Alten Testament, Göttingen
HSM	Harvard Semitic Monographs
HTR	*Harvard Theological Review*

HTIBS	Historic Texts and Interpreters in Biblical Scholarship
IB	Interpreter's Bible
ICC	International Critical Commentary
IDB	*Interpreter's Dictionary of the Bible*
Interp	*Interpretation*
JAAR	*Journal of the American Academy of Religion*
JBL	*Journal of Biblical Literature*
JNES	*Journal of Near Eastern Studies*
JSOT	*Journal for the Study of Old Testament*
JSOTS	Journal for the Study of Old Testament Supplement
JSS	*Journal of Semitic Studies*
JTS	*Journal of Theological Studies*
JWH	*Journal of World History*
KHCAT	Kurzer Hand-Commentar zum Alten Testament, Tübingen
LB	Late Bronze Age
LXX	Septuagint
LXXL	Lucianic Recension
MT	Massoretic Text
NCBC	New Century Bible Commentary
NT	*Novum Testamentum*
OBT	Overtures to Biblical Theology
OLZ	*Orientalistische Literaturzeitung*
OTL	Old Testament Library
OTM	*Old Testament Message*
OTWSA	*Die ou Testamentiese Werkgemeenskap in Suid-Afrika*
PP	*Pastoral Psychology*
RevBib	*Revue Biblique*
SBLDS	Society of Biblical Literature Dissertation Series
SBT	Studies in Biblical Theology
STT	*Studia Theologica Teresiana*
TDOT	*Theological Dictionary of the Old Testament*
ThZ	*Theologische Zeitschrift*
TS	*Theological Studies*
TSK	*Theologische Studien und Kritiken*
TSN	Throne Succession Narrative
VT	*Vetus Testamentum*
VTSup	Supplements to Vetus Testamentum
WBC	Word Biblical Commentary
ZAW	*Zeitschrift für die alttestamentliche Wissenschaft*

Chapter 1

ROST'S THEORY OF A THRONE SUCCESSION NARRATIVE AND ITS PROPONENTS AND OPPONENTS

1986 marked the sixtieth anniversary of the appearance of Leonhard Rost's monumental work on the material from 2 Samuel 6, 7, 9–20; 1 Kings 1–2 in which he advocated his theory of a throne succession narrative (TSN). Since that publication an enormous amount of literature has been produced to either support, expand, modify or replace his theory.

Given the broad appeal and simplicity of Rost's presentation, most challenges to the theory have not received very serious consideration. Similarly, most modifications, with the exception of the question of 2 Samuel 9 as the beginning of the work, have attracted little attention. For the most part challenges culminated in long survey notes reviewing the literature, accompanied by the notation that, given the mass of literature, only a few 'major pieces' will be examined.

In this chapter we shall review the literature to examine the entire range of arguments related to the issue of a TSN and to assess the viability of Rost's theory.

1. *Rost's Theory of a TSN*

In 1926, Leonhard Rost published his *Die Überlieferung von der Thronnachfolge Davids*,[1] initially submitted to the University of Erlangen as a *Habilitationsschrift*. In this work, Rost argued for the existence of a unified document now found in 2 Sam 6.16, 20-23; 7.11b, 16; 9–20; 1 Kings 1–2. He sought to demonstrate the unity of these materials by concentrating not only on vocabulary and the 'use of traditional forms and formulas',[2] but also more importantly on the matter of style. He emphasized the latter, since he felt

> style is and will remain a person's most individual creation—which
> is always being fashioned anew, creatively producing singularity
> and stubborn idiosyncrasy, the more singular and stubbornly
> idiosyncratic the writer's own nature.[3]

Rost's work is divided into four parts, with the first three being
geared toward clearly delimiting the bounds of three narrative
complexes and establishing their original independence from the
Succession Narrative. First, he seeks to demonstrate the unity of the
'Ark Narrative' (2 Sam 4.1b–7.1; 2 Sam 6.1-20a) and argues for the
exclusion of the David–Michal materials (2 Sam 6.16, 20-23) from
consideration as part of this source.[4]

With regard to the Ark Narrative, Rost reaches the following
conclusions:

1. The ark narrative comprises: 1 Sam 4.1b-18a, 19-21; 5.1-
    11bα, 12; 6.1-3bα, 4, 10-14, 16; 6.19–7.1; 2 Sam 6.1-15, 17-
    20a.
2. Through its vocabulary and style it can be shown over
    against its context to be independent and uniform, and
    through its structure to be self-contained and complete.
3. The narrative is to be regarded as the *hieros logos* of the
    sanctuary of the ark in Jerusalem, its author a member of
    the community of priests who took care of the ark during the
    latter part of David's reign or at the beginning of Solomon's
    reign.
4. As a cult legend it has only a limited interest in political
    events. It can lay a certain claim to historical reliability as
    regards the broad relationships and many of the individuals,
    but does not represent historical reality in every detail.
5. Yahweh appears as the all-powerful—but not arbitrary-God
    who normally brings ill fortune, but also salvation; accordingly,
    religious devotion is characterized by fear, but also by joyful
    adoration.
6. Yahweh's interventions are partly related by the narrator
    himself and partly placed as comment in the mouths of the
    active or passive participants.[5]

Secondly, he examines the prayer of David and the prophecy of
Nathan in 2 Samuel 7. He argues that there was an early version of
the prophecy of Nathan that the seed, *zr'*, of David would be great and
that vv. 11b and 16 belong to a separate stratum from the other

materials as their concern for the dynasty of David, *byt dwd*, indicates.[6]

Thirdly, he considers the material on the Ammonite War[7] and reaches the following conclusions:

1. The account of the Ammonite wars is shown to be an independent source incorporating 10.6–11.1 and 12.26-31.
2. The beginning of the account has been replaced by a more detailed introduction coming from the author of the interpolated passage 11.2ff., the same person who wrote the succession source.
3. Apart from this the source has been preserved in full.
4. The style is simple, concise and terse; the action pushes continually forward; there are speeches only at decisive points.
5. The account is entitled to be treated as trustworthy and is very close to the events; it seems to have been a war report intended for the state archives.
6. Its contribution to a description of the theological climate of the early monarchic period is meagre; however, the figure of Joab provides us with an interesting picture of a devout person.[8]

The Ammonite War Story was utilized to provide a setting for the killing of Uriah in ch. 11, and into it the David-Bathsheba-Nathan complex and the narratives about the birth of Solomon have been interpolated.

In all of these instances his methodology is to follow the same five-step procedure.[9] First, he examines each of the specific blocks of materials in Samuel in terms of traditional source critical criteria. In so doing he reviews the literature and presents the various scholarly positions on dividing each block into sources.[10] He then discusses the inadequacies of these criteria for solving the problems of authorship and date. Secondly, he examines the block of material to 'establish the text' by removing what he deems to be later additions to the 'story'. Thirdly, he argues for the unity of the remaining materials in the block based upon stylistic variables, such as the use of dialogue, syntactical similarities, affinities of phrases and the like. Fourthly, he then speculates on the identification of the probable author and date of the remaining block. All this leads him to his main concern, the formulation of the 'religious ideas' promoted by the writer.

After the treatment of these three literary complexes, Rost begins

his examination of the Succession Narrative proper. He first seeks to
establish the limits of the text, which he does in three major stages.
In the first stage his concern is the beginning and end of the block in
2 Samuel 9–20. According to him, the differences in theological
outlook between 2 Sam 21.1-14 and 2 Samuel 9f. are obvious, the
former presenting a more focussed role for Yahweh in the course of
the events than the latter. Thus, he argues for a break in the material
between 2 Samuel 20 and 21.[11]

He next briefly touches on the internal unity of chs. 9–20. After
arguing against the views of Caspari and Gressmann who postulated
different *Novellen* in chs. 13ff.,[12] he posits his thesis that

> just one look at the uniform style or the structure of the succession
> story proves that there is a unifying plan underlying the whole text
> which does not owe its origins to the industrious hands of some
> editor. To pursue this point somewhat further will be our next task.
> *For then we can work backwards* to reach some conclusion about
> the extent of the source, which, if it is to be properly established,
> must be supported finally by the investigation of the stylistic
> characteristics and religious conceptions.[13] (emphasis added)

Rost then proceeds to the second stage in establishing the text of his
Succession Narrative, namely, the coherence of 1 Kings 1 with 2
Samuel 9–20. He justifies the turn of attention to 1 Kings 1 to find
'information about the writer's wishes and intentions', since this
chapter 'is the key to understanding the whole work'.[14] His focus in
this section concerns two issues. First he asks where we find the
antecedents to the events and personalities introduced in this
chapter. Secondly he asks where we find the logical conclusion to the
narrative in 1 Kings 1. He answers the latter question first by
positing 1 Kings 2.13-25 as the continuation of 1 Kings 1.[15] Rost
maintains that the central question in 1 Kings 1 is, 'Who will sit on
the throne of my lord', which is finally answered in 2.46 with the
affirmation that Solomon is secure on the throne. Having reached
this conclusion he moves to the designation of the Deuteronomistic
additions to the text of 1 Kings 2.[16]

There are three major phases in his attempt to answer the question
of the antecedents to the events described in 1 Kings 1 and, thereby
'pursue the source in 1 Kings 1 back to its beginning'.[17] Rost first
turns to the David–Bathsheba story in 2 Samuel 11f. His argument is
that 'II Samuel 13–20 tells a story of the background to the
succession, while II Samuel 11 and 12 tell such a story of the one who
was to succeed'.[18]

In his examination of the 'Nathan scene', he eliminates the first two oracles of judgment (vv. 7b-10 and 11-12) as secondary additions and, thus, as not being part of the original story. He admits that since they are not Deuteronomistic in tone, one cannot be certain as to when they were added.[19] He then concedes that though the remaining unit (vv. 13-14) appears to be self-contained and could be totally removed, it serves the function both of directly addressing the immorality of David's actions and of heightening the tension for the reader. In addition, it allows the writer to introduce Solomon in the positive light of Yahweh's acceptance of him (v. 25). Thus, on the basis of content, it must be considered as part of the original source.

Having established the intention of 2 Samuel 11-12 as introducing the successor anticipated in 1 Kings 1, Rost completes phase two of 'establishing his text' by turning his attention to the stories found in 2 Samuel 13ff. He does this again by returning to 1 Kings 1 and identifying the people and events alluded to there and then seeking to find their antecedents in 2 Samuel 13ff. He notes the similarities of style and wording found in both units.[20]

He again counters the arguments of others[21] that there are separate *Novellen* in this material by arguing that none of the individual scenes can provide a 'key to the understanding of the whole' nor do they individually bring closure to the fate(s) of all of the actors involved in them.[22] He further argues that this is only found in 1 Kings 1. As noted above, for the most part his arguments rest upon his reading of the story line (content) and whether what precedes necessitates or supports what follows.

Having thus established the interconnection of 2 Samuel 9-20 with the question of the succession to the throne raised in 1 Kings 1, Rost enters the third and final stage of 'establishing his text'. In so doing he turns his attention to showing that the David-Michal episode found in 2 Sam 6.16, 20-23 is the beginning of the 'succession story'. He then argues that 7.11b is related to the speech of Solomon in 1 Kgs 2.24 and that both are, therefore, part of the source.[23] It is here that one sees why he began with examination of the Ark Narrative and the Nathan prophecy in an attempt to argue their dating during the reign of David or Solomon, for he now argues that 2 Sam 6.16, 20-23 were probably separated from the succession story proper and added to the other units, which were already in existence and known to the narrator.

Having 'established the text', fundamentally on the basis of content, Rost next moves to the examination of the style of the source for the purpose of establishing its individuality. He first compares the 'terse style of the Ark Narrative' to the 'fuller. . . richer. . .[and] more sonorous' language of the succession source.[24] He notes the use of groups of verbs to describe the actions of individual characters, as well as groups of nouns as objects. He terms these instances of 'graphic descriptiveness'. Additionally he makes note of the use of speeches to move the action along. He then compares the structure of the scenes of the succession story with those of the Ark Narrative. For example, he notes the attention given groups of people as the actors in the latter, as opposed to the attention to individuals in the former. Similarly the use of messenger speeches is different in both.[25] He then traces what he calls an 'unbreakable chain' from scene to scene in the succession story building the tension from Michal's barrenness to Solomon's coronation.[26] In so doing he pays attention to plot, the manner in which characters are introduced and described, and the structuring of the scenes. In this manner Rost argues for unity of the source.

Having established the text and having examined the style of the writer, Rost then turns to the subject of author and date of the succession story. He argues for one who was close to the Davidic-Solomonic court, writing at the beginning of the reign of Solomon with the intention of producing a work 'in majorem gloriam Salomonis'.[27] He then presents the 'theological ideas' present in the succession story.[28] In this regard he concentrates on the themes of human submission to Yahweh's will and of Yahweh as protector of the moral law.

2. Analysis of Research since Rost

Since its initial presentation, Rost's theory has played a major role in the study of the book of Samuel. It has been a cornerstone to the theory that the composition of the book of Samuel is best explained by a so-called 'fragmentary hypothesis'. In this approach it is argued that there were a series of independent collections, a 'History of the Rise of David', an 'Ark Narrative', a 'Throne Succession Narrative', an 'Appendix', and the like which have been loosely joined together to produce the present work.[29]

Enjoying wide acceptance, in many circles Rost's theory has largely gone unchallenged. In fact the only consistently negative critic of Rost's theory has been Eissfeldt.[30] In the last two decades, however, there have been sustained attempts at disproving various parts of the theory. We now turn to a review of this literature and an examination of the assessments of Rost's theory.

There are many reviews of the literature on the TSN.[31] Within these reviews there are those who fundamentally agree or disagree with Rost's position. In the same manner there are those who agree with Rost on most issues, but disagree on one of the variables. Similarly, there are those who basically disagree with Rost, but who agree with him on one of the variables. Thus, neither a scholar by scholar review nor one organized on form critical lines does justice to the various positions with regard to Rost's theory.

Thus, we shall attempt to examine the literature in terms of the four major positions of Rost: (1) limits of the work, (2) literary unity, (3) genre and intention, and (4) date and authorship. All the literature will be assessed in terms of how each piece relates to each of these variables. There will then be an evaluative statement as to the state of the question in each instance.

a. *Limits of the Work*

By way of summary, there were four major points to Rost's argument on the boundaries or limits of the materials to be included in the TSN. First he argued for the inclusion of 2 Sam 6.16, 20-23, the confrontation between David and Michal on the occasion of the ark being brought into Jerusalem. He included this material because of its connection to the question of succession, ending, as it does, with the notice of Michal's barrenness.[32] Secondly, he argued that 7.11b, 16, because of their mention of succession, belonged to the TSN.[33] Thirdly, Rost argued that the theological focus of 2 Samuel 9-20 differed from 2 Samuel 21 and, thus, there was a break at 2 Samuel 20.[34] Fourthly, he argued that 1 Kings 1-2 contained the continuation of events begun in 2 Samuel 9-20, and brought them to a conclusion with Solomon sitting on the throne.[35]

Of all the issues, Rost has received least support for his conclusions about the limits of the TSN. Pfeiffer is the only scholar to support the inclusion of the Michal materials of 2 Samuel 6.[36] Others exclude it because it either does not have a succession theme[37] or because it is not a self-contained unit, but is dependent upon the Ark Narrative for its context.[38]

The picture is a little different in the case of the passages in 2 Samuel 7. Although some reject Rost's position outright,[39] Hertzberg states, 'Rost has discussed this chapter in detail.... We may take Rost's views as basically correct without following him in every detail'.[40] Noth wholeheartedly accepts Rost's position.[41] On the other hand Ridout goes beyond Rost's position and argues that almost all of 2 Samuel 7 belongs to the TSN.[42]

The consensus, however, is not to include the materials in 2 Samuel 6-7 in the TSN. While Whybray argues that 'anything before nine is not absolutely certain',[43] Gunn cites 2 Samuel 9 as the 'least common denominator' for a beginning of the TSN.[44] In support of this Ackroyd and Bowman have argued that the list of 'court officials' in 2 Sam 8.15-18 signals a new beginning.[45]

The major point of disagreement with Rost in regard to the limits of the TSN is on the question of its beginning. Within the past two decades, a number of scholars have adopted Wiener's[46] and later M. Smith's[47] contentions that parts of the materials in 2 Samuel 2-4, the reign of Ishbosheth and the death of Abner, belong to the TSN. The most common reason for the inclusion of these narratives centers around the references in 1 Kgs 2.5, 31-35 to the death of Abner (2 Sam 3.30).[48]

The second major reason presented for including 2 Samuel 2-4 within the TSN revolves around the war narratives found in these chapters. Van Seters argues that the structure of the war narratives in 3.23-27 is very similar to the war narratives of 2 Samuel 18 and 20. In particular he notes that both Abner and Sheba are killed in the same manner, 'by stabbing the unsuspecting victim in the stomach, *ḥomeš*'.[49] He also argues that in both the 2 Samuel 2-4 and 2 Samuel 9-20 complexes David remains home while his men fight, and, thus, is shown not to be in control of 'his own men and affairs'.[50] Similarly Gunn argues for similarities in the war narratives of 2 Samuel 2 with those of 2 Samuel 18.[51]

A third point of argument for connecting 2 Samuel 2-4 with the TSN is the attention given to the psychological motivation of the characters in both complexes and the style of writing.[52] Similarly, the theme of succession has been noted to function both in 2 Samuel 2-4, as well as in the TSN.[53]

A fourth reason for assuming a connection between 2 Samuel 2-4 and the TSN is the mention of Mephibosheth in 2 Sam 4.16. Since he also appears in 2 Samuel 9, 17, 19, and 21, it is argued that these passages are interrelated.[54]

Thus, there is a strong case for connecting the materials in 2 Samuel 2-4 with those of 2 Samuel 13-20 and 1 Kings 1-2 as being from the hand of the same author. Therefore, it appears that Rost's beginning point should be extended to include 2 Samuel 2-4.[55]

On the other hand there has also been disagreement with Rost's position regarding the end of the TSN, most notably on the relationship between 1 Kings 1-2 and 2 Samuel 9-20. In this instance, however, the move has been to shorten the limit of the narrative, rather than extending it. Mowinckel has argued that 1 Kings 1-2 and 2 Samuel 9-20 are not part of the same unit for several reasons. First, there is nothing in the Samuel accounts to prepare the reader for the depiction of David as an aged invalid, as he is portrayed in 1 Kings 1. Similarly the presentations of the inner working of the royal court in both blocks are radically different.[56]

Flanagan has also argued for a separation between the units and distinguishes two different sources, a 'Court History' and a 'Succession Document' which have been secondarily interrelated.[57] He also argues that the two lists of the court officials of David in 2 Sam 8.15-18 and 20.23-26 signal a narrative which begins in 9 and ends in 20.[58] He thus argues that the duplication of the list has the editorial function of stating that the situation is the same at the end of the Absalom Revolt as it was in the beginning.[59]

Most recently P.K. McCarter has argued against the inclusion of 1 Kings 1-2 into a TSN with the materials in 2 Samuel. While Rost had pinned part of his claim for connection between the units on the basis of the similarities between the wording in cases such as 2 Sam 15.1 and 1 Kgs 1.5,[60] McCarter argues that this is best explained by the fact that the writer of 1 Kings 1 had 2 Samuel as a source.[61]

Finally, Carlson maintains that all of 2 Samuel 10-24 is a unified composition arranged by a D-group under the theme of 'David under the curse'.[62] Similarly, he argues that there is a three-fold curse of 'sword, famine, and pestilence' found in Deut 28.15ff., which explains the connection between all of 2 Samuel 13-24.[63] Carlson maintains that the function of 2 Samuel 10-12 is to introduce the curse, which is carried out in 2 Samuel 13-24. While he also maintains that the story line jumps from 2 Samuel 20 to 1 Kings 1,[64] he goes to elaborate lengths to demonstrate verbal similarities between 2 Samuel 20 and 21.[65] Finally he argues that, though the events described in 2 Sam 21.1-14 are closely associated with those in 2 Sam 24.1-25 and probably precede the events in 2 Samuel 9, their current location is to ensure that there is no confusion between the altar built by David in 2 Sam 24.1-25 and the future *byt* described in 2 Samuel 7.[66]

We see, then, that while there has been a tendency to extend the beginning limit of the TSN to include 2 Samuel 2-4, there has been an equal push to limit its ending to the material in 2 Samuel, most notably with 2 Samuel 20 as the preponderant view. These arguments have raised serious questions about the basis of the relationship of the David materials in 2 Samuel to those in 1 Kings. Similar to the arguments for inclusion of the materials in 2 Samuel 2-4, because of their affinity to the materials in 9-20, the arguments for a separation between 2 Samuel and 1 Kings have demonstrated the lack of affinity of these two latter blocks of materials.

Our next concern will be with the questions raised about the unity which Rost saw in the narrative.

b. Unity of Composition

Rost's argument that the TSN is a unified composition from the hand of one writer is predicated on 'content'. In other words, the story line of the narrative flows from one scene to the other. This is one of the most appealing aspects of his theory. In summary, his contention is that there is an 'unifying plan underlying the whole text which does not owe its origins to the industrious hands of some editor'.[67] He argues that 1 Kings 1 provides the 'key to understanding the whole work',[68] and he moves from there to find the antecedents and forward to find the conclusions to the events presented in 1 Kgs 1.1-2.5.[69] He buttresses his position by examining stylistic variables such as usage of verbs and nouns,[70] speeches,[71] and story line.[72] His main argument in this analysis is the conclusion that the subunits cannot stand alone, since none brings closure to the whole.[73]

Support for Rost's position is reflected in Wiener's statement that the TSN is 'the finest specimen of *continuous prose narrative* in the Old Testament'[74] (emphasis added). Similarly, Noth calls it the '*traditional story* of the Davidic Succession'[75] (emphasis added). Even Van Seters states, 'On matters of unity and style I have little argument with Rost's treatment'.[76]

In response to the concept of unity of composition, many scholars have attempted to articulate a 'unifying scheme' over and above that of the succession theme which Rost proposed. Brueggemann argues that the arrangement of the TSN, in terms of the sequence of events, provided the model for the J writer of the Pentateuch in arranging the events of the primeval history in Genesis 2-11. Thus, he equates the David-Bathsheba episode with that of the Garden in Genesis 3. He then equates the fratricide of Amnon (2 Sam 13) with the Cain and Abel incident (Genesis 4).[77] The Absalom revolt (2 Sam 15–19) is compared with the flood narrative (Gen 6–9) and the accession of Solomon (1 Kgs 1–2) with the tower of Babel (Gen 11).[78]

Wharton argues that identification with 'David's feelings' is the organizing scheme. As he states, 'the narrator is not content simply to report the fact . . . here we are expected to experience with David an elemental human reality'.[79] The passages he cites as portraying this reality (e.g. 2 Sam 11.27b; 15.25), however, are deemed by most to be redactional.[80]

Several scholars argue that sex is the major organizing, or unifying, theme of the work. Thus, Blenkinsopp[81] argues that sexual sin leading to death is the key to the TSN. In so doing he states that the most prominent of the sexual motifs is the foreign 'woman who brings death'.[82] He writes

> The motif bears within it two elements: that this kind of woman seduces the heart; that this leading astray is worked out to its conclusion in the kind of children who are born of the ensuing union.[83]

He grounds the motif in the Genesis 3 account of *h'šh* and in the warnings against the foreign woman in Prov 6.29-31, which he argues is the basis for the Nathan-David confrontation in 2 Sam 12.1-15a.[84] Thus, Bathsheba is the foreign woman who seduces David, and this act leads to the death of David's children.[85]

In this regard Fokkelman[86] argues that 'David four times loses a son through a violent death following and *elicited by* the unjustified sexual possession of a woman (women)'[87] (emphasis added). He then cites the instance of Bathsheba leading to the deaths of the unnamed child of adultery. The rape of Tamar leads to the death of Amnon. The taking of the harem by Absalom leads to Absalom's death, while Adonijah's request for Abishag leads to his death.[88]

Carlson offers a variation on sex as an organizing principle in the TSN. He argues that the laws of sex in Deut 22.22–23.1 provide a 'compositional pattern which is of direct traditio-historical interest'.[89] He notes the following pattern:

2 Samuel	10–12	13–14	15–20
Deuteronomy	22.22	22.28-29	23.1[90]

Thus, the David–Bathsheba affair is one of adultery. The Amnon–Tamar episode is one of rape. Finally, the Absalom–concubine incident is one of 'uncovering the nakedness of one's father'.

Therefore, he concludes that in these units 'we are dealing with a given order of tradition which simply happened to coincide with a Deuteronomic pattern of association'.[91]

Similarly, Whybray and Fontaine argue for wisdom, *ḥkmh*, as a major organizing scheme. While Whybray appeals to the statements in Proverbs on the 'foreign woman',[92] however, Fontaine concentrates on interpreting the actions of David as the antithesis of the positive role of wisdom.[93]

Gunn argues that the theme of rebellion in David's public and private life is central. As he states,

> It is a story about David and his kingdom, which explores the complex interaction, generating a sequence of tensions, between the political and private (especially family) worlds of David'.[94]

He then identifies subthemes of the 'gaining, displacement and bestowal of authority or status'.[95] He divides the narrative up, therefore, in terms of a series of conflicts which need to be resolved and which are joined together by various transitions.[96] As with the other such theories, his argument is that the story-line or plot fits within the theoretical framework of public/private acquisition tensions and that these narratives are interrelated in subject matter. For example, the Ishbosheth (2 Sam 2-4) and Mephibosheth (2 Sam 9) narratives depict David's acquiring the kingdom from the Saulides. They also 'prefigure' his acquisition of Bathsheba (2 Sam 11) from Uriah.[97]

Another 'unifying scheme' which has been proposed for demonstrating the unity of the TSN is presented by Hagan. He argues that the motif of deception is used in the TSN and that 'this factor is organized to produce a configuration of plot which is played out five times in the course of the story with new situations and new characters'.[98] He then seeks to demonstrate how the subthemes of counsel, faithfulness and death recur in the five parts of the narrative.[99]

What Hagan really demonstrates is that there is a consistency within the various complexes in the TSN, such as the David–Bathsheba–Uriah–Nathan and Amnon–Tamar–Absalom complexes. He does not, however, demonstrate that these units are necessarily interconnected. Secondly, he presents data which show that the motif of the weak resorting to deception as a tool to redress grievances is found in other parts of the canon.[100] The question then arises as to how useful the concept of deception is for proving unity of a narrative.

As this multiplicity of 'organizing themes' demonstrates, unity about the plot line is open to a variety of interpretations. The analysis of these 'organizing themes' has also demonstrated that the attempt to tie down one theme forces one to ignore important differences between motifs and units. Finally it must be noted that continuity of plot is not a sound basis for unity, since redactional seams may help produce the coherence.

Several writers have concentrated on literary techniques to argue for unity in the narrative. Ridout argues for a series of chiasms, irony, and repetitions within the narrative as being evidence for unity.[101] Sacon furthers this argument by demonstrating the existence of inclusios, which he argues point to the existence of a coherent composition.[102] He examines the components of the story line and concludes that 'a coherent story is found in 2 Samuel 2-4, 9-20 and 1 Kings 1-2'.[103]

He first argues for a 'balanced structure' in 2 Samuel 15-19. He then examines 2 Samuel 10-14 and argues,

> Our structural analysis shows that there repeatedly is found the same composition of the concentric structure with the sharp contrast and ambivalence at the central and chiastic point, which is generally expressed in two sentences put side by side.[104]

He, therefore, argues that the adultery and death in 2 Samuel 11 is replicated in 2 Samuel 13. The main problem with this analysis is that he is comparing consenting sex (11.4) with rape (13.12-14), as well as assassination of the victim (11.14-16) with revenge on the perpetrator (13.28). It would appear that most scholars who utilize 'sex' as a key variable for the analysis of the TSN ignore the nuances just noted and group all sexual behaviors into one category. Most recently Hauser has argued convincingly that the analog to the rape of Tamar (2 Sam 13.8-14) is the plot and murder of Uriah.[105] We would agree, since rape is an act of violence and violation and should best be compared with other heinous acts, such as assassination.

Finally it must be noted that the major work on unity of structure, however, has occurred in the chapters dealing with the Absalom and Sheba revolts (2 Sam 15-20). For example Gunn has argued that there is a chiastic arrangement to be seen in these chapters.[106]

A major point of agreement with Rost, even among those who are his most ardent critics, is in his designating the Ammonite War

materials found in 2 Sam 10.1–11.1 + 12.26-31 as a unified source
taken from annals that date from the time of David and, thus, are
considered to be historically reliable. Similarly, there is agreement
that the David–Bathsheba–Uriah–Nathan complex has been interpolated into this complex.[107]

Another major point of agreement among both followers and
opponents of Rost is in regard to the Nathan oracles in 2 Sam 12.7b-
14. First is the sentiment that there are additions to these oracles,
most probably vv. 7b-12. Similarly, there is agreement that it is the
Nathan material which becomes the unifying element for the
TSN.[108] There is not unanimity, however, on when these additions
to the text were made nor when to date these additions. As Gunn
states,

> ...it is more than likely that the pronouncements by Nathan
> against David in 2 Samuel 12 have been reworked (probably at the
> stage of incorporating the King David Story into the history as a
> whole). I doubt that the extent of the reworking can be defined with
> any certainty.[109]

It must be noted, however, that the unity of the story line is in large
part predicated on the prophecy-fulfillment scheme of the oracles in
2 Sam 12.7b-12 being carried to fruition in 2 Samuel 13-20, 1 Kings
1-2.[110] Similarly, Eissfeldt's critique of arguing for unity on such
literary grounds holds merit. As he notes,

> in spite of its detailed examination of stylistic criteria, this defining
> of the limits of an apparently fixed and complete historical work
> rests ultimately not upon literary criteria but upon consideration of
> content, as to whether the narratives reveal relationships to the
> theme of the succession to David or not; and the conclusions are
> anything but certain.[111]

There are three major points used to argue against coherent unity
in Rost's TSN. The first revolves around the Nathan oracles in 2
Samuel 12. Würthwein raises two objections to the unity of the TSN
on the basis of events narrated in 10-12. First he argues that, since
the characterizations of Nathan in 2 Samuel 12 and 1 Kings 1 are
radically different, reproaching prophet vs. court intriguer respectively,
these units were written by different hands.[112] Secondly, he argues
that the actions of David in response to the illness of the child
conceived in adultery (12.15b-23) are most problematic, since they
presuppose no knowledge of the preceding prophetic pronouncement

(12.13-14). In other words, David's life has been spared with the punishment being 'averted' to the newborn child. Thus, his actions of seeking healing for the child, if answered, would have the effect of rescinding the grace. Therefore, Würthwein argues that 2 Sam 12.1-15a has been interpolated into the David–Bathsheba account.[113]

Similarly Dietrich begins his attack on the unity of the TSN at the point of the Nathan materials. He argues that 2 Sam 11.27b, *wyr' hdbr b'yny yhwh*, reads as similar to the Dtr negative evaluative formula for the kings of Israel and Judah employed in the regnal formulae in 1 and 2 Kings.[114] Similarly, he argues that the variation on the formula, found in 2 Sam 12.9, betrays the hand of the DtrH.[115] Thirdly he notes a connection between the motif of a judgment upon the king being passed on to the next generation found in 2 Sam 12.14 with the analogous motif found in 1 Kgs 21.20.[116] Finally he argues that 2 Sam 12.15b is best understood as the continuation of the David–Bathsheba incident in 2 Sam 11.1-27a, with the *ngp* in 12.15b being the deity's response to the adultery. Given the role of Nathan in this unit, he therefore designates the unit in 11.27b-12.15a as coming from the hand of DtrP.[117] He is followed in this respect by Veijola.[118]

While Rost opened the door to speculating on the authenticity of various verses within the Nathan speech in 2 Sam 12.7bf., the above arguments have gone further and challenged the authenticity of the whole unit. Thus, the implication of Dietrich's, Veijola's, and Würthwein's arguments was to undermine the whole concept of a TSN by eliminating the very unit which Rost argued tied together the narratives in 2 Samuel 10–12 with those of 13-20 and 1 Kings 1-2.

A second type of argument against the unity of the TSN is presented by Flanagan, Würthwein, Veijola, and Langlamet. All of them argue for extensive redactional processes.

Würthwein argues that passages other than 2 Sam 12.1-15a within the so-called TSN are redactional. In essence his argument is that these are passages within the TSN which are duplicates of other passages in the narrative. These duplicating passages differ and/or disagree with each other in content and function. A few examples will suffice to demonstrate his line of argument.

Most notably he designates as redactional 2 Sam 14.2-22, the narrative of the wise woman of Tekoa. In so doing he claims it differs from 13.39, where David appears already to have forgiven Absalom for the murder/death of Amnon.[119] Thus, since the narrative in 14.2-

22 appears to have no knowledge of the sentiment in 13.39, he sees it coming from another hand.

Similarly he argues that in 15.27-28 there are instructions for Zadok, Abiathar, and his two sons to return to Jerusalem to get word for David. In 15.24-26, 29, however, there are pious statements of David about the return of Zadok and the ark to Jerusalem.[120] Since the latter texts show no knowledge of the so-called spies, he designates them as secondary.

Würthwein further argues that 15.31, David's prayer that the advice of Ahithophel be thwarted, is best seen as being answered in the incident in 16.20-23, the incident with the concubines on the roof.[121] He claims that this advice is not of the caliber of the advice given in 17.1-3, to pursue David immediately, nor are these two sets of advice compatible.

In the same manner he argues that the reaction of David to the curse of Shimei in 16.5-14 is theologically different from the response David makes in 19.7-23 and the response Solomon makes to Shimei in 1 Kgs 2.36-38.[122] Thus, he argues that since the pardon given in 19.23 presupposes no knowledge of the response given in 16.11-13, the unit in 16.5-14 is secondary.

Similarly he designates 17.5-14, 15b, the narrative of the advice of Hushai over against that of Ahithophel[123] and the notice of the suicide of Ahithophel in 17.23[124], as secondary. He also so designates 18.2b-4a, the interaction between David and the soldiers about his staying in Jerusalem during the war with Absalom, and 18.10-14, the dialogue with Joab and the 'certain man' who found Absalom hanging in the tree but did not kill him, because of David's request to protect the young man.[125] Also in this category is the assassination of Amasa by Joab (20.8-13).[126]

In all of the above instances Würthwein has identified passages which present David in a favorable light in terms of piety, and has argued that they are secondary because of their conflicts with other units which present David acting ruthlessly. In similar fashion he designates 1 Kgs 2.5-9, 31b-33, 44-45, the units which exonerate Solomon for the ruthless assassinations of Joab and Shimei, as being secondary.[127] Further he argues that it was an exilic redactor attempting to argue for the idealized Davidic lineage who made these editions.[128]

Langlamet and Veijola use similar approaches to that of Würthwein in their examination of the TSN. They both designate verses and units as redactional because they pose inconsistencies within the

TSN. They disagree, however, as to the designation of the redactors. As noted above, Veijola follows Dietrich in his designation of redactional stages by a DtrG, a DtrN, and a DtrP.[129] Langlamet argues for a priestly redaction during the time of Hezekiah.[130]

Flanagan takes issue with Rost's method of beginning at the end of the TSN and then moving forward to the beginning, since the units which are so designated as being the antecedents to the events in 1 Kings 1-2, have their own beginnings. He thus argues that it would be better to ask which stories could be excluded without 'destroying the unity of the entire account'.[131] Thus, he concludes that

> behind the present narrative of 2 Samuel 9-20 and 1 Kings 1-2 there is an earlier literary unit, a Court History, that was intended to show how David maintained legitimate control over the kingdoms of Judah and Israel. Only later was the Court History given a succession character when a *skillful redactor* added the Solomonic sections [132] (emphasis added).

Flanagan argues on the basis of the structure in the so-called TSN, that the material was given a symmetrical ordering. Most notably he first argues for a symmetry in the portrayal of David's difficulties in governing his kingdom, with him first portrayed as secure in Jerusalem (2 Sam 9-14), then fleeing (2 Sam 15), and then reestablished (2 Sam 19). This portrayal is balanced by that of Merribaal who first gains (2 Sam 9), then loses (2 Sam 16), and then regains (2 Sam 19) his fortune. Similarly Flanagan argues for a symmetry of people met by David on the flight from Jerusalem during the Absalom revolt with those met on the return (2 Sam 15-19).[133]

In order to achieve this symmetry, however, he argues that one must remove the David-Bathsheba-Nathan-Solomon materials in 2 Sam 11.2-12.25.[134] Similarly he argues that the Ammonite War materials in 2 Sam 10.1-11.1 + 12.26-31 are integrally tied to the 'Court History' through their connection with the incidents in 2 Sam 17.24-29.[135]

A final type of argument against the unity of the TSN is represented in the work of Conroy. He argues on the one hand that the materials in 2 Samuel 13-20 are self-contained, and do not presuppose the events in 10-12. On the other hand he argues that there are inconsistencies between the portrayals of David in these two blocks.[136] In this line of argument he is followed by McCarter.[137]

In summary, the major claims in support of Rost's position of unity have been on the level of the story line. In these instances, however, there has not been unanimity in designation of the theme(s) which unite the material nor has there been close attention paid to discrepancies and unevenness within the narrative. On the other hand, there has been within the last two decades much attention paid to the contradictions within the various narratives, as well as discrepancies between blocks within the TSN. It would appear that since the crux of the unity argument is predicated on the oracles in 2 Sam 12.7b-12 and on continuity between the events in 1 Kings 1-2 with those in 2 Samuel,[138] that a major crack has been made in the dike of Rost's argument for unity.

Interestingly, there has been very little acceptance of any of the redactional theories proposed by Dietrich, Würthwein, Veijola, and Langlamet.[139] For the most part there has been rejection of such close readings in favor of the overall plot and sequence. It appears that the appeal of the story-line of the 'true exploits of the rich and famous' is a very difficult barrier to cross. On the other hand, while the exact explanations proposed for the observed discrepancies may not be acceptable, it does appear that the matter of ignoring and/or fighting them needs to be rethought.

c. *Genre and Intention*

Rost argued that the TSN was 'historical narrative' in which 'fact and fiction intertwined'.[140] He further argued that the intention was twofold. First it was written 'in majorem gloriam Salomonis', and second it was intended to explain why Solomon and none of the other possible heirs came to the throne.[141]

While Rost was not prepared fully to designate the work as 'history', others took that extra step.[142] In this regard von Rad led the way when he termed it the 'earliest form of ancient Israelite historiography'.[143] Noth reinforced this notion by excluding consideration of the issue in his *DH* and by referring to the TSN as the 'traditional story of the Davidic succession'.[144]

Similarly Rost receives support on his designation of the intention as the glorification of Solomon and an explanation of the succession. For example von Rad argues that the focus of attention is on the resolution of the tension between 'charismatic leadership' and 'dynastic succession'.[145] Interestingly those who have followed Rost in this regard have done so primarily on appeal to his thesis with no additional evidence to support the position.[146]

More than even boundaries and unity, this aspect of Rost's theory has received the most negative critique and challenge from all sides. First Pfeiffer, in his presidential address, argued that the genre was biography on the basis that the 'story centers around the main characters, and national events are narrated in connection with personal history'.[147]

In the early 1960s Mowinckel challenged the designation of the genre as history. His basis for argument is that since there is no mention of a *spr dbry dwd*, and, since the *soper* was added to the administrative structure in Solomonic times, such historiography could not have been written during David's time. Thus, he designates the genre as 'family story'.[148] His was only the beginning of the attack.

Next Delekat took issue with Rost's treatment of the TSN and his designation of the intention of the narrator as being 'in majorem gloriam Salomonis'.[149] Delekat argues that the work provides a negative critique of both David and Solomon and is intended as a polemic against the monarchy on the order of 1 Samuel 8 and 10.17-27.[150] Thus, Delekat raised the possibility of a political intention in the writing of the narrative.

Thornton, while in general agreement with Rost on most points, added a minor twist to the issue of the political nature of the narrative. Instead of glorifying Solomon, Thornton argues, the narrative is intended to exonerate Solomon for the negative actions attributed to him in 1 Kings 2.[151] Thus he proposes that the main question is not, 'Who will sit on the throne?' Rather it is 'Why is Solomon on the throne?'[152] Thus, while he agrees with Delekat that there is a political intention in operation, he sees it as positive and not negative.

Delekat's view of the intention of the narrative as negative critique is advanced by both Würthwein and Langlamet. While Delekat concentrated upon the discrepancies between the actions of the TSN and Israelite law,[153] as noted above, Würthwein and Langlamet concentrated on inconsistencies within the TSN.[154] In both of their theories they envisage an original negative, anti-Davidic intention which was redacted and overlaid with a pro-Davidic/Solomonic presentation. In this manner they speak of 'political propaganda' as the genre of the material.

Gunn correctly objects to this designation of the genre as 'political propaganda' since he feels it is too broad a category. He is quick to note that there are political implications to the narratives in the

TSN, but suggests that the use of the term propaganda suggests that the effect of the narrative was to alter the political opinions of the reader, which he feels is too narrow a focus for interpretation of these narratives. Similarly, as he notes, the fact that one can argue a pro or con political intention makes the category useless.[155]

Whybray argues that the TSN should be designated as a wisdom novel, with the main intention being didactic.[156] While he also notes the political overtones of the work,[157] he draws heavily on comparisons between *mᵉšālîm* in the book of Proverbs and events and personalities in the TSN.[158] He divides the discussion into three parts: wisdom and folly, education of children, and the king. Finally he compares the TSN with the genre of 'political novel' in Egypt.[159] As noted above, others, such as Fontaine, have followed him in exploring the impact of wisdom upon this narrative.[160]

Whybray's thesis has received negative reviews by Crenshaw. He states the following regarding the trend to designate wisdom influence on the basis of the affinity between proverbial sayings and various blocks of literature:

> This trend has caught on so widely that the entire Hebrew canon is in danger of being swallowed... Clearly, such widening of the net threatens to distort the meaning of wisdom beyond repair. In every instance these claims rest upon circular reasoning.[161]

He is supported by Gunn's contention that 'Most of the correspondences between the narrative and Proverbs are generally stated themes which might belong to almost any piece of literature'.[162]

The third major designation of genre for the TSN is offered by Gunn, who argues for 'story'.[163] He objects to the designation of 'novel', since that term does not allow for or suggest the use of oral traditions as precursors to the final work. He has been negatively critiqued on this aspect of his thesis.[164]

As regards intention Gunn also differs with Rost. He first suggests that the major intention of story is to entertain.[165] Similarly he disagrees with the view that the function is the legitimation of the Solomonic reign. As he states,

> ... this is above all else a story about *David* and not any successor or potential successor.... We get little if any hint that we are to view either Amnon or Absalom as *Solomon's* rivals, nor that what is taking place in chapters 13–20 is a steady movement bringing us significantly nearer to the point where only Adonijah... will stand between Solomon and the throne.[166]

Thus some of those who have most ardently supported Rost on the issue of unity are the ones who have taken issue with him on the question of genre and intention. Apparently the TSN is a work which can lend itself to disparate interpretations of genre and intention, with each theorist using a different set of verses and subunits as the crux for a theory.

Finally it is interesting to note that there are those who argue for differing intentions of 2 Samuel 10-12 from 2 Samuel 13-20 and from 1 Kings 1-2. While Rost saw 10-12 as serving the purpose of introducing the successor to the throne,[167] Conroy points out that the absence of any mention of Solomon in 13-20 makes a 'Solomonic glorification' difficult to substantiate. Rather he argues that an 'unprejudiced reading of 2 Sam 13-20 shows that these chapters deal with the causes and outcome of an attempted coup d'état, not with the question of succession. . .'[168]

Similarly, as noted above, Flanagan argues that 2 Samuel 13-20 should be designated as a 'court history' while 2 Samuel 10-12 functions to overlay a succession theme on the former.[169] In the same manner, McCarter argues that 2 Samuel 13-20 is a 'royal apology' in which David's actions during the Absalom Revolt are defended,[170] while 2 Samuel 10-12 serves as an 'interpretive preface' to the events to follow.[171] Finally he argues that the birth of Solomon is not the apex of the complex. Thus it is incorrect to see an interest in Solomon as the concern of the unit.[172]

Maintaining a single or widely accepted intention for the total TSN has proven an impossible task. Similarly, the marked differences between the subject matter of 2 Samuel 10-12 and that of 2 Samuel 13-20, such as the presence or absence of Solomon, makes finding one intention difficult. In addition the fact that so many different designations can be given for genre, especially by those who are proponents of Rost's theory, makes his theory appear to be more and more untenable.

d. *Authorship and Dating*

Rost had wavered between whether the use of private details in the TSN suggested that the writer was an eye-witness of the events described, or whether, given the marked use of dialogue, the writer may have been one 'of particular sensitivity'.[173] He favored, however, the first option and was supported in this by several scholars. For example Wiener[174] and Ishida[175] argued that it was written by Nathan, since there are favorable portrayals of him and since 1

Chron 29.29 mentions *dbry ntn*. Segal argued it was written by Jehoshaphat, the *mazkîr*, mentioned in 2 Sam 8.16,[176] while Pfeiffer argued it was written by Ahimaaz, on the assumption that priests were the only truly literate persons in that time.[177]

Rost also argued that, since 1 Kings 1–2 covers the first three years of Solomon's reign, the work could not have been written during David's time. Similarly, since the end of the narrative suggests a time of relative peace, Rost suggests that it was written early in Solomon's reign, prior to the tensions with the north.[178]

Along with the notion of unity, Rost's position on authorship and dating is one of the most popular and agreed upon aspects of his theory. As Hertzberg notes, 'we are listening to the words of contemporaries'.[179] The most compelling reasons for this notion were given by von Rad who argued the point on two fronts. First he noted that the negative details about David and Solomon could only have been written at a time close to the events, when the readers would have been familiar with them, and, thus, would have expected them in a history work. Secondly he based his argument on the concept of a 'Solomonic Enlightenment Period'.[180] In this regard he is followed by many scholars.[181]

As in other matters related to Rost's theory, there are those who disagree with him. Eissfeldt continued to argue that 2 Samuel 9-20 was written by J because of the parallel nature of the narrative to the materials in 2 Samuel 2-6 and 8 and the positive reaction to Mephibosheth, Jonathan's descendant, which he likewise attributes to J.[182] He has not been supported much in this designation.

Carlson, as noted above, has argued that there was an oral prehistory to the materials on David, which he speculates were circulated either by women or Zadokite priests. He bases the first possibility on the fact that women play important roles in many of the narratives in 2 Samuel 10-24. He bases the second suggestion on the possibility that by circulating these stories, which present the royal family in a negative light, the priests would be attempting to show their independence from and scorn of the royal antics. He maintains, however, that the final work in 2 Samuel was compiled by the D-group.[183] He further argues that the materials have been arranged in terms of portraying David under the blessing (2 Sam 1-9) and David under the curse (2 Sam 10-24).[184] This D-group is considered to be Josianic in its time frame and in accord with the Deuteronomic reform and the Deuteronomic Code in its theology.[185]

McCarter, on the other hand, argues that while 2 Samuel 13–20 was written contemporaneously with the Davidic-Solomonic period,[186] 2 Samuel 10–12 was produced by a prophetic writer attempting to demonstrate that the king was not immune from divine judgment and was responsible to the law.[187] In the same manner he argues that the similarities between the wording in 1 Kings 1–2 with the narratives of 2 Samuel 10–20 are best explained by the notion that the writer of the Kings material had access to the Samuel materials and fashioned the latter correspondingly.[188]

The most radical proposal concerning the date of the TSN has been put forward by Van Seters, who argues for a post-exilic dating of the materials in the TSN. He argues that since the TSN contains materials negative to David, and since the Dtr presents David as the primary example of ideal kingship, it is difficult to explain the former's inclusion within the DtrH. This incongruity is heightened since the Chronicler does not include the materials found in the TSN.[189] Thus, he concludes that these materials were incorporated into the DtrH at a much later time by an anti-monarchic writer in the post-exilic era.[190] Similarly he argues that the eyewitness account thesis must be abandoned, since there was no historiography in Israel prior to the DtrH.[191]

Van Seters has indeed pointed to a pithy problem in terms of the negative portrayal of David in some of the scenes of the TSN, and the apparent inconsistency of these portrayals with the Dtr-idealized David. There are, however, two alternative ways of looking at the portrayal of David. As will be discussed below,[192] the David who abuses power in 2 Samuel 11 is different from the pious David of the flight from Absalom. Thus, there is not merely a negative, but a complex portrayal of David in the TSN.

Secondly, the complex in 1 Samuel 8–12, with its alternating positive and negative views of the kingship, illustrates how the Dtr presents a subject in an ambivalent fashion. The ambivalence in 1 Samuel 8–12 centers around the public or political need for a king, which must be balanced against the private tendency to abuse power (1 Sam 8.4-18). What is most interesting about the 1 Samuel complex is that Van Seters argues that this is a clearly Dtr construction.[193] Nonetheless, he overlooked the fact that this same ambivalence is an organizing motif in the Court History, which could lead also to its attribution to the DtrH.

As one looks at this listing of alternatives for dating and authorship, both those of Rost and his supporters and those of his detractors, one factor becomes very evident. All of these positions about dating and authorship are predicated upon particular views about the genre and function of the materials. For example, those who argue for historiography seek an earlier date. Similarly, those who argue for a legendary nature to the materials seek a later dating.

On the other hand, a major argument for an early dating was the use of negative details regarding David. As Carlson, McCarter, and Van Seters have demonstrated, this variable may lead to an alternative explanation. Thus, a major underpinning for Rost's dating has been challenged on several fronts.

3. *Conclusions*

The above discussions have demonstrated that major details about Rost's theory of a coherent, unified, historically reliable TSN including 2 Sam 6.16, 20-23; 9-20 and 1 Kings 1-2, composed during Solomonic times and explaining how he came to the throne has been challenged by both supporters and detractors. On the level of boundaries for the unit there is almost universal rejection of Rost's claims of a lost beginning which included parts of 2 Samuel 6 and 7. Similarly, there has been growing acceptance of a connection between the Ishbosheth complex with the Absalom complex. In the same manner there are more questions as to whether the materials in 1 Kings 1-2 are from the same hand as those in 2 Samuel or whether they are merely based upon the 2 Samuel materials.

Rost's theory of a coherent narrative has been challenged on the basis of close readings of the text. Those who have tried to maintain the thesis have done so primarily on the basis of the plot or story line, often glossing over rough spots in the text in favor of narrative threads. While this type of reading is appropriate to explaining the final form of the text, it does not meet the test of proving original unity and coherence. This is most notably demonstrated by the plethora of so-called 'unifying schemes' explaining the unity. Finally as noted above, within these schema we have seen broad categories, such as sex, which have tended to lump together such diverse issues as consenting adultery and rape.

The issue of genre and intention in Rost's theory has been most challenged. Some of his proponents have tried to push his designation of 'historical novel' into the realm of 'pure historiography'. Others have argued over political vs. wisdom settings. Similarly his opponents have argued over negative vs. positive intentions of the narrative.

Finally, on the issue of date and authorship, the above analysis has demonstrated the circular reasoning between genre and intention in setting the scope for the discussion. Most notably the main linchpin of Rost's theory, the use of negative details about David, has become a key issue in the arguments of his opponents. Thus, while on a broad, surface level of a final reading, Rost's theory has potential for applicability to the text, on the issues of unity, genre, and dating so many arguments have arisen as to necessitate a reinvestigation and reinterpretation of the complex.

Chapter 2

2 SAMUEL 10-12 AND THE REMAINDER OF
THE THRONE SUCCESSION NARRATIVE

In the previous chapter we reviewed the four major tenets underlying
Rost's theory of a Throne Succession Narrative and examined the
research which has appeared either in support of or in opposition to
each of his major tenets. In so doing we noted in general the types of
arguments and debates which have occurred in the past six decades
concerning this body of literature. It became clear that Rost's specific
conclusions have all been called into question in various ways by
both his supporters and his opponents.

It is our intention in this chapter to argue that the materials found
in 2 Samuel 10-12 are distinct from the other materials thought to be
part of the TSN. We shall first briefly review and critique the works
of those who have previously argued against the coherent unity of the
materials in 2 Samuel 9-20, 1 Kings 1-2, as well as those who have
argued against the initial inclusion of 10-12 within the TSN as
originally demarcated by Rost. We shall then demonstrate the
existence of marked stylistic and thematic dissimilarities between
2 Samuel 10-12 and the other units thought to be contained in the
TSN (i.e. 2 Sam 2-4, 13-20, and 1 Kgs 1-2). Next we shall examine
the prophecy-fulfillment schema presented in 2 Samuel 12 to
demonstrate the redactional character of much of this chapter and to
raise the question of the implications of this redaction for the
coherence of the unit and the interrelationship of 10-12 with 13-20.
Finally we shall demonstrate the existence of historical illusions
within 2 Samuel 10-12 which make its present location in the text
problematic in terms of the events described in chs. 13-20. Having
accomplished this, the case will then be made to warrant an
examination of 2 Samuel 10-12 as a composite unit originally

separate from 2 Samuel 9 and 13–20 and to argue for its interpolation at a time far removed from the events described.

1. *Previous Arguments against the Unity of 2 Samuel 9–20, 1 Kings 1–2*

As noted in the previous chapter, in 1963 Sigmund Mowinckel became the first scholar to attack the connection Rost sought to make between 2 Samuel 9–2 and 1 Kings 1–2. He based his argument on four dissimilarities between the materials and themes found in 2 Samuel 9–20 and those found in 1 Kings 1–2. First of all, Mowinckel noted the lack of continuity in the description of the age of David:

> [1 Kings 1–2] in no wise gives the impression of having been conceived as a continuation of 2 Samuel 9–20. Nothing in these chapters prepares us for the information in 1 Kings 1.1 that David was old and stricken in years; on the contrary, even in 2 Samuel 14–20 we have the impression that he still stands in his full strength. 1 Kings 1–2 gives the impression of having been written as the beginning of a history rather than as a finale.[1]

Secondly, he argued that the major focus of 1 Kings 1–2 is not so much the succession of the Davidides as it is the legitimacy of Solomon as the successor.[2]

Thirdly, in reconstructing the stages of composition he argued that, since there is mention of the 'scribe' *(soper)* in the administrative list of Solomon (1 Kgs 4.3) and of the *spr dbry šlmh* (1 Kgs 11.41), but no corollary mention of *spr dbry dwd*, then the Solomonic materials were the first monarchic traditions committed to writing.[3] Finally, he speculated that the collection of traditions on Solomon spawned an interest in collecting the traditions about David and Saul, with an eye toward the legitimation of David on the throne as the rightful successor to Saul.[4]

Thus, Mowinckel placed a wedge between the materials in 2 Samuel 9–20 and those in 1 Kings 1, primarily on the basis of the content and function of these blocks of narrative. Though he did not raise the issue of the unity of 9–20, he did open the door for re-examining this question. He has not been given the credit he deserves for reopening the door to critical investigation of the blocks of material in Rost's thesis. This is probably due to the fact that his claims were presented in sweeping categories and without sub-stantiated data to buttress his arguments.[5]

Almost a decade later James W. Flanagan argued against the original unity of 2 Samuel 9-20 and 1 Kings 1-2.[6] He presented a case for a Court History containing 9.1-11.1,[7] and 12.26-20.22 which was overlaid with a Succession Document now found in 2 Sam 11.2-12.25 and 1 Kings 1-2. Similar to Mowinckel, his starting point was a demonstration of the differences in the way the court functioned in 2 Samuel 9-20 when compared to 1 Kings 1-2. He noted such things as the difference between the vibrant David of 9-20 and the 'man too feeble to continue as monarch'[8] in 1 Kings 1-2. He also noted the differences in the way the narrators presented the resolution of problems, namely in 2 Samuel 9-20 the drama is played out to its conclusion in normal fashion, while in 1-2 the issues are resolved by executive order.[9] Similarly he contrasted the Absalom 'planned coup' with the 'straightforward assumption of power' by Adonijah.[10] In so doing he concluded that Absalom's revolt is better contrasted with the revolt of Sheba (2 Sam 20) than with Adonijah's succession.[11] Flanagan pointed to the lack of a narrative notice of the deity's concurrence with the course of events in 1 Kings 1-2, a feature found in 9-20.[12]

He also noted similarities to be found between the narratives of 2 Sam 11.2-12.25 and 1 Kings 1-2. He pointed to the appearance of similar characters in both sections and the presence of the theme of Solomonic succession, a connection which he claims 'needs no proof'.[13] However, he did not deal with the dissimilarities between 1 Kings 1-2 and 2 Samuel 10-12, for example, the passive role of Bathsheba in 2 Samuel 11-12, as opposed to her active involvement in the succession drama in 1 Kings 1-2, the adversarial vs. the advisory roles of Nathan, and the manipulative vs. the manipulated David. In fact, except for the similarity of the characters, the connection between the narratives in 2 Samuel 11-12 and those in 1 Kings 1-2 is as remote as what Flanagan finds in the other blocks of material.

The major argument advanced by Flanagan in support of the existence of a 'Court History' is a chiastic structure which he claims exists in 2 Samuel 9-20.[14] This chiasm begins and ends with the list of David's officers (8.16-18; 20.23-26) with its center being David's prayer in 16.23 that Ahithophel's advice be thwarted.[15] He argued that the intention of the 'Court History' is to record 'how David maintained the powers of office and continued to be the legitimate king of Israel and Judah'.[16]

Flanagan appears to be correct in his discernment of a marked difference between the Bathsheba–Nathan–Solomon complexes and the Absalom materials. His analysis thus had the effect of strengthening and expanding the work of Mowinckel. His theory, however, does not provide a satisfactory explanation of the origin and function of the unit in 2 Samuel 10–12. Similarly he does not resolve the issues of why the so-called 'succession document' was divided up and placed in 2 Samuel 10–12 and 1 Kings 1–2, nor did he specifically address the question of the relationship between this succession material and 2 Samuel 13–20, other than to state, 'Only later was the narrative used as a basis for the story of Solomon's succession'.[17]

A decade and a half after Mowinckel, Charles Conroy argued against the unity of the narrative in 2 Samuel 9–20 by positing that 2 Samuel 13–20 was a coherent unit which could and should be analyzed separately from both 2 Samuel 10–12 and 1 Kings 1–2.[18] He argued that 2 Samuel 13–20 warrants study as an independent story since it contains 'the basic narrative unity of a beginning, a middle, and an end'.[19] Thus, he took issue with Rost's contention that 'chapters 15–20 seem in no way to form a self-contained narrative. For on the face of it, there is lacking any well-wrought start and finish'.[20]

In addition to noting dissimilarities between materials in 2 Samuel 13–20 and those in other parts of the so-called TSN,[21] Conroy argued most convincingly for the unity of 13–20 in terms of the literary techniques of narrative patterns, plot action, and theme.[22]

Conroy's most convincing arguments came when he took issue with Rost's claim that the theme of succession is pervasive throughout the narrative. In particular he argued that in 2 Samuel 13–20, isolated from the remainder of the traditional TSN, this theme is not readily apparent. Specifically he argued that the Amnon and Sheba episodes are 'subordinated structurally and thematically to the story of Absalom's revolt', which is best described as a coup d'état, as opposed to a question of succession.[23] Additionally, in addressing the allusions to events in 2 Samuel 13–20 found in 1 Kings 1–2 he argued that this

> only shows that it needs 2 Samuel 13–20 as a preparation; it does not show that 2 Samuel 13–20 needs 1 Kings 1–2 as an indispensable continuation. . . .

The succession thematic proper to the writer of 1 Kings 1-2 englobes 2 Samuel 13-20 by *reinterpreting* those chapters in a way not directly contrary to, but still at variance with, their original intrinsic scope.[24](emphasis added)

Finally he argued that 'when the reader arrives at 20,22, narrative tension is at an end for the first time since 13,1'.[25]

Thus, the wedge between 2 Samuel 13-20 and the other parts of the so-called TSN was firmly and definitely lodged by Mowinckel, Flanagan, and Conroy. First, Mowinckel demonstrated the inconsistencies between the portrayals of David in 2 Samuel 9-20 from those in 1 Kings 1-2. Next, Flanagan demonstrated the inconsistencies between 2 Sam 11.2-12.25 and other materials in 2 Samuel 9-20. Finally, Conroy demonstrated the coherence and independence of 2 Samuel 13-20.

Building upon the above studies, McCarter, in his recent Anchor Bible commentary on 2 Samuel, has argued for the separation of 2 Samuel 10-12 from 13-20. In essence he concluded that the Absalom Revolt narrative in 2 Samuel 15-20 is pro-David in intention, while the Solomonic Succession narrative in 1 Kings 1-2 is pro-Solomonic in intention, and that while the latter relies heavily upon the former for its content, it was written by another hand.[26] Similarly he concluded that the narrative in 2 Sam 11.2-12.24 comes from a pre-Deuteronomistic prophetic strand of material[27] which was added to the Absalom materials as an 'interpretive preface'.[28] First of all, he bases his argument on the internal unity of the narrative in 11.2-12.24 contending that the Nathan-David confrontation in 2 Sam 12.1-15a was deemed to be necessary to resolve the moral ambiguities of 2 Sam 11.2-27a, the David-Bathsheba-Uriah incidents.[29] Secondly he points to differences in the portrayal of characters in the various blocks. For example, he noted that the depiction of David in 2 Samuel 11 is of a more active king than the passive depiction in 2 Samuel 13-20.[30] Thirdly he argues on the basis of his theory of the composition of the book of Samuel that since the structure of this narrative in which a king commits a sin, is rebuked by a prophet, and then confesses is similar to that found in 1 Samuel 15, this must be the work of a pre-Deuteronomistic prophetic hand.[31]

While in agreement with the direction in which McCarter has built upon the works of these previous scholars, I find myself in disagreement with his final conclusion. McCarter has furthered the work of demonstrating that the materials in 2 Samuel 11–12 are different from the materials in 2 Samuel 13–20 and 1 Kings 1–2. He does not, however, account for the use of the materials on the Ammonite Wars in chs. 10 and 12 other than to speculate that the prophetic redactor accepted them from an old annalistic source.[32] Similarly, his theory does not account for the origin of the narrative on the David–Bathsheba–Uriah incident and how it was incorporated into the narrative as a whole. These latter points will be explored throughout the remainder of this book.

2. *Thematic Dissimilarities between 2 Samuel 10–12 and the Remainder of the TSN*

As noted in the previous chapter, the major argument in support of Rost's thesis of a coherent narrative in 2 Samuel 9–20 + 1 Kings 1–2 is that of the story line.[33] Many works have concentrated on this dimension of the complex and sought to reveal the story's 'unifying themes and motifs'.[34] The fact that so many differing schemata can be proposed, each highlighting a different aspect of 10–12, which is supposedly developed in the remainder of the work, suggests the lack of any such unifying motif in the original materials. Similarly, the suggested motifs appear to be more pervasive in one block than the other (10–12 or 13–20), depending upon the particular schema being presented. In these discussions it is obvious that questions of boundaries, unity, genre, intention, and date can best be posited for the entire complex if one speaks of general motifs and avoids specific analysis of the text.

Several examples demonstrate that the existence of a proposed motif is preponderant primarily in either one section of the narrative (10–12) or in another (2–4, 13–20, 1 Kgs 1–2) but not in all. Brueggemann's attempt to show that the Succession Narrative is the basis for the organization of the J primeval history in Genesis 2–11 drew analogies between the David–Bathsheba incident and the Adam and Eve incident. In so doing, however, he had continually to qualify his position with disclaimers. For example,

> Though [Genesis 3] shows the woman taking the initiative, that *does not seem to be a significant departure*. . . . The *nuances* of the story are *different*. In 2 Samuel 12, the central motif is confession whereas here it is fear. But the reactions are not unrelated.[35] (emphasis added)

Such qualifications are not as numerous in the remaining sections of his article. As noted above, however, Brueggemann gave primary attention to the broadest motifs rather than to the nuances of the text.

Blenkinsopp ran into similar difficulties in his attempt to draw parallels between the pentateuchal source J and the TSN. He cited the designation *yph* for royalty, which appears in 2 Sam 13.1; 14.25, 27; and 1 Kgs 1.6 (compare Gen 2.4-9 and Ezek 28.12), as well as the theme of fratricide as similarities.[36] We must note, however, that these terms and motifs do not appear in chs. 10–12. Similar to Brueggemann, Blenkinsopp tried to connect Bathsheba with Eve under the motif of the 'woman who brings death',[37] but again we must note the dissimilarities of the active Eve in Genesis 3, as opposed to the seemingly passive Bathsheba in 2 Samuel 11–12.[38]

Another instance of this tendency to establish a unifying motif but one which is primarily found in chs. 13–20 is Whybray's argument for wisdom influence on the TSN. He stated: 'Every incident illustrates either the application of wisdom and/or counsel to a particular situation, or the consequences of not applying it: the folly of acting without it'.[39] He then proceeded to illustrate how this functions in the text. All but one of his examples, however, occur in chs. 13–20.[40] In the same manner, while he analyzed the use of such terms as *ḥkm* and *ʿṣh*, and the similarities between war and royal motifs found in Proverbs,[41] he did not take note of their absence in the Ammonite War story within the David-Bathsheba-Uriah incident (11.14-25). On the other hand, he interpreted the prophecy/fulfillment motif of 2 Sam 12.11-12 and 16.20-22 as an example of wisdom.[42]

Most recently, Carol Fontaine[43] has argued for wisdom influence on 2 Samuel 11–12. In so doing, she argues for a parallel structure of the narrative in 2 Samuel 11–12 with that of 1 Kings 3.

As with the case of Whybray, all of her specific examples of wisdom in the TSN are outside of 2 Samuel 10–12.[44] In order to overcome this hurdle she compares Solomon asking for *ḥkmh* in 1 Kings 3, with David's inquiring about Bathsheba (11.3), which she calls folly, the antithesis of wisdom.[45] In another example, she compares David on the roof (11.2) with Solomon on the high place of Gibeon.[46] Similarly, she claims the prophetic speech in 2 Samuel 12 is the corollary of Solomon's judgments in 1 Kings 3.[47] All of the parallels are strained and none of the vocabulary to support her claim is found in 2 Samuel 11–12. Thus, one sees that while wisdom may be a valid designation of *Sitz im Leben* for 1 Kings 3, none of the indications are found in 2 Samuel 11–12.

Sexuality has been one of the major organizing motifs proposed as functioning in the TSN. While the traditional pre-Rostian view of the materials in 2 Samuel 9–20 concentrated on David's lust and its consequences for his family,[48] Carlson was the first contemporary scholar to argue that these materials were organized around the theme of sexual misconduct.[49] He argued that the materials in 2 Samuel 10–20 were arranged so that they correspond with the sexual laws of the D-group[50] found in Deuteronomy 22–23, which he termed a '*šākab* Composition'. Specifically he drew parallels between 2 Samuel 10–12 and Deut 22.22 (adultery), 2 Samuel 13–14 and Deut 22.28-29 (rape), and 2 Samuel 15–20 and Deut 23.1 (sex with a step-mother).[51] He did not, however, make the claim that the unity of the materials was the product of the D-group. Rather he first argued that 2 Samuel 13–14 was interconnected and interrelated with 15–20 by catchwords and themes associating the Amnon and Absalom incidents, which already reflected the '*šākab* Composition' contained within them. The association of 13–14 and 15–20 was pre-Deuteronomic and '*naturally* connected with the D-group's arrangement of such laws in Deut 22.28-23.1'[52] (emphasis added).

In the same manner he argued that 2 Samuel 10–12 was pre-Deuteronomistically associated with 13–20 on the basis of the '*šākab* Composition' pattern. These chapters served as a prelude to the depiction of David as having 'weakness over against his sons' in 13–20.[53] He noted, as he did with the previous units, that catchwords interconnected the two and that in both instances the *šākab* led to the death penalty.[54]

While Carlson is correct that there is the presence of sexual activity within each of the units, the treatment of it is radically different in each. As will be noted below, the treatment in ch. 11 is almost businesslike,[55] while that in ch. 13 is described in erotic terms (cf. 13.9-11). Similarly, though he speaks of the penalties exerted in all three instances, they do not in any one of them coincide with the casuistic formulations for penalties to be exacted in these instances of *šākab* as prescribed in the Deuteronomic Code.[56] In the same manner, while sex plays a part in all three of these units, there is more to the narrative threads than just this.[57] Thus, his theory is called into question at the organizational level as well as on a redactional level.

The latest scholar to argue that sexuality is a major organizing schema for the TSN is J.P. Fokkelman. As noted above,[58] he picked up on this theme in his depiction of the pattern whereby 'David four times loses a son through a violent death following and elicited by the unjustified sexual possession of a woman (women)'.[59] In this manner he points to David and Bathsheba, whose adultery leads to the death of their firstborn child; Amnon, whose rape of Tamar leads to his being killed by Absalom; Absalom's 'going to the concubines of his father', which leads to his death in battle; and Adonijah's request for Abishag, which leads to his death at the altar of Yahweh.[60]

One must note, however, in regard to this scheme that not all the women are possessed, since Adonijah never has his request honored. Similarly, the one to die is not always the one who perpetrates the sexual act. Furthermore, given David's flight and abandonment of the capital city and his harem, one could not technically call Absalom's appropriation of the harem, 'unjustified'.[61] In the same manner, to term his death the result of this sexual act, as opposed to seeing this sexual act as an appropriate manifestation of the rebellion motif, distorts the narrative and raises a subtheme to the level of the main theme. Finally, as noted above,[62] in the last three examples the major dynamic is one of power play in which the one attempting to exert influence over the other uses the woman as a ploy and/or legitimizing agent.[63]

Thus, we see that attempts at positing one unifying scheme for the whole narrative of 2 Samuel 9–20 + 1 Kings 1–2 fall into either one or another of two pitfalls. One is that the schema is either preponderantly present in one of the segments and either lacking in another or the claim for its existence is subject to the charge of 'stretching the point'. The second is that the organizing schema is so general that it either misses the nuances of the narrative or raises subthemes to the level of major themes.

3. *Literary Dissimilarities between 2 Samuel 10–12 and the Remainder of the TSN*

As we have noted, those who argue for similarities in subject matter *and* style between 2 Samuel 2–4 and the Succession Narrative proper[64] draw almost all of their parallels from chs. 9, 13–20 and 1 Kings 1–2, and not from chs. 10–12.[65] For example, the mourning behavior of David over the death of Abner (2 Sam 3.31-39) is quite similar to that expressed at the news of the death of Absalom (2 Sam 19.1), but they are both markedly different from the response to the death of the child in ch. 12.[66] In the same manner, the conflict with the 'sons of Zeruiah' in ch. 3 is similar to that in ch. 19,[67] but this aspect of David's relationship to the sons of Zeruiah is opposite to the cooperative and non-competitive ventures between David and Joab depicted in chs. 10–12.[68]

An example of those who extend the boundaries of the TSN to include the 'Ishbosheth story' (2 Sam 2–4), finding primary similarities between it and chs. 13–20, is represented by Van Seters' latest work. He makes the claim that in chs. 2–4

> David sits at home in Hebron while his men do all the fighting, a
> pattern that is consistent in the Court History. David is also no
> longer in complete control of his own men or affairs. He begins to
> show that weakness so characteristic in the Court History.[69]

Again we must note that this is not the picture of David found in chs. 10–12. While Van Seters notes the difference in the war story in 10.15–19a, which he excludes from the Court History,[70] he nevertheless ignores the fact that the picture of David in ch. 11 is of one who manipulates the contingencies until they suit his own ends. He sends (*šlḥ*) for Bathsheba and Uriah, as well as sending Uriah with his own death warrant. Similarly, his mourning behaviors in ch. 12 are to manipulate the deity and, as he shows in his response to his servants, they are totally under his control. Thus, while such arguments have sought to extend the boundaries of the narrative, they also have had the effect of raising the question of whether the complex in chs. 10–12 derives from the hand of the writer of 2–4 and 13–20, as he maintains.[71]

Other dissimilarities exist between the portrayal of both the characters and events depicted in 2 Samuel 10–12 and those presented in 13–20 and 1 Kings 1–2 in addition to the ones just mentioned. For example, while Rost[72] and von Rad[73] make a point of the great attention given to explicit psychological details with regard to the characters' motivation for their actions within the narrative, such details of psychological analysis are not to be found in ch. 11. For example, Gunn stated,

> It is striking how the emotions and actions of chapter 13 are
> heightened compared with those of the chapters 11 and 12. David's
> dealings with Bathsheba have a curiously matter-of-fact character.

... There is nothing here about David's emotions, nothing about 'love' or other feelings for Bathsheba. ... Likewise we hear nothing of Bathsheba's response, ...

The contrast with the Amnon and Tamar episode could not be more marked.[74]

He then went on to argue for a 'broad connection between the two episodes... even if it is not quite so obvious how precisely the one can be the *consequence* of the other'.[75] On the one hand, to argue that there is marked dissimilarity in the units, and then to argue there is definite unity ignores the implications of the first observation. It is as though the interpreters take the presupposition of unity for granted and then impose this on all the possibilities for interpreting the data.[76]

In similar fashion Alter characterized 2 Samuel 10–12 as a narrative 'dense with moral and psychological meanings and possibilities' which must be interpreted by what the characters 'repeat, report or distort of the speech of others'.[77] The 'psychological meanings and possibilities' were elaborated upon by Berlin who argued in regard to 2 Samuel 11–12 that

> Throughout the entire story the narrator has purposely subordinated the character of Bathsheba. He has ignored her feelings and given the barest notice of her actions. The reader can *feel the whole range of David's emotions*: sexual desire, frustration... indignation... shame... grief.... The only emotions ascribed to Bathsheba are mourning at the death of her husband and grief at the death of her child[78] (emphasis added).

What is significant in these statements is that all of these emotions must be *'felt'* by the reader, since the writer does not specify these.[79] Similarly, to decry the absence of attention to Bathsheba's emotions, and then to discuss psychological portrayal is to ignore the data in favor of a predisposed position.

The latest attempt to resolve the tension between 'psychologized' readings of 2 Samuel 11 and the lack of specifically related narrative and dialogical notations within the text itself is to argue that ambiguity is the major intention of the writer. As Perdue correctly noted,

> One of the major difficulties in assessing the David character results from the type of narrator in the Succession Narrative.... When one examines the narrator's stance in the Succession

Narrative, it is obvious he *does more 'showing' than 'telling'*....
What is more, he usually declines to provide the motives behind
the characters' actions . . .[80] (emphasis added).

Perdue proceeds to argue that the key to this lack of 'providing
motives' is the author's intention to present the David character as
ambiguous.[81] Thus, when it became apparent that arguments built
on the importance of character portrayal to the narrative were seen
to be lacking in 10–12, this has been turned into an argument for
ambiguity.

A further example of dissimilarity between 2 Samuel 10–12 and
2 Samuel 2–4, 13–20 is the make-up of the characters in the scenes.
In the former we have David, Joab, Bathsheba, Uriah, Solomon,[82]
and Nathan as the major characters. With the exception of Uriah,
who dies, and David and Joab, the other main characters do not
appear in the narratives in 13–20. Interestingly, in the two lists of
David's officials found in 2 Sam 8.16-18 and 20.23-26,[83] which are
generally taken to be historically reliable data,[84] there is no mention
of Nathan as having a function at the court, while 2 Samuel 7, 12 and
1 Kings 1 present him as an integral part of the court life with access
to the king and with a divine mediatory role. Given this access to the
court and his role in ch. 7, one wonders why he is not mentioned in
the retinue which fled Jerusalem with David during the Absalom
revolt.[85] In his place we have the *yoʿeṣ*,[86] the advisor, and the *ḥakam/
ḥakamah*,[87] the wise person, as the ones upon whom the king is
dependent for his course of action.[88] Thus, there is a marked shift in
the characters who appear in 10–12 in comparison with those who
appear in 13–20. In addition there is a marked shift from prophetic to
wisdom-led characters.

A third set of differences comes in the theological perspectives of
the units. With the exception of 2 Sam 12.15b-23, the illness and
death of the first child born to David and Bathsheba,[89] there is no
suggestion about David's actions that Yahweh is either watching or
caring about what goes on, either in the battle reports or in the
Bathsheba affair. In the flight from and return to Jerusalem,
however, we see repeated references to Yahweh's control and
favoritism for David's side.[90] The latter references read like a litany
of faith affirmation. In the one scene where David does turn to
Yahweh in chs. 10–12, we see him functioning more in a manipulative
way. Thus, in the flight from Jerusalem materials (15.16–17.28),
David is presented as a beleaguered and positive character,[91] while in

the Bathsheba–Uriah affair (11.2–12.25) he is the 'ruthless despot'. Though modern-day scholars raise questions about the efficacy of David's administrative skills in his response to the challenges from Absalom,[92] 2 Samuel 15–20 presents him as the pious king who has ultimate trust in Yahweh. This on the other hand must be contrasted with the David of ch. 11, who is shown to be less 'pious' than Uriah (v. 11).

Thus, there are marked contrasts between the materials in 2 Samuel 10–12 and the remainder of the segments argued to be part of the TSN. These differences are on the level of character portrayal, subject matter, and cast of characters. In the same manner, however, the very areas of dissimilarities find common expression in 2 Samuel 2–4 and 13–20. Therefore, the data suggest that 2 Samuel 10–12 should be treated as a separate unit from the other sections.

4. *Prophecy-Fulfillment Schema of 2 Sam 12.1-15a*

We now turn our attention to the argument that the unity of the TSN is based on the fact that chs. 13–20 and 1 Kings 1–2 are part of a prophecy-fulfillment schema fulfilling the Nathan oracles in 2 Sam 12.7b-14.[93] Those who maintain this position do so while arguing that the first two oracles in vv. 7b-12 are most probably secondary to the text (these texts will be discussed in detail below, see Chapter 4§4).

As we noted above[94] these positions are contradictory. In other words, the claim to a coherent narrative rests upon the evidence provided by material which is deemed to be secondary to the text. Once these verses (i.e. the judgments that 'the sword will never leave your house', 2 Sam 12.10, and that 'your wives will be despoiled in the sunlight', 2 Sam 12.11) are admitted to be secondary to the speech, then the claim that they are '*the* unifying elements' which bind the narrative together begs the question of unity. At the same time, it poses the possibility that the unity of 2 Samuel 10–12 with chs. 13–20 is not original but redactional.

In looking at the ways in which previous writers have attempted to handle the tension of maintaining these seemingly contradictory positions, two major patterns become obvious. The first is to deny that the redactional nature of the material necessitates its lateness. Thus, Hertzberg argued that, 'The punishment fits the crime. This need not, of course, be a sign of late composition, but the passage will certainly be a later development'.[95] The problem is that he did not speculate as to when 'later' could be. Thus, while he affirmed the redactional possibilities, he attempted to mute the implication that the connection between the larger blocks may also be late.

Gunn provides the classic example of the second pattern, which is to disclaim any hope of identifying the redactional materials. Thus, he argued,

> while it is more than likely that the pronouncements by Nathan against David in 2 Samuel 12 have been reworked (probably at the stage of incorporating the King David Story into the history as a whole) I doubt that the extent of the reworking can be defined with any certainty.[96]

In this pattern, while the redactional possibilities are affirmed, the methodological pursuit of them is discouraged, thereby pushing for a final reading as the only viable option.

In contrast to these positions, several arguments have been advanced for identifying the time and extent of the redactional elements in 2 Samuel 12. The first set is represented by the work of Smend,[97] Dietrich,[98] and Veijola,[99] who argue that the Nathan materials are in part or wholly the work of DtrP. In the same manner Meadows has isolated specific deuteronomic wording in ch. 12.[100] In contrast to this, Campbell has lately argued that it is a pre-Deuteronomic prophetic redactor at work.[101]

That the unity of 2 Samuel 10–12 and chs. 13–20 has been created by redactional interpolations in the Nathan oracles of judgment is reinforced by several features in the research noted above. Thus, the door was opened further to the possibility that the continuity between chs. 10–12 and 13–20 is the result of the redactional addition of 2 Sam 12.7b-12 in an attempt to join these separate and possibly previously unrelated blocks of material. None of these scholars maintains such a position. Rather, they focus upon which verse(s) in ch. 12 was/were added to an already existing 'Succession Narrative'. It is our contention, however, that once there is raised the possibility of these connective pieces being redactional, the question of unity and arrangement of the materials in the TSN must be reopened.

5. Problems Raised by the Historical Allusions in 2 Samuel 10–12 in Relation to 13–20

Thus far the arguments have centered on literary dissimilarities between 2 Samuel 10-12 and the other parts of the TSN. The current location of this block also raises thorny questions for historical reconstruction. As noted previously[102] the prevailing view of the narratives of the Ammonite Wars found in 2 Sam 10.1-11.1, 12.26-31 was that of Rost, namely that these were taken from an annalistic source contemporaneous with the events described and, thus, are historically reliable. Similarly it was argued that they function only to provide a backdrop into which the David-Bathsheba-Uriah-Nathan narrative is interpolated.[103] In this he has been followed by most scholars,[104] with few exceptions.[105] In so doing, however, interpreters have ignored the war story found in 2 Sam 11.16-17. Similarly they have run into difficulties in relating the historical allusions[106] in these war narratives to references to the same individuals and locations in other parts of the book of Samuel.

Difficulty arises, for example, in the mention of the death of Nahash, king of the Ammonites in 2 Sam 10.1 and the mention of some *hesed* which he demonstrated toward David. First of all, most scholars have argued that these texts must refer to the same Nahash who was Saul's enemy and who attacked the people of Jabesh-Gilead (1 Sam 11). Secondly they argue that this *hesed* must refer to the way Nahash treated David during his fugitive years in flight from Saul.[107]

One difficulty with this interpretation, however, is that the stories of David's flight from Saul (1 Sam 19-29) place him in Judahite territory, the Negeb, and in Philistia. The only reference to him in a Transjordanian context is in the story of the relocation of his parents in Moab (1 Sam 22.3-4). None of these stories connect him with Ammon. Thus, the text of Samuel gives no evidence for the positing of a David-Nahash alliance during his renegade years.

A second set of problems associated with the historical allusions within 2 Samuel 10-12 and other parts of the book of Samuel concerns the relationship between the Ammonite War narratives of 10.1-11.1 and 12.26-31 with those of 2 Sam 8.3-8. In both of these accounts David is in conflict with Arameans and there is a mention of the king of Zobah, who is soundly defeated and, in ch. 8, humiliated. One way of interrelating these texts is to see them as describing the same situation.[108] Another is to see them as sequential, but with the wars in ch. 10 preceding those in ch. 8.[109] A third alternative is to view them as sequential events.[110]

A third historical allusion which appears in 2 Samuel 10–12 and which must be interrelated with another within 2 Samuel 13–20 is the reference to David's refuge and reception in Mahanaim during his flight from Absalom.[111] The text states that 'Shobi the son of Nahash from Rabbah of the Ammonites' along with others met and greeted David and his retinue with supplies. This is generally explained as the act of a 'political official' or 'colonial administrator' appointed by David after the siege of Rabbah.[112]

One problem with such an interpretation is the irregularity of such behavior. By this we mean that when an occupying regime experiences political turmoil and strife, the tendency is for the vassal states to rebel, rather than giving comfort. Given the depiction of the conquest, humiliation and subjugation of the Ammonites,[113] the last action one would expect is that described in the greeting of Shobi. It is for this reason that McCarter raised the possibility that the Absalom revolt preceded the Ammonite War materials and this act of Shobi is the *ḥesed*[114] referred to in 2 Sam 10.1.

A fourth historical allusion found in 2 Samuel 10–12 which needs to be interrelated with references outside this unit is found in 2 Sam 11.3, where Bathsheba is identified as the 'daughter of Eliam'. An Eliam is mentioned in 2 Sam 23.34 as the son of Ahithophel the Gilonite. The question arises as to whether these are the same individuals. If they are, the question arises why Ahithophel, Bathsheba's grandfather, would support Absalom,[115] her child's rival to the throne. Or might this be a further indication that this unit is out of chronological order?[116]

Given the general consensus that the 'exact chronological sequence [of events in the reign of David] eludes us',[117] one is surprised by the rigid adherence to the ordering of the events in 2 Samuel 9–20 for the retelling of the history. In addition, the general consensus that the 'writer sometimes groups his subject matter more in terms of content than chronological order'[118] would make one wonder why there has been so little scholarly questioning of standard interpretations of these historical allusions. At any rate the historical difficulties produced by the present location of chs. 10–12 indicate that we cannot accept Rost's assumption that the TSN represented an historically reliable and an eyewitness account of events.

6. *Conclusions*

2 Samuel 10–12 is composed of the Ammonite War Narratives (10.1–11.1), the story of the David–Bathsheba adultery and marriage and the murder of Uriah (11.2-27a), the account of a confrontation between David and Nathan with the judgment speeches of Nathan (11.27b-15a), the story of the death of the child conceived in adultery and the birth of Solomon (12.15b-25), and the account of the end of the Ammonite Wars (12.26-31). The question arises as to how this block of material was so organized and placed in its current location.

We have seen that there are marked thematic and literary dissimilarities between 2 Samuel 10–12 and the blocks of material in 2 Samuel 2–4 and 13–20. Such differences would suggest a different origin for the materials. In addition, we have noted that the passage which presently provides structural continuity between these blocks (2 Sam 12.7b-12) is secondary to the units. This suggests a literary development in which the blocks of materials were secondarily edited. Finally, we have seen that there are historical allusions to events within 2 Samuel 10–12 which presuppose events described in 2 Samuel 13–20. This raises the question of whether the narratives in 2 Samuel 11–12 are found in their chronologically correct location or whether this is additional evidence of redactional activity in relocating units out of chronological sequence to fit a theological schema. The latter alternative appears to describe the situation better. Such a position goes completely counter to Rost's theory of a unified TSN originating from one hand contemporaneous with the events.

On the other hand the question arises as to whether 2 Samuel 10–12 itself is a coherent block of material or a compilation. The issues of the development of this unit and its incorporation into its present location must now be our concern.

Chapter 3

THE AMMONITE WAR MATERIALS
2 SAMUEL 10.1–11.1; 12.26-31

Gressmann appeared to have given the classical formulation for dealing with the so-called Ammonite War materials in 2 Samuel 10–12, when he stated:

> In comparison with other contemporary war reports, here we are dealing with an excellent 'historical narrative'. For whereas usually only those individual sections are selected which have arrested the attention of the popular narrator, here we gain a real insight into the whole course of the campaign, whose main stages are clearly indicated.[1]

Having designated the genre of the material as 'historical narrative', he also concluded that it should be dated close to the occurrence of the events, and that the material is a unity. The latter point is seen in his outline of the narrative:

Introduction—cause of war—10.1-5
First campaign—with the Arameans—10.6-14
Second campaign in another year—10.15-19
Third campaign—11.1; 12.26-31[2]

The designation of the events in this material as the 'Ammonite Wars' suggests the appropriateness of this division and analysis. His analysis has been adopted by almost all commentators and historians of Israel.[3]

Gressmann's view has not gone unchallenged, however. H. Smith,[4] Winckler,[5] and most recently Van Seters[6] have argued against the unity of the materials by designating the 'second campaign' (10.15-18) as being from another source on the basis of the mention of Hadadezer (from *'br hnhr*), the presence of David at the battle site, and the section's affinity to 2 Sam 8.3-8. Though in disagreement with this contention, Rost argued that the so-called 'Introduction' to the Ammonite Wars (10.1-5) was similar in style to 2 Samuel 11, and thus not part of the original war materials.[7] Finally, Flanagan connects these narratives with the reference to Shobi son of Nahash in 2 Samuel 17.27 rather than with the David–Bathsheba–Uriah incident, and thus sees them as part of the 'court history' and not the TSN.[8]

Similarly, there is still debate as to how, when and by whom these war narratives were gathered. Rost maintained that the writer of the TSN rewrote an introduction to the Ammonite War materials to make for a smoother interpolation of the David–Bathsheba incident.[9] Van Seters has argued that the writer of the 'Court History' used Dtr materials from ch. 8 in order to integrate his narrative into an existing narrative sequence.[10] McCarter has argued that a pre-Dtr prophetic redactor had knowledge that the David–Bathsheba adultery occurred during the siege of Rabbah and, therefore, constructed these materials from annalistic sources.[11]

In the following discussion, we shall demonstrate that these so-called 'Ammonite War narratives' are not a unity. We shall also argue that the structure, style, and arrangement of these materials have affinity with similar passages within the DtrH, and that it was the Dtr redactors who produced the final form of these materials.

As the story is presently told, David, upon hearing of the death of Nahash, the Ammonite king, sent a delegation with a gift to the heir apparent, Hanun, at Rabbah. Hanun's advisors persuaded him that David was really sending spies. The Ammonite king thereupon disgraced the messengers, an act which precipitated a war between Israel and Ammon (10.1-5). Ammon secured assistance from several Aramean states, but they were no match for the Israelite army commanded by Joab and Abishai (10.6-14). As a result of this defeat Hadadezer gathered more forces to engage once again in battle with David, this time at Helam, but the Arameans were again defeated and ended their coalition with Ammon (10.15-19). In the following year Joab was sent to besiege Rabbah (11.1), and upon its capture David subjugated the Ammonites (12.26-31).

The following detailed structural outline of the text manifests several dissimilarities and discontinuities of wording, syntax, style, and concepts, which militate against the above unified reading and interpretation of the text. As we shall see, first of all, sections of the narrative contain vague and general references to personalities and locations whereas other portions utilize specific names and localities.

Secondly, the names of the actors and groups change from unit to unit. Thirdly, the transitions from one section to another are awkward. Fourthly, the structure of the narratives indicates rather striking dissimilarities in the form and intention of the various battle reports. The suspicion, therefore, arises that we have neither a unified source nor a progression of events, but rather a compilation of different traditions.

1. *The Introductory Narrative (2 Sam 10.1-6a)*

Outline of 2 Sam 10.1-6a

I. Unsuccessful diplomatic exploit (1-6a)
   A. The precipitating event (1)
      1. Introductory formula—*wyhy 'ḥry kn*
      2. Report of the death of an unnamed Ammonite king
      3. Report of succession to the throne by Hanun
   B. Response of David to the death of the king (2)
      1. Speech of David (2a)
         a. Designation of speaker
         b. Statement of intention—*'‘śh ḥsd*
         c. Reason for intention—*k'šr ‘śh 'byw ‘mdy*
      2. Report of David's gift—*wyšlḥ lnḥmw*
      3. Report of arrival of David's servants—*wyb'w*
   C. Response of Ammonites to gift (3-4)
      1. Speculation of Ammonite officers (3)
         a. Designation of speaker and addressee
         b. Questioning of David's sincerity—*hmkbd. . . ky šlḥ*
         c. Reinterpretation of David's actions—*hlw' b‘bwr ḥqwr*
            . . . *wlrglh wlhpkh šlḥ*
      2. Response of Hanun to David's Servants (4)
         a. Seizure—*wyqḥ*
         b. Disgrace—*wyglḥ . . . wykrt*
         c. Dismissal—*wyšlḥm*
II. Responses to Hanun's actions (5-6a)
   A. David's response (5)
      1. Report of telling David—*wygdw*
      2. Report of intercepting—*wyšlḥ lqr'tm*
      3. Reason for interception—*ky hyw. . . nklmym*
      4. David's Message
         a. Designation of speaker
         b. Instructions
            (1) Present action—*šbw*
            (2) Location—Jericho

          (3) Time span—*'d yṣmḥ*
          (4) Future action—*wšbtm*
   B.   *bny 'mwn's* response
        1. Assessment—*wyr'w*
        2. Reason—*ky nb'šw*

The outline of these verses indicates that it is possible to view the narrative as a self-contained unit. It begins with the formula *wyhy 'ḥry kn*, which signals a break with the preceding and the beginning of a new narrative.[12] Similarly the subject has changed from Mephibosheth in 9.13[13] to Hanun. In the same manner v. 5 contains David's response to Hanun's actions, namely, care for the messengers, with no suggestion that there is need for any further action.[14] The question arises, therefore, as to whether the unit ends in v. 5, or in v. 6a as our outline suggests. In v. 6 there are three verbs in the third person masculine plural imperfect with *waw*-consecutive, all of which have the same subject, *bny 'mwn*. In addition to this observation is the fact that the name, *bny 'mwn*, appears twice in the sentence as the subject of consecutive verbs, which is syntactically unusual.[15] Were both of these verbs relating sequentially causal actions (i.e. they feared, and therefore they sent), there would be no need for the second appearance of the *bny 'mwn*. This point is best demonstrated by the lack of repetition of the subject in the third clause, *wyśkrw 't*. . . . Thus, it appears that v. 6a should be seen as the reaction of the *bny 'mwn* to the actions of Hanun, while 6b begins a different unit.[16]

The narrative of 10.1-6a begins with a problem, the death of an unnamed Ammonite king, presumably Nahash, and a description and reason for David's response. It continues with recording the hostile response of the new monarch, and descriptions of David's and the Ammonites' responses to his actions. In both situations the reader is struck by the consistency of the presentation of David's responses. He begins by demonstrating care for Hanun *''śh ḥsd*, and he ends by demonstrating care for the messengers, *šbw . . . wšbtm*. Thus, the consistency of his portrayal holds throughout the unit.

The unit beginning in 10.1 opens with the introductory formula, *wyhy 'ḥry kn*. This expression appears as an introductory formula four other times in 2 Samuel (2.1; 8.1; 13.1; 21.18).[17]

This introductory copula, *wyhy 'ḥry kn*, usually translated 'after this', implies a chronological or sequential ordering of the materials preceding and following the formula. Commentators have maintained that it is a loose 'link' between the units and that it has no usefulness as a chronological tool.[18] While Rost dismisses any attribution of significance to the formula,[19] others have long noted its occurrences in 2 Samuel, but they have not come to a consensus as to its function or origin within the total work. Most, however, agree that it is redactional.[20]

Since, with only two exceptions,[21] the formula only appears within the Deuteronomistic History and in parallel passages in Chronicles,[22] some scholars have suspected it to be of Dtr origin. The difficulty in arriving at consensus about the origin of the formula rests in a disagreement as to its function in the text. With regard to the passages in 2 Samuel, Carlson has argued that

> one characteristic of Deuteronomic history is that it is divided into different periods, marked by discourses, legal edicts and the like; the temporal function of this copula is entirely in accordance with this general principle in 2 Samuel.[23]

Meadows takes issue with him on this point in arguing that unlike the Dtr formula *wyhy 'ḥry mwt*, which denotes specific periods in the history of Israel, such is not the case for this formula.[24] Similarly, Rost had argued that the formula was 'purely temporal (and not causal)';[25] thus its function was less defined than Carlson would want to suggest. In fact Carlson himself refrains from giving the copula the stamp of the Dtr when he states:

> Analysis of the structure of the complex [2 Samuel 10-12, 13-14, and 15-20] shows that these three sections cannot be regarded as three separate narratives, combined by the D-group to form 2 Samuel 10-20 by the use of the copula in question. The copula is rather used to mark the boundaries of three integral sections in an original compositional whole.[26]

In addressing the question of function of the formula, Gunn has argued that the formula designated major breaks in the narrative.[27] Conroy agreed but noted that 'the formula does not. . . mark a completely new beginning but rather a new episode which shares something with the foregoing'.[28] Since it does not join similar materials, however, according to him, it functions differently in the various contexts. Because of this, and since it does not appear in 1 Samuel, he also does not ascribe a Dtr origin to it.[29]

The occurrences of the formula within 2 Samuel all appear during the presentation of the reign of David.[30] In the units divided by the formula, there is no uniform closing formula preceding its use. It does, however, give the impression that the events described are presented in chronological order.

In the previous chapter, we saw that, with regard to the historical reconstruction of events in the reign of David, the events in 2 Samuel do not appear to be presented in chronological order. For example we noted that several scholars have argued that the battles in 2 Samuel 10 predate those in 8.3-8.[31] In the same manner most hold that the famine described in 2 Sam 21.1-14 probably predated the bringing of Mephibosheth to the court of David, described in 2 Samuel 9.[32] Similarly it has been argued that the battles with the Philistines in 2 Samuel 5 are neither sequential nor do they postdate the capture of Jerusalem.[33] Thus, we see that the formula, *wyhy 'ḥry kn*, is utilized to introduce various stages within the reign of David in order to give the impression of sequential ordering. The introductory apostasy/ oppression/liberation formulae in Judges and the regnal formulae in 1 and 2 Kings, which all ascribe to Dtr authorship,[34] often function similarly. This fact alone, however, is not enough to tie our formula unquestionably to the work of the Dtr.

The formula occurs, outside of 2 Samuel and corollary passages in 1 Chronicles, three times within the DtrH (Judg 16.4; 1 Sam 24.6; 2 Kgs 6.24) and twice in 2 Chronicles (20.1; 24.4). With the exception of 1 Sam 24.6, a text embroiled in controversy over its secondary nature,[35] all other instances appear at the beginning of episodes in the accounts of the reign of a particular individual (as either *šopeṭ* or *mlk*). In addition to this, both of the passages in Judges and Kings appear to sequence units which are from different hands and whose arrangements are chronologically suspect.[36]

The two passages in 2 Chronicles in which the formula appears introduce narratives of events occurring within the reign of one *mlk*, giving the impression that the events are being presented in chronological sequence. Neither of these narratives mentions events discussed in the DtrH, and this were probably composed by the Chronicler. Because of their theological concern, these two narratives have been judged historically suspect.[37]

Thus, we see that there is consistency in the utilization of the formula in terms of function and intention. When the compilers presented materials, perhaps from different sources, describing events purported to have occurred within the reign of an individual and which they wished to represent as being sequential, the formula, *wyhy 'ḥry kn*, could be utilized.[38] In other words, the formula's function is controlled not by the genre of the material it introduces, but rather by the redactor's intention, positing a sequence of events internal to a reign.

The question of the origin of the formula still remains. Is it pre-Dtr, or does it originate with the Dtr? The question, then, is whether the formula existed in a pre-Dtr form in the David material and was subsequently employed by Dtr in the Samson and Elisha materials. Given its limited but consistent usage, it appears that the evidence would weigh more on the side of a Dtr origin. The expression was specific and technical enough for the Chronicler to adopt in limited usage.

Following the introductory copula, we find the announcement of the death of an unnamed Ammonite king and a dynastic succession formula in which he still remains anonymous.[39] It is not until v. 2, in the speech of David, that the Ammonite king is identified as Nahash.[40] Various Old Testament narratives involve anonymous kings, such as the king of Moab,[41] the king of Edom,[42] the king of Aram,[43] the king of Israel,[44] and the king of Ammon.[45] In several of these instances the anonymity of the king is explained as the result of the loss of a name in the transmission of the material, either prior to its incorporation into the DtrH or as the result of the Dtr's attempt to place material within a chronological time frame to suit the particular theology of the redactors.[46]

By itself, these data do not specifically point to the Dtr. There is, however, one unit which is clearly Dtr and noted for its references to anonymous kings.[47] This is the list of kings conquered by Joshua and 'all Israel' in the conquest narratives in Joshua 6–11, now found in Joshua 12. This listing, in which none of the kings is named, enables the writer to describe the destruction of various localities of which some apparently were not simultaneously inhabited.

Following the introductory copula and the announcement of the death of the anonymous king of Ammon, the clause, *wymlk ḥnwn bnw tḥtyw*, 'and he reigned, Hanun, his son, in his stead', appears. This dynastic succession formulation, in which the name and genealogical designation of the incumbent appear *between* the verb and adverb, is unique to the biblical regnal formulae found in 1 and 2 Kings and their parallel passages in 2 Chronicles,[48] which we have already noted come from the hand of the DtrH.[49]

This dynastic succession formula is not limited by the Dtr to Israelite and Judean kings, but also appears in other passages in the DtrH in reference to monarchs of other ancient Near Eastern kingdoms,[50] as is the case in our unit. In both of these other instances, it is important to note that these units are designated as coming from the hand of the Dtr.[51]

There is only one other succession list using *wymlk*, that of the Edomite kings in Gen 36.31-39, which is in most instances not designated as having any Dtr influence.[52] The formulation in the Edomite king list differs from 10.1 in that *wymlk* is followed by the adverb *thtyw*, which is then followed by the name and genealogy of the king.[53] The list in Gen 36.31-39 does not deal with dynastic succession, but since there is both a regnal name and a genealogical notation in both listings, this becomes a moot point. Thus the dynastic formulation using *wymlk* in 2 Sam 10.1 is best seen as a case of Dtr wording. One immediately recognizes the significance that the adverb is not in the same location within both formulations. Thus, the dynastic formulation using *wymlk* in 2 Sam 10.1 is best seen as identical to the Dtr wording in the regnal formulae in 1 and 2 Kings.[54]

Thus, each phrase and clause in 2 Sam 10.1 possibly points to the hand of the Dtr. The first two phrases, *wyhy 'hry kn* and the mention of an anonymous king, are characteristic of Dtr introductory formulae in narratives which may have been placed out of logical chronological order. The third, the regnal succession formula, is unique to Dtr regnal formulae.

In 10.2, reference is made to the *hsd* which David sets out to perform for Hanun to repay the *hsd* done for him by Hanun's father. The passages in the DtrH which employ the term *hesed* display an interesting although somewhat confusing situation. In the narratives there are generally two groups and/or individuals, A and B, engaged in conflict. At some point in the working out of the conflict, a member of group A, or an individual closely associated with individual A, switches loyalty and helps B in the conflict. This switch of loyalty and the reciprocal protection/payback offered are both termed *hesed*. Some examples will illustrate the phenomenon.

In the conflict between the *bny ysr'l* and the people of Jericho (Josh 2) Rahab's speech in vv. 9-11 conforms to Dtr Salvation History. This is followed by the negotiation between Rahab and the spies in which her treasonous actions, termed *hesed*, are to be repaid by safety for her family, also termed *hesed*.[55]

In the conflict between the House of Joseph and the people of Bethel in Judg 1.22-26, there is a situation similar to that in Joshua 2. A local inhabitant is induced to be traitorous to his own people, in repayment for the safety of his family. The action of the tribe in allowing the person to live is termed *ḥesed*.[56] Although unstated, the man's willingness to aid the house of Joseph would have constituted his act of *ḥsd*.

In the narrative of the battle between Saul and the Amalekites in 1 Samuel 15 the text describes protection being given to a people in a situation when *ḥerem* has been declared on an area, and an acceptable deviation is reported. The Kenites are warned to flee the region, because they had shown *ḥesed* to the people of Israel when they came up out of Egypt (1 Sam 15.6). Saul's action is thus his *ḥesed* in repayment for the Kenite's *ḥesed*. In this sense, the *ḥesed* is similar to that in Joshua 2.[57] The context of the reference to *ḥesed*, namely in a Dtr statement about the exodus from Egypt, would indicate that much of the image of *ḥesed* in this text is Dtr.

Finally, in the narrative of the conflict between Saul and David, Jonathan is described as giving *ḥesed*[58] to David by being traitorous to his father and in return seeks *ḥesed* from David (1 Sam 20.8, 14).[59]

What is common to all four of these situations is that even though the actions of the persons would otherwise be termed treason,[60] the narratives describe them as *ḥesed*. In fact it is only our own theological predispositions which keep us from naturally viewing these acts negatively (i.e. Rahab helped God's people, and is therefore termed a hero, and this explains why not all the inhabitants were put under *ḥerem*).

In 2 Sam 10.2, Nahash is said to have performed an act of *ḥesed* for David and David is planning to reciprocate. In the preceding chapter, David states that he is going to return *ḥesed* to Jonathan by taking care of his son, Mephibosheth, and giving him a place at his table (2 Sam 9.1). Thus *ḥesed* could be repaid to the next generation, as is also the case with David's repayment of *ḥesed* to Nahash. In the other examples of *ḥesed*, the reciprocal offer is protection at a point of vulnerability. David's messengers sent to Hanun were to bring assurance[61] to Hanun that at this point of regnal transition, a point of possible international turmoil, protection was available. This would also help clarify why David's ambassadors were mistaken for spies.[62]

Another passage in the DtrH which mentions *ḥesed*, and which sheds light on our unit, is 1 Kgs 2.7, when David charges Solomon to repay *ḥesed* to the sons of Barzillai, in repayment for his actions of *ḥesed*. All commentators note that the reference is to Barzillai's presence in the delegation that received David at Mahanaim during the king's flight from Absalom (2 Sam 17.27-29).[63] It is generally assumed that Barzillai's name is Aramaic and thus, that he was probably a non-Israelite, from Aramean extraction,[64] who assisted David, the enemy of his people, when the Judean king was in need of protection. Commentaries, however, have failed to note the similarity between this type of *hesed* and the examples just discussed.[65] In other words we have an Aramean, one from group A, giving aid and assistance to David, king of group B, at a point when the latter is in trouble.

One final unit to be explored, which is clearly from the hand of the Dtr, but in which *hesed* does not appear in direct discourse, is Judg 8.35. This verse is the closing formula for the narrative of Gideon, who is also called Jerrubbaal.[66] In this unit Israel is charged with not reciprocating *hesed* in exchange for what he did for them. The basis of the charge is generally accepted to be the assassinations of his children in ch. 9.[67] If the accusation is understood as referring to the mistreatment of his children, then for the Dtr, *hesed* could be used to designate political acts which humans are expected to reciprocate, even in the next generation.

Thus, it would appear that we have more than ample evidence to suggest that the usage of *hesed* in 2 Sam 10.1-6a is consistent with that in other passages within the DtrH. *Hesed* is used by the Dtr in several texts to refer to acts in the political sphere in which a member of the enemy betrays his/her own people to help Israel/David at a point of extreme vulnerability. In the same manner, this act of betrayal is to be repaid with reciprocal *hesed* by the recipient/ beneficiary of the first act, not by Yahweh, as 2 Sam 2.6 suggests,[68] but by the beneficiaries themselves, as Judg 8.35 asserts. Similarly, this obligation to reciprocate with *hesed* in the political sphere involves an offer of protection for the other individuals at a point their vulnerability.

Finally, our analysis would suggest that the antecedent of the *hesed* mentioned in 2 Sam 10.2 was the aid granted David by Shobi the son of Nahash in 2 Sam 17.27-28. This would suggest that the events described in 2 Sam 10.1-6a are out of chronological sequence with other events in the book of 2 Samuel and probably relate to a time after the Absalom Revolt.

2 Sam 10.1-6a may have been given its present placement because of the catchword *hesed* in ch. 9 and the similarity of repayment, namely, to the second generation in both cases. This further

substantiates our interpretation of the introductory copula *wyhy 'ḥry kn* as a Dtr expression; not only is the introductory verse from the hand of the Dtr, but also the conception of *ḥesed* within the unit in comparison with its usage in Joshua 2, Judg 2.22-26, 1 Samuel 15, and 1 Kgs 2.7.

Our unit ends with a notation that the *bny 'mwn* realized that they had 'become odious', *nb'šw*, to David. Thus use of *b'š* in the *niph'al* only appears two other times in the canon,[69] and only one of these uses the preposition *b*.[70]

Other attestations of the verb in the *qal*[71] refer to a 'stinking odor', while the *hiph'il* is primarily used to describe conflictive relationships between parties.[72] Thus, several commentators suggest that the *niph'al* should be understood as functioning in the same way as the *hiph'il*.[73]

We would contend, however, that this peculiar use of the *niph'al* of *b'š* with *b* raises a flag.[74] The other instance of *b'š* in the *niph'al* is in a unit fraught with difficulties. First, the occurrence in 1 Sam 13.3-4 attributes the capture of a Philistine garrison to Jonathan and Saul,[75] respectively. Most recently, McCarter has argued that v. 4 functions to prepare the reader for the unit in 1 Sam 13.7b-15, which is almost universally viewed as redactional.[76] Thus, both 1 Sam 13.4 and 2 Sam 10.6a appear to be redactional seams between units, both of which employ the peculiar usage of *b'š* in the *niph'al* followed by *b*. This suggests they both stem from the same hand.

2. *War with the Ammonites and Arameans (2 Sam 10.6b-15)*

Having argued that vv. 1-6a form a separate unit, we now turn our attention to the particular units about the Ammonite War(s). A structural outline of the passage will be followed by an analysis.

II. The Ammonite War (6b-15)
    A. The Ammonites engage mercenaries—*wyšlḥ . . . wyśkrw* (6bf)
        1. Arameans
            a. Location—*byt rḥwb* and *ṣwb'*
            b. Number—20 *'lp rgly*
        2. King of *m'kh*—*'lp 'yš*
        3. Men of *ṭwb*—12 *'lp 'yš*
    B. David's muster (7)
        1. Reason for preparation—*wyšm'*
        2. Engaging the troops—*wyšlḥ*
            a. Designation of commander—Joab

        b. Designation of troops—*ḥṣb' hgbrym*
    C. The battle report (8-14)
        1. Position of the enemy—*wyṣ'w . . . wy'rkw* (8)
            a. Ammonites in *ptḥ hš'r*
            b. Others *bśdh*
        2. Position of Israelites (9-10)
            a. Assessment of enemy lines—*wyr'. . . pny hmlḥmh*
            b. Positioning *bḥwry yśr'l* opposite Syrians
            c. Positioning *ytr h'm*
                (1) Designation of Abishai as commander
                (2) Location—opposite Ammonites
        3. Joab's instructions—*wy'mr* (11-12)
            a. Strategy (11)
                (1) Contingency if Syrians attack
                (2) Contingency if Ammonites attack
            b. Words of inspiration (12)
                (1) *ḥzq wntḥzq*
                (2) National pride—*b'd 'mnw*
                (3) Divine sanction—*yhwh y'śh*
        4. Description of Israelite victory (13-14a)
            a. Joab attacks Syrians—*wygś*
            b. Reports of enemy flight
                (1) Syrian flight—*wynsw*
                (2) Ammonite retreat—*wynsw . . . wyb'w*
    D. Post-war summary (14b-15)
        1. Report of Joab's return to Jerusalem—*wyšb . . . wyb'*
        2. Report of Aramean reassembly
            a. Battle assessment—*wyr' . . . ky ngp*
            b. Regrouping—*wy'spw*

The unit is comprised of four major sections. The first two (v. 6b-7) describe incidents which lead up to the battle, the Ammonite-Aramean musters and David's responses to these. The third and major portion of the unit reports the battle scene itself. Within this section primary attention is given to describing the preliminary particulars of the battle scene in terms of positions assumed by the various armies (vv. 8-10), the strategy to be employed by the Israelites (v. 11), and a patriotic pep-talk given by Joab (v. 12). In fact the battle itself is described only in terms of enemy flight when faced with the threat of Israelite attack (vv. 13-14a). In the fourth section the unit closes with the notation that Joab returned to Jerusalem (v. 14b), while the Arameans reassembled (v. 15). Thus, the unit can stand alone as an independent entity, with a clear beginning[77] and end, with the details in between leading to a climax and resolution of the problem posed in the beginning.

In the account, the war begins because of Ammonite aggression, namely their engaging the Aramean forces as mercenaries (v. 6b).[78] As the text states, it is this muster which causes David to send troops to the area (*wyšm'*, v. 7a). One might question, however, the abrupt beginning of the unit with v. 6b, *wyšlḥw . . . wyśkrw*. In other words, a disjunctive introductory formula, such as *wyhy*, would make clear that a new unit begins. Without such a formula, one might see v. 6a as providing the 'reason' for the Ammonite-Aramean muster, as do most commentators.

In defense of our position, we have maintained that the function of v. 6a is to close out the account of the 'Davidic emissaries to Hanun', by reporting the Ammonite response to the humiliation. Similarly, the awkward grammatical construction of v. 6a, with the use of the *niph'al* of *b'š + b*, as opposed to the *hiph'il*, which is customary for describing negative human interaction, suggests the possibility that v. 6a is a later redactional seam.[79] Thirdly, as will be noted below, this follows the tendency of the other two Ammonite war narratives in Judges 11 and 1 Samuel 11, where unprovoked Ammonite aggression begins the war. Fourthly, the hyperbole of Joab's speech in v. 12, suggesting that national and divine honor rested on this battle, goes far beyond the proportions of the events described in vv. 3-4, as well as beyond the bounds set by David's instructions of v. 5.[80]

As evident in the structural outline, we see the end of the unit in v. 15, generally viewed as the beginning of the third unit of ch. 10.[81] In terms of the structure of other units, this verse is better seen as paralleling the conclusions of other units. In the first place, contrary to Ridout, who argues that the wording of v. 15a is parallel to that of v. 19a and thereby forms a chiasm in vv. 15-19,[82] we would argue that v. 15a functions in relation to vv. 6b-14 as does v. 19a to vv. 16-18, namely both provide reports of Aramean responses to battle. Secondly, like v. 6a which ends the first unit, so v. 15 contains the verb *r'h*. Thus, it appears that the threefold use of this verb in this chapter[83] is part of a compositional technique in which the enemies of Israel assess the damage that has been done to them by their aggressive actions against Israel. Thirdly, while there is a statement as to the location of the Ammonites and the Israelites after the battle (vv. 13b-14), there is no such locating of the Arameans until v. 15b.[84] Thus, rather than opening the next unit, v. 15 is better understood as closing out the unit in vv. 6b-14 with a note about the Aramean response to the war and their geographical location.[85]

In examining these Ammonite war narratives of 1 Samuel 10, it is necessary to look briefly at the biblical materials about this eastern neighbor of the ancient Israelites. The traditions about these people are diverse. Pentateuchal references present them as ethnologically kin to Israel.[86] The oracles against foreign nations in the prophetic literature present them as enemies of Israel,[87] while in other prophetic pronouncements they are generally grouped with the Edomites and Moabites as adversaries of Israel.[88]

The traditions about the Ammonites found in the DtrH are close to the prophetic traditions in their adversarial tone.[89] On the other hand it is interesting that none of the conquest traditions, either in Numbers, Deuteronomy, or in Joshua, contain any reference to conflict between Israel and Ammon.[90]

There are two other narratives (Judg 11; 1 Sam 11),[91] besides 2 Samuel 10, which concern specific wars between the Ammonites and Israel. All three of these narratives contain certain similarities. The first is the fact that all three narratives present the Ammonite king as acting in a seemingly irrational manner.[92] Secondly, they are all introduced by chronologically useless introductory phrases, *wyhy mymym* (Judg 11.4), *wyhy kmḥryš*[93] (1 Sam 10.27b), and our *wyhy 'ḥry kn*.[94] Thirdly all three wars are placed within the story line to give the appearance that they occur in the formative years of an Israelite *r'š/mlk*.[95] Fourthly, in all three there is the recognition that the victory is to be credited to Yahweh (*wntn yhwy 'wtm lpny*, Judg 11.10; *hywm 'šh yhwh tšw'h*, 1 Sam 11.13b; *wyhwh y'šh hṭwb b'ynyw*, 2 Sam 10.12b). Fifthly, all three wars result in a great defeat of the Ammonites.[96] Sixthly, there is no narrative suggesting the Ammonites regained their independence after any of these defeats.[97] All of these similarities raise the possibility that we are dealing with a standard Dtr Ammonite War tradition.

Interestingly in the Jephthah unit, we have an anonymous king of the Ammonites, as we do initially in 2 Samuel 10.[98] In the Saul and David units, on the other hand, though the Ammonite king is named, the name can be considered a pun, which reflects the royal behavior in the instigation of the war.[99] It is also only in these two passages plus 2 Sam 17.27 that Nahash is mentioned. This could possibly further suggest a literary setting for our unit.

In order to assess this point we must turn our attention to 1 Sam 14.47 and 2 Sam 8.12 where we find Dtr[100] summaries of the successful military exploits of Saul and David. As the following chart suggests there are great similarities in these two units:[101]

Chart 1. Military Exploits of Saul and David

1 Sam 14.47	*2 Sam 8.12*
Moab	Aram
Ammonites	Moab
Edom	Ammonites
Kings of Zobah	Philistines
Philistines	Amalek
	Hadadezer son of Rehob king of Zobah

Along with the similarities of names, one notes discrepancies between these lists and the war narratives found in Samuel. For example there are no narratives which describe wars between Saul and the Moabites, the Edomites, or the king of Zobah.[102] Similarly, the narrative of David's wars with the Ammonites not only comes after this Dtr summation, but also goes unmentioned in ch. 8,[103] which appears to be a composition demonstrating the consolidation of the Davidic empire. This is difficult to explain, especially since in ch. 8 the war with the Arameans is twice noted, as is also the case in ch. 10. In the same manner there is no mention of a war between David and Amalek during his reign as king, and even its mention in 1 Sam 14.48 is problematic.[104] What can be concluded from these lists is that, according to the Dtr, these nations comprise an idealized conquest or consolidated imperial territory (see Isa 11.14). The question arises, however, how historically reliable these traditions are. Given the similarities among Judges 11, 1 Samuel 11, and 2 Samuel 10–12 noted above, it may well be that Dtr sees a victory over the Ammonites as a traditional means for the authenticating of kingship. Conquest over the Ammonites affirms one's right to rule.

There are some similarities between 10.6b-15 and 10.1-5a. The major similarity is the anonymity of characters and locations. For example, with the exception of the Judeans, David, Joab, and Abishai, all the characters are anonymous.[105] Similarly, with the exception of the closing statement, which mentions Joab's return to Jerusalem, the geographical locations are ambiguous. For example the battle takes place with the *bny 'mwn* in the *ptḥ hš'r* (v. 8ab) and the other armies *bśdh* (v. 8bb).[106] Similarly, while the location of this battle is generally assumed to be Rabbah,[107] it is not until 11.1b that we read any mention of that specific location.[108] The lack of specific details, such as names of kings and geographical locations, suggests that these war stories are best designated as legend, rather than as historiographical narrative.

In 10.6b-15, there appears to be a pattern of reversal of traditional themes and motifs. For example, in Chapter 2 above we noted that there was discontinuity between the 'sons of Zeruiah' tradition as presented in other parts of 1 and 2 Samuel and that presented here in ch. 10, namely that elsewhere in Samuel, there is conflict with David over their activities,[109] while here there is no such conflict.[110] In fact, instead of the mere absence of such a conflict, we have here a 'reversal' of the tradition.[111]

Other elements in the unit suggest reversals. For example, the use of *rgly*, foot-soldier, is elsewhere reserved for Israelite troops,[112] while here it is used for Aramean troops.[113] Similarly, with the exception of the Syro-Ephraimite War narratives, Aram is presented as the ally of the southern kingdom and as the enemy of the northern.[114] Here it is presented as entering a coalition against David.

Elements of the Holy War, enumerated by von Rad, most noticeably the depiction of the Israelite troops as being outnumbered (vv. 6b, 9a), and emphasis on trust in divine intentions, are present in the unit (v. 12b). As he states,

> The stories intentionally exaggerate the numerical disparity in order to give the honor of the victory to Jahweh alone... the fighters' chief duty was to submit confidently to Jahweh's sway and not to be afraid in face of the enemy's superior numbers.[115]

Given this perspective, one is surprised to see alongside the plea of *ḥzq wntḥzq* (v. 12) the mention of *gbwrym* (v. 7),[116] the mighty men of war, 'who had already distinguished themselves by performing heroic deeds'[117] and *bḥrym* (v. 9), the elite trained core.[118] Such a troop make-up flies in the face of the faith affirmation, *yhwh y'śh*.

Similarly, within the Holy War traditions, it is the king,[119] as opposed to the general, who seeks the divine assurance through some oracular means.[120] Thus, what appear to be appropriate pious statements in line with the tradition are balanced by their antithesis in troop composition and strategy (vv. 7b, 9b) and are pronounced by the 'wrong' party. Such ironic interplay of motifs supplements our contention of reversals of traditions.

Finally, the only other references to most of the particular nations mentioned in this narrative are found either in the other narratives which contain Ammonite traditions and/or in Dtr summary passages.

For example, the only other mention of Tob is found in the Jephthah narrative, as the place where he sought refuge (Judg 11.3, 5). In the same manner, in addition to the war narrative in 2 Sam 10.6bf., Josh 12.5 and 13.11 (Dtr summaries of conquest in the Transjordan) are the only other ones which mention Ma'acah as a geographical location. Other than Judg 18.28[121] this is the only passage which mentions Beth Rehob as a geographical location.[122] Similarly, Zobah appears in 1 Sam 14.47, the Dtr listing of nations conquered by Saul,[123] as well as in 2 Sam 8.3 and 1 Kgs 11.23.[124] In the same manner, most attempts to locate these cities geographically have been unsuccessful.[125] In light of this, it is surprising that so much reliability is given to this unit for the purposes of historical reconstruction.

In summary, we have shown that in terms of structure 10.6b-15 can stand on its own as an independent unit, separate and apart from vv. 1-6a. We have also noted a literary/compositional pattern which closes out units in vv. 6a, 15a, and 19a. Thirdly, we have noted that the use of anonymous designations suggests that we are dealing more with legend than with reliable historiography. Finally, we have noted that the use of traditions and traditional materials, in many respects, can best be understood as reversal of their standard usage. These arguments would suggest a literary origin, setting, and intention for this unit and indicate that it in no way represents an archival or eye-witness narrative.

3. *War with the Arameans and Concluding Etiology (2 Sam 10.16-19)*

An outline for the third unit in the Ammonite War materials, vv. 16-19, is as follows:

III. Report of Syrian War (16-19)
    A.   Report of Syrian aggression (16)
        1. Report of Transjordanian help—*wyšlḥ . . . wyṣ' . . . wyb'w*
        2. Designation of general—Shobach
        3. Location of muster—*ḥylm*
    B.   Report of Israelite response (17a)
        1. Report of informing David—*wygd*
        2. Report of muster
           a. *wy'sp*
           b. Report of entering Transjordan—*wy'br*

        c. Location of battle—*ḥl'm*
        d. Designation of general—David
    C. Battle report (17b-18)
        1. Report of engagement—*wy'rkw ... wylḥmw* (17b)
        2. Report of Syrian flight—*wyns* (18a)
        3. Casualty report—*wyhrg* (18b)
            a. 700 *rkb*
            b. 40,000 *pršym*
            c. Shobach
    D. Report of consequences of war (19)
        1. Assessment by *kl hml kym 'bdy hdd'zr*
        2. Peace—*wyšlmw ... wy'bdwm*
        3. End of Syrian-Ammonite alliance

As in the preceding unit, this war narrative begins with a statement about an aggressive act of a foreign power, *wyšlḥ hdd'zr* (v. 16a). Secondly, David responds defensively to the muster (*wygd ... wy'sp*, v. 17a). Thirdly, as in the previous war unit, characters and geographical localities are mentioned which appear nowhere else in the canon, namely, Shobach[126] and Helam.[127]

There are, however, several significant differences between vv. 16-19 and 6b-15. First, unlike v. 6, which specified the particular Aramean groups mustered, this unit uses the general designation *'rm 'šr m'br hnhr*.[128] Secondly, unlike the previous unit, which never specifically mentioned the location of the battle, this unit gives a geographical location, *ḥylm*.[129] Thirdly, while the previous unit presented the Arameans as a mercenary force hired by the Ammonites to fight with them against David, in this unit there is no mention of the Ammonites in the battle report. Instead it appears that we have here a 'Syrian War Narrative'.

Not only are there differences between these two units, but also there are interesting reversals on the previous unit. For example, in vv. 6b-15 Israel was led by a general and the foreign armies were led by kings, while in this unit Israel is led by King David and the Arameans are led by a general, Shobach. In the same manner, David assembles *kl yśr'l*, while in the previous unit Joab uses an elite professional force.[130] Finally, while the previous unit assigned the victory to Yahweh, there is an absence in vv. 16-19 of any such pious pronouncements similar to those put in the mouth of Joab. Instead the victory is assigned to David.

The verbs describing the movements of David's armies are in the 3ms (*wy'br ... wyb'*, v. 17). Similarly the Arameans are said to fight *'mw* (v. 17d), and the casualty report is attributed to him (*wyhrg*, v. 18). Thus in this unit, the emphasis is placed upon the glorification of David, who almost 'single-handedly' defeats the enemy.

Because of the many differences noted above, some scholars argue that vv. 16-19 come from another hand than that of vv. 6a-15.[131] In addition, given the similarities between this unit and 2 Sam 8.3-8,[132] there are those who argue that the events described in this unit precede those described in ch. 8.[133] Others argue that these two units are parallel accounts of the same war.[134]

In order to assess which of these options, if either, is the most feasible, we must look more closely at the structures, wording, and ideas of 8.3-8 and 10.16-19. The differences between 8.3-8 and 10.16-19 outnumber the similarities.

First of all, 8.3 portrays David as the aggressor, while in 10.17 he is responding to external aggression. Secondly, although Hadadezer is mentioned in both units, it should be noted that in 10.16-19 he is mentioned as summoning *'rm 'šr m'br lnhr*,[135] while in ch. 8 he is identified as being *bn rḥb mlk ṣwbh*. The latter site is often assumed to be a geographical location in the anti-Lebanon mountain range.[136] The link between these two references is seen to be in 10.6b, in which the Arameans of *byt rḥb* and of *ṣwb'*[137] are mustered, but in which Hadadezer is not mentioned. Thus, while similar names for the Aramean king occur in 8.3f. and 10.16f., these kings do not seem to control the same territory. Similarly, we note that the verse which seems to relate to a similar territory as that mentioned in 8.3 (10.6b) is not in agreement with 8.3 in two respects. One speaks of *ben* Rehob (8.3), the other of *bet* Rehob (10.6b). Secondly, the orthography of Zobah is different (*ṣôbā'* and *ṣôbāh*). Because of this we would suggest that what we have in 8.3 is a late synthesizing of the data in 10.6b and 16a.

A third difference between the two units is the fact that in 10.16-17 Shobach, the general, is in command, while in 8.3-4 Hadadezer is in control. Fourthly, there is no battle report at all in 8.3-9, while 10.16-17 goes through elaborate detail not only about the muster but also in describing the battle array.[138] Fifthly, while both reports have elaborate casualty reports, in 8.4 and 5b and 10.18, there is neither a direct match of the numbers nor ordering of the military organs, *rkb*, *'yš rgly*, and *prš*. Nor is there a match in the verbs which introduce them, *wylkd*, 8.4, and *wyhrg*, 10.17.[139]

At the end of the unit in 8.3-9 there is an extensive description of the nature of the political subjugation after the war in 8.8-9, while there is no such corollary in ch. 10.[140] Finally, 8.9b attributes the success of the campaign to Yahweh, while, as we have noted above, this is not the case in 10.16-19.

Thus, we would have to conclude that if 10.16-18 relates in any way to 8.3-9, they cannot be from the same hand, since neither the structure nor vocabulary is the same. At best they could be corollary reports, but not interdependent either in term of sequencing or intention.[141]

In 10.16-19, the primary attention is given to explaining the circumstances of the musters (vv. 16-17c) and the size of the casualties lost by the enemy (v. 18).[142] The threefold conclusion in v. 19 does not directly relate to the events described in vv. 16-18. Instead, two of the statements which relate to the events in vv. 6b-15 seem to have the function of tying together vv. 16-18 and 6b-15.

In the conclusion, there is first a reference to an evaluation made by various Aramean kings (v. 19a). In this regard, v. 16 refers to a muster under the control of Hadadezer and his general, Shobach. On the other hand, v. 6b also mentions a muster headed by various Aramean kings. Thus, there appears to be an attempt in this clause in v. 19a, to create a connection between the events described in vv. 6b-15 with those described in vv. 16-18 by linking v. 6b and v. 16b.

Verse 19b reports the end of the mercenary relationship between Aram and Ammon. As noted there is no mention of Ammon in vv. 16-18. The relationship is characteristic of vv. 6b-15. Thus, v. 19b is also a redactional move to link vv. 16-18 and 6b-15.

It would appear that, given the account of the war and subjugation of the Arameans found in 2 Samuel 8 and the mention of their mercenary status again in 10.6bf., the compiler of ch. 10 needed once again to subordinate them to Davidic control. Thus, vv. 16-18 were added to the tradition in 6b-15, and then v. 19 was composed to bring the whole narrative to a close.

A clue to the identity of this compiler is seen in the second clause in v. 19. This clause speaks about a process of peace-making and subjugation (*wyšlmw . . . wy'bdwm*). The only other instance of these two verbs in this combination is in the 'law of war' found in Deuteronomy 20.[143] In this regard it is striking that Deut 20.15 notes that this is the law in regard to *kl h'rym hrḥwqwt mmk*. The dependence of 10.19b on the Deuteronomic law points to the Dtr as the arranger and redactor of ch. 10.

The pattern of reversals noted above would suggest there is also a conscious literary device at work in ch. 10. As the three units now stand, there is a progression from 10.1-5a, in which David sends *'bdyw*, to 10.6b-15, in which he sends Joab, to 16-19, in which he himself *'br 't-hyrdn*.[144] Thus, there appears to be a broad compositional technique utilized here.

In v. 5 we get a piece of data useful in dating our unit. This is the mention of Jericho. The verse states that David sent instructions for the *ml'kym* to remain there until their beards grew back. The verse implies that Jericho was a habitable city at the time. Archaeological excavations suggest that the site was not inhabited during the tenth century or during the time when the TSN was composed according to the classical Rostian theory.[145] In spite of this archaeological evidence many commentators cite 2 Sam 10.5 in support of such an occupation of Jericho in the tenth century.[146]

According to Kenyon's studies, the LB settlement at Jericho was 'followed by some six hundred years of abandonment'.[147] This would mean that contrary to expectations, there was no city in which the Davidic messengers could stay on their return from Ammonite territory.[148] These data would suggest that 10.1-6a was most likely not written during the time of David or Solomon, since the instructions to the messengers would have posed problems for the reader of that day in light of Jericho's abandoned status. The unit with its reference to Jericho probably dates from a time when Jericho was inhabited, but far enough removed from Davidic times that there would be among the readers little historical recollection of its non-habitability in the tenth century.

In seeking to date this passage more closely, some attention should be given to the orthography of the term Jericho. As Driver correctly noted,[149] the way Jericho is spelled *and* pointed in our unit, *yᵉrēḥô*, is paralleled in the DtrH only one other time, namely, in 2 Kgs 25.5.[150] In all other references to the city and/or vicinity of Jericho, which are found in the DtrH, the pointing uses a *ḥīreq* or a *ḥīreq yod* combination in place of a *ṣēre*.[151] This would suggest that the author of 2 Sam 10.1-6a is the same as that of 2 Kings 25.[152] This would fit the assumption that the writing derives from a time when Jericho was inhabited (post-seventh century), which was also far removed from the time of David.

4. *The Battles at Rabbah (2 Sam 11.1 + 12.26-31)*

The fourth unit in the so-called 'Ammonite War Narratives' is found in 2 Sam 11.1 + 12.26-31. An initial reading of the text raises a number of questions: is this unit a continuation of the narratives found in ch. 10? What is the relationship between this text and the David-Bathsheba-Uriah complex? What is the relationship between 11.1, 12.26-31 and the traditions and compiler of ch. 10? To answer these questions, we shall first analyze the structure of the narrative.

In the story, David sent Joab to wage war against the Ammonites in Rabbah, while he remained in Jerusalem (11.1). Once Joab laid siege to Rabbah and was about to capture it (12.26), he sent word to David to come and lead the assault (12.27-28), which David did (12.29). David then subjugated the people (12.30) and returned to Jerusalem (12.31). With this in mind the following outline of the unit is presented.

IV. Ammonite War at Rabbah (11.1; 12.26-31)
    A. Initiation of the war (11.1a)
        1. Temporal setting
            a. Time of year—*ltšwbt hšnh*
            b. Military campaign—*l't ṣ't*
        2. Designation of actors
            a. David—*wyšlḥ*
            b. Joab, servants, 'all Israel'
    B. Battle Reports (11.1b; 12.26-29)
        1. Victory report over the *bny 'mwn* (1b)—*wyšḥtw*
        2. Location of parties
            a. Joab *et al.*—Rabbah—*wyṣrw*
            b. David—Jerusalem—*wyšb*
        3. Battle-victory report at *'yr hmlwkh*—*wylḥm . . . wylkd* (v.26)
        4. Report of informing David of results (27-28)
            a. Commissioning messengers—*wyšlḥ*
            b. Message
                (1) Battle-victory report at *'yr hmym*—*nlḥmty . . . lkdty* // v. 26
                (2) Instructions to act
                    (a) Identification of other actors—*'sp 't-ytr h'm*
                    (b) Desired action—*wḥnh . . . wlkdh*
                (3) Motive clauses
                    (a) *pn 'lkd h'yr*
                    (b) *wnqr'*
        5. Report of David in battle (29)
            a. Report of muster—*wy'sp . . . kl h'm*

        b. Battle-victory report at Rabbah—*wylk . . . wylḥm*
           . . . *wylkdh* // 27b // 26
  C. Subjugation report (30-31a)
      1. Report of humiliation (30)
        a. Act of humiliation—*wyqḥ 'trt*
        b. Description of crown
        c. David crowned—*wthy 'l r'š*
      2. Report of despoilage—*wšll. . . hwṣy'*
      3. Report of subjugation of the people (v. 31)
        a. Report of torture—*h'm . . . wyśm bmgrh*
        b. Forced labor—*wh'byr . . . bmlkn*
        c. Statement of general practice—*kn y'śh*
  D. Report of David's and the army's return to Jerusalem (31b)//29a

The unit begins with the disjunctive *wyhy*.[153] This is followed by the formula, *ltšwbt hšnh* (11.1a). The shift in time suggests that a new unit is beginning and the *wyhy* suggests that it is different from that which precedes.

Since 11.1 ends with Joab and the army encamped at Rabbah and 11.26 begins with him fighting there, the latter is, therefore, taken to be the continuation of the war account begun in 11.1. Similarly, since 11.1 ends with a notice of David remaining in Jerusalem, and 12.27 contains the bringing of a message from Joab summoning David to Rabbah, the continuation theory is strengthened. Thus, 11.1 and 12.26-31 are traditionally designated as a coherent whole into which the David-Bathsheba marriage narrative has been interpolated.[154]

As the above outline demonstrates, the unit is composed of four major divisions. The first is a short introductory segment which identifies the time, actors and mission (v. 1a). This section concludes with a notice of the location of the principal actors, which functions as a transition to the events in 11.2f.[155] and presumably to the events of 12.26ff. The last section is an equally short report of the actors returning to their previous positions once the mission was accomplished (v. 31b). This notice of return, however, is only related to 11.29a, the muster of David, and not to 11.1a, the sending of Joab and his soldiers.[156] Thus, there is a different set of actors in the introduction from those described in the conclusion. The former speaks of Joab, his servants, and *kl yśr'l*. The latter speaks of David and *h'm*. This variation in terminology suggests that 11.1 plus 12.26-31 may not be a coherent unit after all.

In addition, there is unevenness in the second section dealing with the battle reports. As we noted earlier within the genre of

Kriegserzählungen one usually finds only one battle report per unit. This unit, however, contains not only a victory report, but also three battle reports claiming victory at the same location.

In this series of three battle-victory reports the same two verbs are repeated: *lḥm* followed by *lkd* (vv. 26, 27, 28). All refer to the same geographical vicinity, namely, Rabbah. The first battle-victory report is of Joab capturing the *'yr hmlwkh* (v. 26b). The second is contained in his message summoning David, after he had already taken the *'yr hmym* (v. 27b). The two descriptions of the town—'royal city' and 'city of waters'—are taken to be synonyms for the same location, since the message to David in v. 27 uses the same verbs found in v. 26, only in v. 27 they appear as 1ms perfect verbs referring back to what was reported in v. 26.[157] The third battle-victory report is preceded by a further muster of the army, *wy'sp* (v. 29a), and contains a report of David taking Rabbah (v. 29b).

On the one hand, v. 26b contains a victory report in which Joab captures *'yr hmlwkh*. On the other hand David is reported in v. 29 mustering *h'm*, fighting against, and capturing Rabbah. Similarly, since the construct phrase *'yr hmlwkh* literally means the city of the kingdom, it appears that the traditional translation for *'yr hmlwkh*, namely, the royal city, is less appropriate than the term 'the capital',[158] and if so, could both vv. 26 and 29 be different traditions referring to the same event?

Unusual repetitions and confusing geographic/topographical terms appear in the message of Joab to David (vv. 27-28), which is also the source of the general understanding that 11.1 plus 12.26-31 reports one 'taking of Rabbah'. In the first place, between the two battle-victory notices in vv. 26 and 29, Joab is quoted as referring to the capture of an *'yr hmym* and in a motive clause (*pn 'lkd h'yr*) refers to *h'yr*. Both of these references suggest that Rabbah has not yet been captured, assuming that *'yr hmym* denotes not the city itself but the external water source.[159] Thus, these two references serve to modify the meaning of *'yr hmlwkh* in v. 26.

Secondly, the mention of a muster in v. 29 appears to be unusual, since Joab is at Rabbah with *kl yśr'l*. To mute the suspicion which this second muster (12.29) might arouse for the reader, Joab's instructions for David to come to Rabbah begin with a call to muster *ytr h'm*. Thus, David's actions are in line with the instructions and not unusual. One even does not readily notice that David's muster in v. 29 is of *kl h'm*.

Finally, Joab's instructions replace *lḥm* with *ḥnh* (12.28a). This change suggests that all that is needed is for David to lead the final charge. After all there is no need for a fight, only the taking.

Thus, it appears that Joab's message uses unusual repetitions of battle-victory reports and unusual geographical citations to give the impression that the military activity was progressive in nature: first the *'yr hmlwkh/hmym* were taken by Joab, the servants and 'all Israel', and then David and *h'm* captured the city proper.[160] In addition it is the use of 'catchwords' in the speech of Joab in vv. 27-28 which forms the basis for the view that 12.26-31 contains a coherent unit on the sacking of Rabbah.

Following the battle-victory reports the narrative turns to the subject of the ritual humiliation[161] of the captured people and their torture and subjugation (vv. 30-31). Such actions are reminiscent of the humiliation reports found in ch. 8 in which David is said to *wymdd šny ḥblym lhmyt* (8.2aβ) and with *wy'qr . . . 't kl rcb*.[162] 12.29-31 only mention David being involved in the capture of Rabbah; there is no mention of Joab and his forces after v. 28. Thus, vv. 30-31 belong with the report begun in v. 29.

This examination of the structure of this unit suggests that we have two different traditions or narratives joined together by vv. 27-28. In other words there is one narrative which speaks of David sending Joab and his forces to Ammonite territory, while he remains in Jerusalem. Joab along with the royal servants and all Israel is successful in capturing Rabbah, the *'yr hmlwkh*, the capital of Ammon (11.1; 12.26). The other narrative describes David's muster of *h'm*, his battle and capture of Rabbah and his ritual humiliation and subjugation of the people (12.29-31). Both of these independent units have been joined by a 'messge from Joab' which uses the catchwords *lḥm/lkd*, *'yr hmym . . .* , and *'sp . . . h'm*. In line with this the broad outline is seen in Chart 2.

Chart 2. Compositional Arrangement in 11.1 + 12.26-31

11.1 + 12.26	Joab's war at Rabbah
12.27-28	Redactional seam—Joab's message
12.29-31	David's war at Rabbah.

Having shown that 11.1 + 12.26-31 is separate from ch. 10 and is composed not of one but two independent *Kriegserzählungen*, we can now turn our attention to the relationship of these units to the Ammonite War narratives of ch. 10.

The first indication that there is a break between the narratives in ch. 10 and what follows is in the victory report found in 11.1b. Since ch. 10 already attests to the Israelite victory over the Ammonites, one wonders what is meant by this second notice. The fact that the victory report is followed by a reference to a siege of Rabbah would indicate that the victory report speaks of outlying areas of Ammon.[163] This narrative, therefore, appears unaware of the events reported in 10.13-19 in which all the Ammonites take refuge in *h'yr* (10.14a). Thus, 10.13-19 and 11.1 + 12.26-31 are probably variant traditions on the David-Ammonite War.

2 Sam 11.1 + 12.26-31 contain some significant differences in presentation, structure, and emphasis from the war narratives in ch. 10. The first difference is in the opening formulae. As has been noted the *wyhy* in 11.1a is a disjunctive beginning, while the use of *r'h* in the narrative seams of the two *Kriegserzählungen* in 10.6a and 15 function as connectives.

A second difference between the presentation of the events in chs. 11–12 and those in ch. 10 is that it is Davidic aggression which begins the conflict in chapter 11 (*wyšlḥ dwd*—v. 1a).[164] As previously demonstrated, the point of view of the compiler of the materials in ch. 10 is that these wars are the result of Ammonite (10.6bf) and Aramean (10.16) aggression[165] to which David responds and which end in a resolution of peace (10.19a).

A third difference between these two groups of narratives concerns the focus of the emphasis in the accounts. In the two narratives in ch. 10 the focus is upon the battle array and the casualty report primarily in terms of the numbers of people involved. In 12.29-31, the focus is upon the ritual humiliation and subjugation of the people. In essence, the David of 10.1-19 acts radically different from the one of 12.29-31.

On the other hand there are some striking similarities between the presentations of the war narratives in chs. 10 and 11–12. The most apparent is that in the first war in both instances (10.6b-15; 11.1c + 12.26) Joab is presented as commander-in-chief and functions alone in the leadership of the battle. Similarly, in the second wars in both collections (10.16-19; 12.29-31) David is presented in command of the army which defeats the enemy.

A second striking similarity in the two collections is the portrayal of Joab. As one recalls, 10.9-12 presents Joab as a crafty strategist and manipulator. As was also previously argued, terms used otherwise in holy war contexts are placed in his mouth as the basis for the strategy (e.g. *yhwh y'śh ḥṭwb b'ynyw*, 10.12b). In the same manner, his message to David in 12.28 ends with the motive clause *wnqr' šmy 'lyh*, which is a phrase often used to describe theological relationships, most notably Yahweh's claim to someone or something.[166]

Such similarities are more than likely not just happenstance but probably denote a similar redactional hand. In other words, the dissimilarities in the two collections probably reflect their origin in different circles and settings, with varying concepts of the Davidic kingship. The similarities, which are found at the level of arrangement of the materials, suggest the hand of a redactor.

The first clue as to who this redactor might be is found in the opening formula of the unit, *ltšwbt hšnh*, for the formula only appears in two other contexts (1 Kgs 20.22, 26 and 2 Chron 36.10).[167] It should first be noted that all three of these occurrences relate to wars and activities of kings in battle. It appears, however, that the first instance is the one which is closest to the unit begun in 11.1.

1 Kings 20[168] is composed of two originally unrelated battle accounts, vv. 1-21 and 22-35, joined together in such a way that they give the impression of being different stages of a continuous war between Israel and Syria in which both accounts follow a similar pattern.[169] The verse which functions as the redactional seam (1 Kgs 20.22) contains the formula *ltšwbt hšnh*. This joining of the two different narratives is generally ascribed to a Judahite[170] or the final editor of the Kings materials.[171] The similarities between the nature and arrangement of the materials in 2 Samuel 10, 11.1 + 12.26-31 with those of 1 Kings 20 are both very obvious and appear to be more than mere coincidence.

In the other occurrence of *ltšwbt hšnh*, 2 Chron 36.10,[172] this formula replaces the ambiguous phrase *b't hhy'*, and is clearly an example of the Chronicler's *Tendenz* for specifying ambiguous dating in the Dtr.[173] It would appear that since the 2 Kings 25 passage speaks of a military campaign, the Chronicler has borrowed the phrase *ltšwbt hšnh* to make his account more specific.[174]

A second clue to who this redactor may be is found in the observations made above that 11.1b (the location of David and the army) paves the way for the events in 11.2-27a and that the depiction of David in 12.30-31 is similar to that found in ch. 8. In the first instance the David–Bathsheba–Uriah narratives have been interpolated into the framework of 11.1 + 12.26. Thus, the notice of

David's remaining in Jerusalem makes possible the transition in the story to the episode of the meeting of David and Bathsheba, and the location of the army provides for the opportunity to have Uriah killed. Thus 1.1aβ is probably to be related to the interpolation of 11.2-12.25. In the same manner, 11.16 describes a battle which Joab lost, but 12.26 functions as his vindication.[175] Thus, as we shall see, the original end of the David–Bathsheba narrative was the battle-victory report of Joab at Rabbah, *'yr hmlwkh*, in 12.26.

The second observation, namely the similarity between 12.30-31 and ch. 8, is noteworthy since ch. 8 contains the narratives of the subjugation of all the nations surrounding Israel and Judah (attested in the list in 8.12) except for the subjugation of Ammon. In other words, though Ammon is listed in 8.12, there is no accompanying narrative to support this mention. While Hertzberg[176] and McCarter[177] note that chs. 10–12 make the Ammonite connection, the above analysis has demonstrated that it is only 12.30-31 which truly relates to the style and intention of the narratives in ch. 8.

5. Conclusions

We have thus demonstrated that the materials commonly referred to as the 'Ammonite War materials' in 2 Samuel 10 are not a coherent unit, nor are they historical narrative taken from archival sources. Rather we have shown that these materials have been edited and arranged by the Dtr (cf. Chart 3 below). In so doing we have argued

Chart 3. The Ammonite War Narratives

Written by Dtr	*Unit*	*Source utilized by Dtr*
2 Sam 10.1-2a, 5-6a	Intro to war	2 Sam 10.2b-4
2 Sam 10.6b-15	Ammonite-Aramean war with Joab	
	Aramean war with David	2 Sam 10.16-18
2 Sam 10.19	Concluding statement and etiology	
2 Sam 11.1a*a*	Transitional seam	
	Joab and the taking of the Rabbah	2 Sam 11.1a*bb*+12.26
2 Sam12.27-28	Speech of Joab calling for David	
	David and the taking of Rabbah	2 Sam 12.29-31

that v. 1, the introduction to the materials, and v. 19a, the closing summary of the materials, have their origin in phraseology which, though not generally thought to be 'deuteronomic,' is found predominantly and/or exclusively in passages within the DtrH and the Deuteronomic Code. We have also argued that these phrases and clauses function in this narrative in the same way as in their corollary units in the DtrH. Thus, we have concluded that these introductory and concluding verses are from the hand of a Deuteronomistic historian.

We have also argued that within these materials there are traditions which are utilized in ways which, on the one hand, are consistent with their usage in corollary units of the DtrH, such as a narrative which details unprovoked Ammonite aggression against Israel which leads to the defeat of Ammonites early within an Israelite ruler's reign. On the other hand there are traditions used which function as literary reversals on their standard usage, such as the Holy War motif in vv. 6b-15. Thus, there is in these materials affinity with and critique of Deuteronomistic themes.

We have also argued that there are structural similarities within these units, which have the stamp of the same writer/compiler. For example the ambiguous use of *r'h* seems to be part of a redactional seam between the various units. Further it appears that clauses introduced by this term, though generally taken to be introductory to the next unit, are evaluative of the actions in the current unit and function as summations of the enemies' positions. In this way, they function as seams between the units, as well as summations.

We have also argued that many of the geographical and historical locations and events utilized in these materials are found predominantly only in this chapter and in Dtr summaries such as the geographical location Ma'acah. We also demonstrated that the other geographical designations only appear in corollary units, such as the similarities between 2 Samuel 8 and 10, but that these are not exact matches. Thus, we have argued that the various attempts to locate them on the map have missed their legendary nature.

In a similar manner we have argued that the references to *hesed* in v. 2 are best understood in relation to the events described in 2 Sam 17.27. Thus, as in other places in the DtrH, chronological sequencing of events has not been adhered to in the placing of 2 Samuel 10 prior to 2 Samuel 20.

Finally, we have argued that the specific reference to Jericho is most helpful in dating these materials in 2 Samuel 10, since they must have been written at a time when Jericho was inhabited. In the same manner, they must have also been written when the historical memory that it was uninhabited in David's days was not prominent. This would suggest an exilic dating.

The above analysis has demonstrated that the narratives in 2 Samuel 10 tend to glorify David and his administration in a somewhat mocking manner. In this way, they appear to critique the materials in 2 Samuel 8, which glorify David's prowess in establishing the empire. In this unit, as we have shown, there is a skepticism which seems to argue that it was only when provoked that David entered battle. Similarly, they tend to critique motifs which may have been central to the late Davidic claim to reestablish the Davidic empire through military might and conquest. Thus, the literary reversals are, as we have argued, stylistically devised to turn accepted traditions on their head.

As regards the Ammonite War narratives in 2 Sam 11.1 + 12.26-31 we have shown that they are a completely separate tradition from the narratives in ch. 10. We have also demonstrated that there is a radically different compositional technique at work in this unit in that two independent narratives are joined together by a speech which uses catchwords from both units as a means of holding them together and which has theological terminology in line with the Dtr. On the other hand the ordering of the narratives in 2 Sam 10 parallels those in 2 Sam 11.1 + 12.26-31, namely a Joab + foreign enemy war narrative and a David + foreign enemy war narrative. This similarity suggests the hand of a redactor.

Finally we have shown that the Dtr had available several independent narratives of the Ammonite Wars. First was the narrative now found in 2 Sam 10.16-18, which paralleled the narrative in 2 Sam 8.3-9 and was incorporated into the narrative in 2 Sam 10 to report the return of the Arameans to a state of subjugation, similar to their status in 2 Sam 8 after their coalition with the Ammonites noted in 2 Sam 10.6b-15. Second was the Joab at Rabbah narrative in 2 Sam 11.1ab + 12.26, which was the original conclusion to the David-Bathsheba-Uriah narrative in which Joab took the city after the unsuccessful battle in which Uriah lost his life. Third the Dtr had the David at Rabbah narrative, 2 Sam 12.29-31, originally probably part of the 2 Sam 8 collection of war narratives about David's consolidation of the kingdom. The Dtr was responsible for the following material: (1) the introduction to the Ammonite Wars in 10.1-6a and the Ammonite War narrative in 10.6b-15 following the pattern of the Jephthah/Saul rise to rulership model (2) the concluding etiology in 10.19 as a means of joining 10.16-18 with the preceding (3) the redactional seam in 11.1a*a* to join the unrelated war traditions in chs. 10–12, and (4) 12.27-28 to join together the Joab and David at Rabbah narratives.

It is now time to turn to the David-Bathsheba, David-Uriah, and David-Nathan narratives in 2 Sam 11.2–12.25.

Chapter 4

THE DAVID-BATHSHEBA,
DAVID-URIAH, AND DAVID-NATHAN COMPLEXES
AND THE BIRTH OF SOLOMON

As was done with the units in the so-called 'Ammonite War Narratives', we shall begin our analysis of the David–Bathsheba–Uriah complex with a statement of the generally told 'story-line'. Then will follow structural outlines of the units and analysis.

As the story and its usual reading go, one evening David was walking on his roof-top and noticed a woman bathing (v. 2). He inquired and was told that she was Bathsheba, the wife of Uriah, the Hittite (v. 3). He was overcome by his lust, sent for her, and the two engaged in sexual intercourse (v. 4). As a result of this encounter she became pregnant (v. 5).

In order to avoid discovery of the adultery, David devised a plan. He recalled Uriah from the battlefield, and twice tried to get him to go home and have sex with his wife in the hope that the pregnancy would then be attributed to Uriah. Unfortunately for David, Uriah refused David's urgings (vv. 6-13).

With no other alternative,[1] David sent Uriah back to the battlefield with a letter to Joab, the commander-in-chief, to have Uriah placed in the thick of the battle, which he did.[2] Once Uriah died, Joab sent word to David, who then married Bathsheba.[3]

As was noted in Chapter 2 §3 above, the attempts to describe the events in 2 Sam 11.2-27 in terms of sexual lust gone awry and to concentrate on the psychological motivation of the characters are predicated upon the reader's speculations. This is the case, since the narrator neither describes the scenes in lustful terms[4] nor does the narrator present any indication of these emotions and motivations. With the exception of Joab's speculation on David's possible anger (v. 20a), which is not realized, there are neither stative verbs nor parenthetical narrative comments which give clues to either the emotions or the motivations of the characters and their actions.

As was also noted, there is currently an attempt to retain and justify primarily psychological readings of the text on the basis of theories of 'ambiguity'.[5] In other words, the fact that these narrative clues are omitted is evidence of a literary device which serves the purpose of heightening the interest of the reader in such aspects. As Yee states, 'Our author achieves the ambiguous tension between character action and motive by *deliberately resisting a description of the characters' feelings in dramatic situations . . . . He focuses upon the action. . .* ' (emphasis added).[6]

In contrast to such a line of argument it would appear more likely that the intention of the writer is definitely not to focus upon a story of feelings—either of 'love' or 'lust'—but rather to point the reader in another direction. In other words, it seems more likely that the lack of such clues would point to a different intention on the part of the author. Instead of concentrating on a story of sexual lust gone awry and then speculating on the internal psychological states of the characters, one should look at the structure of the narrative and at the choice of words utilized and see if there is an alternative reading of the narrative presented. In other words, by examining the particular words which *are* utilized in terms of their standard usage and by examining the narrative structure as it is presented, one can more probably determine the clue to the intention of the narrator.

1. *The David–Bathsheba Affair (2 Sam 11.2-5)*

The following is a structural outline of the unit.

    I. David-Bathsheba adultery (vv. 2-5)
      A. Scene set (2-3)
        1. Temporal designation (2aα)—*wyhy l't 'rb*
        2. Actions of the king (2aβ)—*wyqm . . . wythlk . . . wyr'*
        3. Introduction of the woman (2b)
          a. description of her activity—*rḥṣt*
          b. description of her beauty—*ṭwbt mr'h*
        4. Identification of the Woman
          a. Actions of David—*šlḥ . . . drš . . . 'mr* (3)
          b. Query of David
            (1) speculation—*hl' z't*
            (2) genealogy
              (a) patronymic—*bt 'ly'm*

(b) marital—*'št 'wryh*
B. Adultery (4)
    1. David's actions—*šlḥ ... lqḥ*
    2. Her action—*wtb'*
    3. Their action—coitus—*wyškb 'mh*
    4. Description of her condition—*mtqdšt mṭm'th*
    5. Her action—*wtšb*
C. Consequences of adultery (5)
    1. Pregnancy—*wthr h'šh*
    2. Notification of David by the woman
        a. Her actions—*wtšlḥ...wtgd ... wt'mr*
        b. Speech—*hrh 'nky*

The unit opens with the disjunctive *wyhy*. This suggests a break between the events in v. 1 and those in 2f. The unit then gives a general temporal designation, *l't h'rb*, which gives the narrative a 'once upon a time' character.

The unit contains three instances of a clustering of three verbs describing the actions of either David or the woman. In v. 2 there is the set *wykm* + *wythlk* + *wyr'* which describes how David found himself in the situation. In v. 3 there are the three verbs *wyšlḥ* +*wydrš* + *wy'mr*,[7] which function to further the plot by depicting David's interest in and speculation about the woman observed. It should be noted that generally this third verb is attributed to an anonymous speaker who 'answers' David's inquiry. The structure of 2 Sam 11.3, however, demonstrates that there is no other subject introduced in the verse. Similarly, there is no use of *l* to indicate David has become the indirect object of the verb. Thus, syntactically it appears that all three verbs have David as the subject. The story line offers further confirmation of the correctness of this interpretation of the verbs in v. 3. The verb *'mr* follows *drš*, which points to an inquiry for information. Similarly it is followed by a 'speculative identification' of the woman (*hl' z't*). It would appear, therefore, that the statement in v. 3b is the 'inquiry' (*drš*) of David in search of confirmation of the identity of the woman. In similar fashion, one would not expect a response to a *drš* of the king to consist of a 'speculation'. In v. 5 the unit ends with the cluster *wtšlḥ* + *wtgd* + *wt'mr*[8] which functions to bring the unit to a close by describing the actions taken by the woman once she becomes pregnant.[9] Both the male and female characters are accorded the same type of syntactical presentation of a threefold verb complex followed by a quotation which affects the narrative which follows.

In each one of these verbal triplets there is a key word which functions as a code for setting the tone of the narrative and foreshadowing the events to follow. In the first instance the use of *wythlk* is most interesting. Most instances of the usage of *hlk* in the *hithpa'el* refer to positive events. They refer to instances of either Yahweh traversing the scene[10] or to others 'walking with Yahweh'.[11]

There are, however, three other instances where this verb is used in relation to David to describe his roaming the countryside with his 'band of men' during his conflicts with Saul.[12] Unlike the above noted instances of *hlk* in the *hithpa'el*, which are all positive in connotation, these latter instances occur in contexts in which David runs a protection racket and thereby has problems with the local inhabitants of Judah.[13] Given the events which take place in this unit, it would appear that *wythlk* in 2 Sam 11.2 functions to indicate to the reader that some questionable conduct is about to occur.[14]

The other two instances of triple verbs both contain the verb *šlḥ*. Both the male and the female characters in the story, who appear to carry similar weight in the narrative, are subjects of the verb (*šlḥ*). Richard Bowman[15] has argued that the use of *šlḥ* in this context denotes the exercise of authority. He bases this conclusion upon the high frequency of the usage of *šlḥ* in 2 Samuel 10–12[16] and also the fact that the objects of this sending are Joab, the army, Uriah, Nathan (by Yahweh), and Bathsheba (sent for).

He has also argued that in ascribing the verb *šlḥ* to Bathsheba, the writer is signalling that she also has authority.[17] Contrary to the contention that the use of this verb is 'expected' in this verse, the story could have simply stated that she went to him. It would appear, rather, that the balanced use of *šlḥ* and *'mr* in vv. 3 and 5 is intentional.

This suggestion is reinforced by the mere fact that the only other women within the DtrH who are the subject of this verb are women of power and influence. It is used in depicting Rahab helping the spies escape (Josh 2.21), Deborah summoning Barak for battle (Judg 4.6), Delilah summoning the Philistines to get Samson (Judg 16.18), and Jezebel plotting against Elijah (1 Kgs 19.2) and against Naboth (1 Kgs 21.8). Thus, Bathsheba is placed within a highly select number of powerful and/or devious women[18] through the use of this verb. These data would not only confirm the contention of Bowman, but they also raise the possibility that this unit, similar to the others just cited, is one of political importance in which a woman is a prime mover. is a prime mover.

A clue to the correctness of this suspicion is found in the identification of the woman in terms of two different relationships, namely patronymic[19] and marital (v.3b). It is also significant that the patronymic relationship comes first, since the order of the identifying items points to their relative importance in the narrative. Johnson notes that, 'Genealogies were used to provide an individual of rank with connections to a worthy family or individual of the past'.[20] In this sense the function is to enhance the status of the individual.

This point is best illustrated by looking at the presentation of three other women who appear in the DtrH. Deborah is identified first as a prophetess and then as the wife of Lapidoth (Judg 4.4). Similarly, Huldah is first identified as a prophetess and then as the wife of Shallum (2 Kgs 22.14). Thus, in these two instances, where two pieces of identifying information are provided on the woman, it is the first piece which conveys her primary importance to the narrative.

In the same manner Michal is identified as either the daughter of Saul (2 Sam 3.13; 6.16f.), where her political connections are paramount, or as the wife of David (2 Sam 3.14), where his claim to her is more important. Thus, one sees that the way in which women are identified in the various narratives is dictated by the importance of these data to the narrative.

In the order of the relationships[21] in the identification of Bathsheba in 2 Sam 11.3, she is first designated 'Bathsheba,[22] the daughter of Eliam'. According to 2 Sam 23.34 an Eliam[23] the son of Ahithophel served among the *gbry dwd*.[24] If these two references are to the same person, this would mean that Bathsheba came from a politically influential family, since Ahithophel is noted as one of David's key advisors, who during the Absalom revolt shifted his allegiance to the latter (2 Sam 16.23). Thus, the implication of the genealogy is that this woman was from an important family.[25]

With this in mind, the significance of the previous argument that the syntax of v. 3 suggests that David is the one who speaks these words becomes clearer. In other words, as presented by the narrator, David observes from the roof a woman bathing and questions whether this is Bathsheba, the daughter of Eliam, and by implication, the granddaughter of Ahithophel,[26] the wife of Uriah. Thus, the narrator points out that David is more concerned about the woman's political connections[27] than her marital status.

This emphasis on his part would not surprise the reader, for 1 Samuel 19 and 25,[28] as well as 2 Sam 3.2-5 relate stories of how David is attracted to and marries women of high social/patronymic status. In this regard, however, perhaps one should rethink whether this unit is a narrative primarily concerned with 'sexual lust gone awry' or rather with a story of political intrigue in which sex becomes a tool of politics. In other words, is this not really a story of 'political marriage'?

In the remainder of the narrative, as outlined above, there is a lack of attention given to sexual details and descriptions. Two important nuances appear in v. 4. The first is a pattern in which David's actions are paralleled by those of Bathsheba.[29] Secondly her actions are not described with *hiph'il* verb forms, which would suggest that she was being 'caused to act'. Rather they are in the *qal*, she comes and returns. Finally the wording for the sexual act in v. 4 is *wyškb 'mh*, which demonstrates that the narrator suggests that she is here as well as throughout the narrative a willing and equal partner to the events which transpire.[30]

The suggestion of 'co-partnership' is further grounded in the interpolation of the clause *why' mtqdšt mtm'th* in v. 4. This activity has correctly been associated with the laws regarding the menstrual cycle and purification in Lev 15.19-24.[31] The Talmudic tractate *Niddah* 31b notes the relationship between the menstrual cycle and conception.[32] Gressmann has argued that the function of these words is 'to emphasize that there can be no doubt as to David's paternity'.[33]

The implication is also that, in the view of the narrator, the actors knew the probable consequences of their deed. This is seen in the fact that the clause is inserted between the statement of intercourse and the woman's return home (v. 4aβ). In other words, the narrator is pointing to the fact that not only is the question of paternity settled by the time designation, but also that the actors knew the 'danger' of such an encounter leading to pregnancy.[34] With this in mind the question is raised as to whether pregnancy is not the desired outcome. In other words, could it be possible that the narrator is suggesting that this instance of *škb* taking place at this time has deliberate political overtones and motivations?

The above possibility may initially appear to be far-fetched. In v. 5, however, the narrator does not provide any indication of distress on the part of Bathsheba once she learns of her pregnancy. Rather, immediately following the statement of pregnancy, *wthr*, there is the calculated triple verb construction, followed by the terse quotation *hrh 'nky*, 'I'm pregnant'.

In order to assess whether this statement is indicative of distress, it is necessary to examine other 'pregnancy narratives' found in the Bible. Noteworthy is the fact that all such narratives relate to the birth of a special individual (e.g. a patriarch, Lot's grandsons, Samson, Samuel, etc.). Similarly some follow particular motifs.[35] In many of the narratives there is a promise made regarding the life of the child as a result of the pregnancy.[36]

Two other pregnancy narratives like 2 Sam 11.2-5 involve illicit relations, Gen 19.29-38, the incestuous relationship between Lot and his daughters,[37] and Gen 38.13-30, the seduction of Judah by Tamar.[38] Both narratives present the woman as devising a plan to get pregnant and carrying out the plan through entrapment.[39] More importantly, in the latter a deal is made between Tamar and Judah prior to the intercourse. Additionally, the narrator depicts her informing him of her pregnancy through the use of the verb *šlḥ* and by the words *'nky hrh*. The reason that Judah is in search of such a liaison is due to the death of his wife, *bt šw'* (Gen 38.12), which interestingly is the name the Chronicler also records for the mother of his children (1 Chron 2.3), as well as the name the Chronicler gives to the mother of Solomon in 1 Chron 3.5.[40]

In summation, pregnancy narratives are told only about the birth of special children. Similarly, there is precedent for deal-making as an integral part of pregnancy narratives. There is also precedent for portraying situations where women engage in sex as a means of improving their status.

In 11.2-5, Bathsheba's bathing in a location which is observable from the palace may be viewed as part of an attempt at improving status.[41] 1 Kgs 1.17, if read straightforwardly, attests to an arrangement concluded at some points between David and Bathsheba concerning David's successor. Could it not be reasonable, therefore, to take the statement, *hrh 'nky*, as a signal that the deal has been 'consummated', there is a new heir to the throne on the way, or so there will be once David can marry Bathsheba?

What, however, would be the basis or necessity for such a deal? In the earlier discussion of *hesed* in 2 Sam 10.2 we noted an allusion to actions which are discussed in 2 Sam 17.27 and thus concluded that the Ammonite War narratives are edited out of chronological sequence. The events of the Ammonite Wars probably followed Absalom's revolt rather than preceded it.

During the Absalom revolt, Ahithophel, Bathsheba's grandfather, switched sides from David to Absalom (15.31) and eventually committed suicide (17.23). If Bathsheba were already a member of David's harem, then her offspring, and Ahithophel's descendant, would be a possible heir to the throne. Similarly, given the chronological notations in 2 Samuel 13–15, if the narratives as they are currently presented are in correct chronological order, Solomon would be at least 12 years old at the time of the Absalom revolt. It seems highly unlikely at the least that Ahithophel would have foreclosed such a possibility as his great-grandson becoming king by supporting a rival candidate's overthrow of David.

Could it not also be that the David–Bathsheba affair took place after the Absalom Revolt? If so the narrative in 2 Sam 11.2-5 could have initially concerned an event in which a deal was struck between David and Bathsheba. The agreement that her son will be the successor is a solution to reinstating her family in good graces with the reigning powers and to recementing David's ties to the Hebronites and other southerners[42] after the defection of Ahithophel to Absalom. Thus her status could be improved by such a liaison.

In this light we would have to look at the David–Bathsheba marriage not only as political in nature but also as another case of David's consolidating political power through marriage. The significance of these observations can be seen in reviewing the way in which many scholars traditionally view this complex. For example, Bowman has argued that the arrangement of the material in 2 Samuel 10–12 is a portrayal of the successful David exercising power in the sphere of public events and the corrupt David misusing power in the sphere of his private life.[43] Similarly, Gunn has argued for the split of public vs. private/familial as the key to the narrative arrangement and that it is the latter area in which David meets trouble.[44]

On the other hand, the case being made here is that another possible scheme for explaining the arrangement of these narratives is that of foreign vs. domestic policy.[45] In other words, while 2 Sam 10.1–11.1 + 12.26-31 relate to David's foreign policy, the narrative in 2 Sam 11.2–12.25 concerns his domestic policy. Similarly, as will be seen in our discussion of 11.26-27a and 12.24-25 below, he is successful in some aspects of his policy (e.g., he marries Bathsheba and Solomon is born). Thus, the organizing principle appears to take its direction from the statements made about kingship in 1 Sam 8.11-18, where the Dtr, speaking through Samuel, argues that both in the areas of military defense and domestic policy the king will be exploitative of the people and will abuse his power.

2. *The David-Uriah Complex (2 Sam 11.6-25)*

Having demonstrated that the narrative depiction of the incident between David and Bathsheba in 11.2-5 could involve a political arrangement, attested in 1 Kgs 1.17, we now turn to an investigation of the David-Uriah narratives of 11.6-25.[46] An important issue will be the question of how 11.2-5 relates to 11.6-25 and, secondarily, whether there is substantiation and reinforcement in 11.6-25 for the above interpretation of 11.2-5.

The following is a structural outline for 11.6-25.

II. Attempts to kill Uriah (vv. 6-25)
  A. Plan A (6-13)
    1. Setting it up (6)
      a. Report of David's actions—*wyšlḥ*
      b. Message to Joab—*šlḥ* Uriah
      c. Compliance of Joab—*wyšlḥ*
    2. Report of interaction between David and Uriah (7)
      a. Uriah's compliance—*wyb'*
      b. David's queries about army—*wyš'l lšlwm*
    3. Instructions of David (8a)
      a. Designation of speaker and addressee (8aα)
      b. Instructions—*rd ... wrḥṣ* (8aβ)
    4. Report of implementation of plan (8b-9)
      a. Description of Uriah's action—*wyṣ'* (8b)
      b. Description of signaler—*wtṣ' ... mś't* (8b)
      c. Description of Uriah's non-compliance—*wyškb ... wl' yrd* (9)
    5. Informing David of results (10a)
      a. Designation of addressee—*wygdw* (10aα)
      b. Report—*l' yrd* (10aβ)
    6. Response of David to information (10b-13)
      a. Dialogue between David and Uriah
        (1) David's questions (10b)
          (a) *hl' mdrk*
          (b) *mdw' l' yrdt*
         (2) Uriah's response (11)
          (a) Designation of speaker and addressee
          (b) Reminders of war
            i. Ark, Israel, Judah—*bskt*
            ii. Joab and servants—*bśdh*
          (c) Interpretation of plan—*w'b' ... l'kl ... wlštwt ... wlškb*
          (d) Oath

          i. *ḥyk*

          ii. *wḥy npšk*

   b. Instructions of David

     (1) Designation of speaker and addressee

     (2) Instructions—*šb . . . 'šlḥk* (12a)

   d. Report of Uriah's compliance *wyšb*

   e. Second attempt at Plan A (13)

     (1) David's summons—*wyqr'*

     (2) Report of Uriah's behaviors *wy'kl . . . wyšt . . . wyškrhw* (13a)

     (3) Report of Uriah's non-compliance—*wyṣ' . . . l' yrd* (13b)

B. Plan B (14-25)

   1. Setting it up (14)

     a. Time designation—*wyhy bbqr* (14a*a*)

     b. Means of setting it up

       (1) *wyktb spr*

       (2) agent—Joab

     c. Compliance of Uriah—*wyšlḥ byd*

   2. Report of letter to Joab—*wyktb* (15a)

   3. Instructions for Joab (15b*a*)

     a. Positioning of Uriah—*mwl pny hmlḥmh hḥzqh*

     b. Actions of army—*wšbtm m'ḥryw*

     c. Anticipated results—*wnkh wmt* (15bβ)

   4. Description of implementation of plan (16-17)

     a. Time and place designation (16a)

       (1) *wyhy bšmwr*

       (2) *h'yr*

     b. Report of positioning of Uriah—*wytn* (16b)

     c. Battle report (17)

       (1) Actions of enemy—*wyṣ' 'nšy h'yr*

       (2) Casualty report

         (a) *'bdy dwd*

         (b) Uriah

   5. Informing David of results (18-25)

     a. Summary commissioning report—*wyšlḥ . . . wygd* (18)

     b. Instructions to messenger (19-21)

       (1) Commissioning report—*wyṣw* (19a)

       (2) Time designation—*kklwtk* (19b)

       (3) Description of possible negative reception (20-21a)

         (a) Possible negative reaction—*t'lh ḥmt*

         (b) Possible questions

           i. *mdw' ngštm* (20aβ)

           ii. *hl' yd'tm* (20b)

iii. *my hkh* (21aα)
iv. *hl' 'šh hšlykh* (21aβ)
v. *lmh ngštm* (21aγ)
(4) Designation of appropriate response—*w'mrt ... 'wryh mt* (21b)
c. Summary messenger report—*wylk ... wyb' ... wygd* (22)
d. Messenger speech (23-24)
(1) Designation of speaker and addressee (23a)
(2) Battle description—*ky gbrw ... wyṣ'w ... wnhyh ... wyr'w* (23b-24a)
(3) Casualty report (24b)
(a) *m'bdy hmlk //* (17bα)
(b) Uriah // (17bβ)
6. Response of David to information (25)
a. Designation of speaker and addressee (25aα)
b. Commission of messenger (25aβ)—*kh t'mr*
c. Message (25b)
(1) Words of assurance—*'l yr' ... hdbr*
(2) Motive clause
(3) Battle instructions—*hḥzq mlḥmtk //* (15b)

As noted from the above outline 11.6-13 and 14-25 are parallel in structure. They both contain descriptions of David setting a plan into motion (vv. 6, 14), oral communication between David and Uriah (v. 7), report of letter from David to Joab (v. 15a), instructions of David (vv. 8a and 15b), report of implementation of the plan (vv. 8b-9 [thwarted] and 16-17 [successful]), a report of informing David of the results (vv. 10a, 18-24), and reports of David's reactions to the information (vv. 10b-13, 25). While each parallel section is not of the same length and internal structure, their similarity in function relative to the narrative is clearly apparent. The major differences between the parallel sections are in the last two parts, the reports of informing David (vv. 10a//18-24) and the responses of David to the information (vv. 10b-13//25). (See below Chart 4.)

While one would expect some difference in the means of informing David, since the locus of the primary action in both plans is different, the length of the instructions in Plan B raises questions. In Plan A there is simply the notation of *wygdw* (v. 10a). This appears to be paralleled in Plan B by a report of Joab informing David of the results of the battle, *wyšlḥ ... wygd* (18). What follows in vv. 19-24 appears to be additions or repetitions in the narrative.

Chart 4. Parallel Structures in 11.6-25

6	Setting plan into motion	14
7[47]	Communication between David and other key actor	15a
8a	Instructions of David	15b
8b-9	Implementation of plan—thwarted/successful	16-17
10a	Informing David of results	18-24
10b-13	David's reactions to information	25

A problem arises in the fact that the initial report to David is then followed by a further account of Joab giving instructions to a *ml'k*, with speculation on David's probable reaction to the news and the way to respond to this reaction (vv. 19-22), and a separate report of the *ml'k* informing David (vv. 23-24).

The original authenticity of 11.19-24 is problematic for several reasons. First, since v. 18 states that David had already been informed, the instructions in this material appear to be after the fact. Secondly, since v. 22 states that the *ml'k* reported (*wygd*) to David, the report of the *ml'k* informing David of the war (vv. 23-24) also appears to be after the fact. Thirdly, the details of the battle descriptions in vv. 17, 20, and 23 do not completely coincide.[48] Fourthly, v. 21 is a quotation from Judg 9.50-53. Finally, Joab's anticipated negative reaction of David does not occur.[49] It thus appears that the text has undergone a series of expansions.

The three battle reports in vv. 16-24 provide a clue to the possible development of the text. In the first battle report, vv. 16-17, there is an ambiguous reference to the location of Uriah ('*l hmqwm*, v. 16b). This is followed by a description of a battle in open terrain (*wys'w . . . wylḥmw*, 17a).[50]

Given these details, it is surprising to read of Joab's instructions to the *ml'k* speaking about 'approaching the walls', with no indication of an open-field battle (vv. 20-21). Similarly, the quotation of material from Judg 9.50-53 in v. 21 suggests redactional activity.

The third battle report in vv. 23-24, however, repeats the *ys'* of 17, as well as the anonymous name for the enemy, '*nšym*, while clarifying the ambiguous reference to *mqwm* by specifying *pth hš'r* (23b) and *ḥwmh* (24a) (see Chart 5).

It would thus appear that vv. 23-24 were added to the narrative in order to clarify the ambiguous references in v. 16a and to provide an opportunity and vehicle for a response by David (v. 25). While vv. 19-21 anticipate the reference to a wall, they also serve the purpose of introducing a *ml'k* to the narrative. Thus, once again a speech of Joab functions literarily to hold together two separate narratives (vv. 14-18, 23-25) as was the case in 12.27-28.

Chart 5. Compositional Arrangement in 11.16-24

11.16-18	—Battle report in which Uriah dies and report of informing David.
11.19-22	—Speech of Joab instructing the messenger and sending him to David.
11.23-24	—Report of Messenger informing David of battle in which Uriah died.

Thus, not only is the report of informing David of the results of implementing Plan B longer and more involved than the report in Plan A, but we have discovered that the same compositional technique employed in 12.26-31 has been employed in this section. This would suggest that the hand of the same redactor is at work, which conclusion is supported by the quotation of parts of Judg 9.50-53 in v. 21.

At this point we need to explore the responses of David to the information in both plans. As noted above the response in Plan A (vv. 10b-12) is much longer and complex than that in Plan B (v. 25). The response of David to the news delivered in 11.18-24 is to try to take the city again (v. 25), which they did.[51] This is the intention of v. 13, since the conclusion to the incident repeats the phrase *w'l bytw l' yrd*. Thus, the actions described in v. 13a, namely getting Uriah drunk,[52] present a variation on the plan described in 8a. Since v. 13 provides a complete parallel to v. 25, the question arises as to the function served by vv. 10b-12 within this section designated 'the response of David to the information'.

In 10b the double question formulation *hl' m...* is followed by *mdw'*. This is significant, since the same pattern in reverse is found in v. 20αβ-b. Similarly in Uriah's response to these questions in place of the the ambiguous term *wrḥṣ rglyk* (8a)[53] the unambiguous *wlškb 'm 'šty* (11aβ) is found. In addition he adds the activities of eating and drinking, which, though not found in the instructions of David in 8a, are found in the parallel material which follows in v. 13. One also notes the reference to *Heilskrieg* in the mention of the *'rwn*, the *yšbym bskt*,[54] and the oath formula, *ḥyk wḥy npšk* (11b). Finally the instructions in v. 12 serve the function of explaining why Uriah does not go right back to the front, thereby paving the way for the second attempt at getting him to 'go home' described in v. 13.[55] Thus, once again two parallel units (11.6-10a and 11.13) are joined together by a redactional seam which contains Deuteronomic themes (Holy War) and in which an ambiguous term in the first unit is clarified by quoting terms from the parallel one (see Chart 6).

Chart 6. Compositional Arrangement in 11.8b-13

11.8b-10a	—First attempt to get Uriah to go home.
11.10b-12	—Dialogue with David and speech of Uriah using *Heilskrieg* motif and clarifying *rḥṣ rglk*.
11.13	—Second attempt to get Uriah to go home.

Clearly, the existence of three examples of the same compositional technique (11.10b-12, David and Uriah; 19-21, Joab to *ml'k*; 12.27-28, Joab to David) in the same narrative complex could not be by coincidence. In addition, the fact that the speeches share *Heilskrieg* terminology and/or quotations from Judges within these speeches suggests the hand of the Dtr as having reworked this material.

As noted in the outline two plans are involved (Plans A and B). The goal of the former is for Uriah to have sex with his wife (*rḥṣ rglyk*, 8b), while the latter is to have him killed in battle (*wnkh wmt*, 15b). Generally the intention of Plan A is taken to be the cover up of the pregnancy announced in 11.5b, and the intention of Plan B is only the unavoidable consequence of the failure of Plan A.

Given their similarity in structure, however, the question arises whether the narrator is signalling a similarity in intention in both units. In other words, has not the narrator structured both units to follow the same format as a way of suggesting that the final outcome, the death of Uriah, should be taken as the intention of both Plan A and Plan B.

The dialogue between Uriah and David in the redactional seam of 10b-11 is most important for the interpretation of the intentions of the narrator.[56] In Uriah's response to David's query as to why he had not gone home, there is reference to a 'soldier's oath' of abstinence during battle (v. 11b). This is generally understood in the light of 1 Sam 21.5, which attests to this taboo.[57] Additionally, Josh 7.6-26 speaks to the consequences for one who violates a taboo of the *Heilskrieg*. Similarly, even though the oath formula found in v. 11b is noted to be tautological,[58] it would appear that its use, coupled with the allusion to 'holy war motifs'[59] implies that *škb* is to be understood as life-threatening. In other words, for a soldier to engage in such behavior places lives in jeopardy,[60] and Uriah was not interested in 'following in the sandals' of Achan.

By the same token, there is nothing in the text to indicate that

David was willing to forgo claims on Bathsheba if only Uriah would have intercourse with her and David could thereby be released from a charge of adultery or illegal paternity. As v. 27 indicates, the issue in the narrative concerns who would 'possess' Bathsheba, not who would be considered the father of her child.

A clue to the significance of these observations is found in the misinterpreted and long-misunderstood term, *mś't hmlk* (11.8b). This phrase is generally taken to mean a 'gift from the king' which in some manner was presumably to serve as an inducement for Uriah to have sex with Bathsheba.[61]

Since Budde[62] there has been appeal to Gen 43.34 to substantiate such an interpretation. In this text, the banquet scene between Joseph and his brothers, the narrator states that *mś't* were given to the brothers, with the *mś'h* of Benjamin being five times that of his other brothers. Since this verse is taken to be part of the execution of the instructions of Joseph to serve the meal,[63] *mś't* in Gen 43.34 is taken to be a 'portion of food from the king's table'.

Such an interpretation, however, is very strained. In other words, why would a 'gift of food from the king' be taken to be an inducement for sex? In the Genesis 43 account, it is clear from the banquet context that *mś't* has something to do with food which is being delivered, since the verb of the clause is a form of *nś'*. In 2 Sam 11.8b, however, the verb of which *mś't* is subject is a form of *yṣ'*, 'to go out', in the *qal*.[64] It would thus appear that the meaning of *mś'h* in 11.8b must be deduced from the other occurrences of the term rather than from Gen 43.34.

In Jer 40.6 it is used in the context of an *'rḥh*; and in Esth 2.18 it is used in the context of a *mšth*; thus, these two instances are close to the meaning of Gen 43.34. In Ezek 20.40 it refers to a type of sacrificial offering and in Ps 141.2 it refers to the lifting of the hands of the priest during a sacrifice, neither of which relate to the 2 Samuel 11 context. In Amos 5.11 and 2 Chron 24.6, 9 it relates to a tax on the poor/levied by Moses respectively. Again, there is no relationship to the context in 2 Samuel 11.

In Judg 20.38 and 40,[65] *mś'h* appears in a context when smoke signals are given to begin an ambush. Similarly in Jer 6.1 *mś'h* is used parallel to blowing the shophar in signalling the people of the 'foe from the North'.[66] Interestingly, the term also appears in the Lachish Letters (iv, line 10) with the same denotation of signals within a war context.

The clause, *wtṣ' 'ḥryw mś't hmlk*, in 11.8b should be rendered, 'and the one to give the signal to the king followed him'.[67] In this regard, it would appear that the intention was to 'catch them in the act', so to speak. More specifically, the intention was to catch Uriah breaking the 'soldier's oath', for then, as his speech in v. 11 confirms, he could be charged with placing the army in jeopardy and possibly be executed.

Thus, the traditional interpretation of Plan A as a cover-up for the adultery and Plan B as a last resort 'assassination' no longer appears plausible. The above reinterpretation of *mś't hmlk* coupled with the speech of Uriah in 11.11 suggest that Plan A should be interpreted as entrapment in which Uriah is sent home to have sex with Bathsheba so that he can be caught and executed, not to cover up the paternity. Thus, David's use of the threefold *šalōm* functions ironically. While David tries to stress peace-time through this statement, Uriah's speech foils the plan by stressing that it is wartime.

Similarly, the fact that the structures of vv. 6-13 and vv. 14-25 are identical adds more weight to the argument that the intention of the narrator was to present the two plans as heading toward the same objective, the death of Uriah. In other words, the identical structures for Plans A and B suggest that there has been no shift in motivation on David's part as the 'traditional' interpretation would have us believe.

In the same manner, given the above interpretation of 11.2-5 as a narrative of 'political intrigue', such an interpretation fits very well into the scheme. In other words, the narrative suggests that once Bathsheba notified David that she was pregnant with a potential 'heir to the throne', he then set into motion plans to kill Uriah so that she could then be free to marry him, which she does as soon as the 'period of grief' has passed (v. 27a). In this regard all of the narrative of 11.2-25 reaches its climax in this action.

Finally, much has been made of the assumed theological significance[68] of Uriah's name and the uniqueness of this for one who is not a Yahweh worshiper. It would appear, however, that in concentrating on this aspect of the character, one misses the fact that Uriah is presented as a non-Israelite who speaks with authority about the will of Yahaweh on Deuteronomic law and custom[69] and who appears to be more pious and God-fearing than David. This observation takes on more significance in light of the fact that the same motif is utilized in the presentation of Rahab in relation to the spies (Josh 2.9-13). As was argued above in the discussion of *ḥesed*,[70] Rahab's speech is clearly from the hand of the Dtr. One could speculate the same about this presentation of Uriah.

In this regard there can be no doubt but that the hand of the Dtr is very active in the final shape of the materials in 2 Sam 11.6-25. Our analysis has pointed to the use of Deuteronomic themes in the redactional seams of 11.11a and 21b. Secondly it noted the unusual usage of *mś'h* in 8b paralleled in Judges 20, which similarly has been claimed to be a Dtr passage connecting duplicate accounts. Finally we noted the similarity in the portrayal of Uriah to that of Rahab in Joshua 2.

3. *The David-Bathsheba Marriage and the Birth of the Child (2 Sam 11.26-27a)*

Following the death of Uriah there is a brief notice of the marriage of David and Bathsheba and of the birth of the child conceived through the adultery. A structural outline of the unit follows.

III. Marriage of David and Uriah's Wife (vv. 26-27)

    A. Response of *'št 'wryh* (26)
        1. Temporal designation—*wtšm' . . . ky mt*
        2. Report of mourning—*wtspd*
    B. Marriage and birth reports (27a)
        1. Temporal designation—*wy'br h'bl* (27aα)
        2. Actions of David—*wyšlḥ . . . wy'sph*
        3. Actions of Woman—*wthy . . . wtld*

As in 11.2-5 there is a symmetry in the way the narrator presents the actions of David and the woman.[71] In v. 27 there is the use of a two-fold verb structure for the actions of David, *wyšlḥ . . . wy'sph*, and for the actions of the woman, *wthy . . . wtld*. This symmetry is similar to that of vv. 3 and 5, as noted above.[72] In other words the symmetry can be seen as the narrator's way of signalling equality of responsibility for the actions taken. In this regard David's sending, *wyšlḥ*, is paralleled by the woman's becoming his wife, *wthy*. Since an alternative reading could have been presented in terms of David as the sole subject of the verbs[73] with the marriage presented as *wyqḥh*, the use of *wthy* in 11.27a clearly signals her independent action.

Ridout has termed this section of the narrative the 'apex' which is the 'fruition of both the adultery and the removal of Bathsheba's husband'. He designates these events 'David's folly'.[74] Thus, in line with what has been demonstrated above, we can say that for the narrator this section of the narrative is the completion of a plan initiated in 11.3-4, carried out in vv. 6-17, and consummated in 11.27.

The references to mourning in 11.26b and 27aα reinforce this interpretation of a plan being brought to fruition. While the first verb, *spd*, denotes wailing and emotion,[75] the second verb, *'bl*, denotes only the customs of mourning[76] (as opposed to the expression of emotions) and a specified period of time for it.[77] Thus, while 11.26 portrays the wife of Uriah expressing the expected grief of a wife over the death of her husband, 11.27 minimizes and may even trivialize[78] this mourning, since the narrator states that as soon as the mourning period passed, *'br*,[79] the marriage took place. In other words, through the use of the phrase, *wy'br h'bl*, the narrator gives the impression that once the required seven-day period was satisfied, they married. Thus, the impression of two persons carrying out a plan is reinforced.

Additional evidence for this 'planful' nature of the events is found in the use of *'sp* (11.27), which is most peculiar in a marriage context.[80] It has been suggested that this verb should be understood as David's giving protection to Bathsheba on the order of Rahab gathering her family together (Josh 2.18).[81] In the case of widowhood, however, the protection/support for her would be given either by her family or her in-laws.[82] Given the context, this marriage of two adulterers could not be understood as David's offering protection.

It would appear that in the use of *'sp* the narrator is suggesting that Bathsheba is one more of the 'harvest' of David's wives who had been married to other men (after Abigail, 1 Sam 25[83] and Michal, 2 Sam 3). Thus, she became one more gathered in/added to his collection of influential women. Though the means of acquiring each was different, the fact that he was married to three women who came from influential families and who were at some previous point married to other men probably helps explain the use of *'sp* in 11.27a.

Finally, Neff has demonstrated that the birth narrative genre usually contains an indication of pregnancy (*hrh*) followed by the announcement of the birth (*yld*).[84] In this unit, however, the *hrh* is missing. Similarly there is no other verb in 11.27 which would suggest sexual contact as a replacement for the *hrh*.[85] Thus, the *wtld* in 11.27 must be understood as going with the *wthr* of 11.5, in which case there is an indication that the goal of the narrative from the beginning was not just the marriage, but also the birth of the child.

In this light there has been a narrative tension held since v. 5. In other words, while the birth narrative genre usually contains the *hrh* followed by the *yld*, in this instance there needed to be reports of a death and marriage before there could be the birth report. So the plan appears to have run its course.[86]

The indication that the plan has been completed, however, is missing in the omission of the name for the child born in 11.27a. Burke O. Long has argued that birth narratives usually contain three verbs, *hrh*, *yld* and *qr'*.[87] As just noted the first of these verbs appears in 11.5 and the second in 11.27a. The third, however, is not found until 12.24b. Thus, since the deal in 11.2-27a leads to an unnamed child, the birth narrative formula has not been completed.

This omission of the name is most unusual. Of all instances of the verb *wtld* in birth narratives, thirty-three are followed by a naming with *qr'*.[88] Eighteen others are followed by the name of the individual born.[89]

There are only five birth narratives other than 11.27 which do not give a name to the child born. In these instances either the individual born is named later as a part of the narrative flow,[90] a child born to a woman after the main character has been born,[91] or the other characters, especially the mother, are also anonymous.[92]

There is a significant difference between two of the above situations and the incidents in 11.2–12.25. In the latter the unnamed child is born prior to the birth of one of the main characters, namely, Solomon. Secondly, the mother is not anonymous; she is Bathsheba. Thirdly, as currently depicted, unlike the Moses narrative, it is not the child born in 11.27 whose name is held in abeyance. Rather it is another child, Solomon, whose name is given as completion of the birth formula.

The question before us, therefore, is whether we have a deviation from the formula with a complete narrative in 11.2-27a, or whether the same technique of narrative tension is to be re-employed. In other words, has an intervening narrative been placed between the second and third elements of the formula to accommodate concerns of the narrator? An answer to this question will have to be held until we examine the units in 11.27b–12.23.

4. *The David–Nathan Complex (2 Sam 11.27b-12.15)*

As noted above, there is almost a scholarly consensus that all or part(s) of the David-Nathan complex in 11.27b-15 is/are secondary to the David–Bathsheba–Uriah complex in 11.2-27a.[93] Similarly, in the previous section we demonstrated that 11.6-27aα now separates two parts of a birth narrative formula, *wthr ... wtld*, by supplying narratives of a death and remarriage as intervening events between the pregnancy and birth. The notations in 11.27bf. also seem to function in the same way. Namely, they intervene between the second and third elements of the typical birth narrative *wtld ... wt(y)qr'*. Thus, in both cases interpolation appears to have occurred. What has to be examined, however, is how much of the inserted material is secondary.

The following is a structural outline of 11.27b–12.15:

I.   Yahweh's reaction to the events reported in 11.2-27a (11.27b-12.1a)
    A.   Theological evaluation—*wyr' hdbr b'yny* (11.27b)
    B.   Report of messenger commission (1a)—*wyšlḥ*
II. Nathan–David Confrontation I (12.1b-7a)
    A.   Report of Nathan's obedience (1bα)—*wyb'*
    B.   Parable of lamb (1bβ-4)
        1.   Introduction of setting and characters (1b)
            a.   *'yr 'ht*
            b.   *'šyr* and *r'š*
        2.   Description of characters (2-3)
            a.   Property of *'šyr* (2)
            b.   Property of *rš* (3)
                (1)   Designation of property *kbśh* (3a)
                (2)   Importance to *rš* (3b-c)
                    (a) Fulfillment of ownership responsibility
                    (b) Extraordinary behaviors—*'kl ... šth ... škb* // 11.11, 13
                    (c) Characterization of relationship—*kbt*
        3.   Introduction of problem situation (4a)
            a.   Precipitation of problem—*wyb' hlk*
            b.   Nature of problem—*wyḥml lqḥt*
        4.   Solution to problem—*wyqḥ ... wy'śh* (4b)
    C.   David's response to parable—(5-6)
        1.   Description of David's reaction—*wyḥr 'p* (5aα)
        2.   Designation of speaker and addressee (5aβ)
        3.   Judgment speech I (5b-6)
            a.   Oath formula—*ḥy yhwh*
            b.   Motive clause designating appropriate punishment (5b)
            c.   Announcement of just punishment—*yšlm 'rb'tym* (6a)
            d.   Motive clauses for punishment
                (1) *'śh 't hdbr hzh* // 11.11b, 25b

(2) *l' ḥml*

D. Nathan's response to David's response—*'th h'yš* (7a)

III. Prophetic Judgment Speeches (7b-12)

    A. *Rîb* (7b-10)

        1. Messenger formula (7bα)—*kn 'mr yhwh*

        2. Recitation of previous divine actions (7bβ)

            a. Divine anointment *lmlk*—1 Sam 16

            b. Salvation from Saul—1 Sam 19-26

            c. Divine gifts (8)

                (1) *byt 'dnyk w't nšy 'dnk*—1 Sam 25

                (2) *byt yśr'l wyhwdh*—2 Sam 2-5

                (3) *w'sph . . . khnh*—2 Samuel 5-8

        3. Charges against accused (9)

            a. Question of motivation—*mdw' bzyt*

            b. Listing of punishable actions

                (1) Killing Uriah—*hkyt*

                (2) Marrying wife—*lqḥt l'šh*

                (3) Killing Uriah—*hrgt*

        4. Announcement of punishment (10a)—*l' tswr ḥrb*

    B. Judgment speech II (10b-12)

        1. Charges

            a. *bztny*

            b. *wtqḥ . . . l'šh*

        2. Announcement of punishment (11-12)

            a. Messenger formula—*kh 'mr yhwh*

            b. General punishment—*hnny mqym . . . r'h*

            c. Specific punishment (11b)

                (1) Divine action—*wlqḥty . . . wntty*

                (2) Human action—*wškb*

            d. Motive clause (12)

                (1) Human action—*'śyt bstr*

                (2) Divine action—*''śh . . . ngd hšmš*

IV. Nathan-David Confrontation II (13-14)

    A. David's response

        1. Designation of speaker and addressee

        2. Confession—*ḥt'ty lyhwh*

    B. Nathan's response to David's response

        1. Designation of speaker and addressee

        2. Divine action—*yhwh h'byr*

         3. Punishment averted—*l' tmwt*

         4. Motive clause for punishment—*'ps ky*

         5. Punishment for child

V. Fulfillment of Prophecy (15)

    A. Departure of Nathan (15a)

    B. Report of illness of child (15b)
        1. Designation of divine causation—*wygp yhwh* (15bα)
        2. Identification of child by circumstances of birth—*'šr yldh*
           'št 'wryh (15bβ)
        3. Report of severity of illness—*wy'nš*

There is disagreement as to whether the theological evaluation in 11.27b is the ending of the unit in 11.2-27a or whether it is the introduction of the unit in 12.1-15. Von Rad has argued that it is the ending of the unit in 11.2-27, since 'the narrator could not allow his reader to pass on to the next event without some comment' of God's hand in the punishments to follow in 2 Samuel 13–20.[94] In this he is followed by Hertzberg,[95] Dhorme,[96] Caird,[97] Simon,[98] Gunn,[99] and Brueggemann.[100]

Budde has argued that this clause introduces the narrative in 12.1f.[101] In this he is followed by Ridout,[102] Bowman,[103] and Smith.[104] McCarter agrees and argues that 11.27b was introduced into the text when the David–Bathsheba–Uriah materials (2 Sam 11.2-27a) were placed before the account of Absalom's revolt to allow the Nathan materials (2 Sam 12.1-15) to function in a prophecy-fulfillment scheme with 2 Samuel 13–20.[105]

Carlson pushed previous discussions a bit further by arguing that 2 Sam 11.27b was introduced by the D-group as a 'typical Deuteronomic commentary'.[106] In this he finds agreement from Dietrich, who argues that it comes from DtrP, since it presupposes an ethical norm.[107] Helga Weippert, in seeking to demonstrate the Deuteronomic usage of the clause as an evaluative mechanism,[108] provides additional support for this position.

Mettinger argues against designating 11.27b as Dtr, since the formula *wyr' hdbr b'yny X* appears in other 'contexts that can hardly be said to be of Dtr origin'.[109] To support his contention, he cites (1) the reaction of Abraham to Sarah's demand that Hagar and Ishmael be exiled (E; Gen 21.11), (2) the deity's negative reaction to Onan's coitus interruptus (J; Gen 38.10),[110] (3) Samuel's negative reaction to the people's request for a king (1 Sam 8.6), and (4) Saul's negative reaction to the singing of the women praising David at Saul's expense (18.8).[111]

It is interesting that in three of these four instances, the *r'h* (displeasure) involves an issue of male-female loyalty,[112] while the other involves a question of the loyalty of the nation to the deity. Similarly, only in one of these instances (Gen 38.10) is the deity the subject of the clause.

In assessing the redactional nature of the expression, *r'h*, one is confronted with its rather limited employment. Simultaneously, there is the marked consistency of its use in contexts of male–female loyalty/shift of loyalty. Weippert and Dietrich present a cogent case for the Dtr usage of the clause in relation to the assessment of royal behavior, while Mettinger makes a case for the clause as a general phrase signalling legitimate anger about an act of disloyalty. Although the David-Bathsheba-Uriah incident is one of shift of female loyalty, given the heavy hand of the Dtr in shaping the narrative in 11.2-27a, the employment here of the formula, *wyr' hdbr b'yny*, is probably a case of the Dtr choosing a formula which could be used to address all aspects of the situation.

There are two other narrative techniques in operation in 2 Samuel 10-12, which may tip the scales in favor of the redactional nature of 2 Samuel 11.27b. The first is the redactional seams in 2 Sam 10.6a, 15a, and 19. As we demonstrated, there is a tendency to construct the seams in such as way as to look backward and forward at the same time.[113] Secondly, it has been noted that there is a compositional technique in operation in the arrangement of 2 Sam 11.2-12.25 in which birth narrative formulae, *wthr ... wtld ... wt(y)qr'*, are divided up into three separate narratives, with narrative interludes used to complete certain actions before the next part of the formula is presented.[114] Thus, 2 Sam 11.27b looks backwards and leads forward, and also introduces the next narrative interlude before the completion of the birth formula. In this way the argument between von Rad and Budde is muted. What is clear, however, is that the clause should be taken as redactional and not part of the original story.

In 2 Sam 12.1-4 there is the 'parable of the ewe-lamb',[115] which Nathan tells to David. Upon hearing the details of the case, David pronounces severe judgment upon the 'culprit' in the case (12.5-6), only to discover that he, David, is the one described (12.7a).

As has been widely recognized, there are a number of dissimilarities between the incidents in the parable and the events described in 2 Sam 11.2-27a which have raised questions about the original and editorial connection of the parable to the story. There are three notable differences between the parable and the David-Bathsheba-Uriah incident. First, there is no indication of adultery nor of murder in the parable. Instead it concerns theft.[116] Second, the rich man acts out of avarice to keep from using his own possessions, while David is depicted in 11.2-27a as acting for definite motives of personal gain and desire.[117] Third, there is a sense of sympathy for the ewe-lamb in the parable. This becomes incongruous since the ewe-lamb is taken to be symbolic of Bathsheba in 2 Samuel 11, who at the very least cooperated with David in the adultery.[118]

Simon, who designates this unit, along with 2 Sam 14.1-20; 1 Kgs 20.35-43; Isa 5.1-7 and Jer 3.1-5, as a 'juridical parable',[119] argues that the differences can be explained as an attempt of Nathan to keep David from easily recognizing the applicability of the parable to himself.[120] Hoftijzer, on the other hand, argues that if one distinguishes between 'basic and non-basic facts' and realizes that the intention of the parable is to 'get either an acquittal or a condemnation', then the differences are minimized in importance.[121] Both of these arguments break down in light of the similarity of detail between the parables in 2 Samuel 14 and 1 Kings 20 and the incidents to which they refer. In other words, in both 2 Samuel 14 and 1 Kings 20, the parable used to get the king to condemn himself is very close to the actual situation in the narrative proper. Thus, the lack of such a fit between the parable in 2 Samuel 12 and the events in 2 Samuel 11 is unusual for this genre.

In contrast to these attempts to focus upon the juridical nature of the parable, Whitelam notes that 'the terms of reference in the case presented by Nathan were so vague that it is unlikely that the king would be bound by any such precedent'.[122] Thus, he argues along with Gunn[123] against a juridical intention. Instead he maintains that the narrative is a literary construction used for the purpose of answering why David was not ultimately brought to justice for his actions.[124]

Similarly Camp argues that the intention of the unit is psychological manipulation. In essence the parable creates two conditions— 'distancing and re-involvement—necessary for a person blinded by proximity to a problem to achieve a new perspective on it'.[125] The problem in these interpretations is the fact that David's response is of a legal nature (2 Sam 12.5-6) and thus there appears to be more than just a literary function to the situation. In other words, since his response is based on a law in the Covenant Code, there appears to be a case law intention lying behind the narrative.

In spite of the differences between the interpretations of Simon and Hoftijzer and those of Whitelam, Camp, and Gunn, they all share one basic presupposition about the unit: the story demonstrates that the king in ancient Israel functioned in a juridical capacity. The question arises, however, as to how one substantiates this understanding, for then we might find a clue as to the source of the unit in 12.1-15 and its relationship to 2 Samuel 11.

While Frankfort states the Israelite king was the arbiter in disputes,[126] Szikszai cautions that in the Deuteronomic Code it is the elders who have this juridical function (Deut 19.12; 21.20) and not the king.[127] Likewise, when a case cannot be solved 'in the gates', it is referred to the 'levitical priests' (Deut 17.8-13) and not to the king.[128] Interestingly, the law of the king, Deut 17.14-20, does not mention any royal juridical functions either as primary judge or as a 'court of appeals'.[129] Similarly neither 1 Sam 8.10-18 nor 12.13-15, where the Dtr view of kingship is discussed, list this as a function of the king. Thus, it appears that the Deuteronomistic sources do not substantiate a juridical function for the king.[130]

2 Sam 8.15b, which claims that David was '*šh mšpṭ wṣdqh*, has been proposed as significant support for a juridical function for the king.[131] It should be noted that this verse is not replicated in 2 Sam 20.23-26, which contains a duplicate list of David's court officials.[132] Thus it is most probably redactional.

Recently Campbell has argued that 2 Sam 8.15 was added by a prophetic redactor.[133] Credence is given to this line of thought, since the phrase in 8.15b appears three times in Jeremiah in relation to the king.[134] It would appear, however, that in these Jeremianic texts the king is described as responsible for maintaining the 'social well-being' of the community, as opposed to a restricted 'juridical function'.[135]

The phrase '*šh mšpṭ* also appears in 1 Kgs 3.28 and 10.9 in relation to the function of the king. In the former it is clearly part of a redactional seam tying the narrative in 3.16-27 to its context. The latter is part of the Queen of Sheba's speech of validation of Solomon.[136] In both of these contexts the sense of the phrase is similar to that of Jeremiah, namely, maintaining a just social order.[137] Thus, it appears that 2 Sam 8.15b is misused when it is employed to ground a juridical function for the king.

The most common means for substantiating that the king in ancient Israel functioned in a juridical capacity comes from five narratives in which biblical kings are so depicted: 2 Sam 12.1-7a; 14.1-17; 15.3-4;[138] 1 Kgs 3.16-28; 20.33-45.

1 Kings 3 presents Solomon's decision, his juridical function, as a means of exemplifying the centrality of *ḥkmh* in the activities of the monarch.[139] Similarly, the narrative in 2 Samuel 14 revolves around a 'wise woman'.[140] This suggests wisdom influence on this notion of a

royal juridical function. As previously argued, however, these
examples are not concerned with a prophet but with women whose
cases allow the king to show his sagacity.[141] Thus, these narratives
are not helpful in grounding 2 Sam 12.1-15 in a tradition of the
'juridical function of the king'.

The narrative closest to the one in 2 Sam 12.1-7a is 1 Kgs 20.35-43
in which a prophet uses a trick to get a king to pass judgment in a
situation. The royal verdict is then turned into a prophetic
pronouncement of judgment on the king himself.[142] While the
narratives in 2 Samuel 12 and 1 Kings 20 do have this deception plot
similarity in common, as Long points out,[143] the narrative in 1 Kings
20 is more similar to the narrative in 1 Samuel 15 in which a prophet
announces judgment on a king for not following the will of Yahweh
in a war situation.[144] Thus, the possibility of prophetic influence on
the shaping of the unit in 2 Samuel 12 seems stronger than that of
wisdom influence. In other words, the unit is used to demonstrate the
role of the prophet in holding the king accountable to the will of
Yahweh.

There may, then, have been a pre-deuteronomistic prophetic
redaction of the narratives in 2 Samuel 11–12 which used as its basis
the prophet/king conflict, as noted in 1 Samuel 8, 13 and 15.
Secondly, given the disparity between the parable and the incident in
2 Samuel 11, this redaction was probably a secondary addition to a
David–Bathsheba–Uriah narrative, in which a commonly known
parable about the rich abuse of the poor was utilized to set up the
self-condemnation, on the model of other such narratives.

Finally, the 'decree' of David in 12.5-6 has a parallel in Exod 21.37
rather than in Deuteronomy. This would suggest that the hand of the
Dtr was not involved in the earliest shaping of the narrative, since in
other instances in 2 Samuel 10–12, where there has been a
connection between the narrative and the law, the connection has
been to the Deuteronomic law code. This would suggest that this
tradition was intact when it was received by the Dtr.

Thus, the above findings argue against Dietrich's and Veijola's
designation of this unit as from the hand of the DtrP. As has been
shown, the notion of king as *špṭ* in a juridical sense is not in line with
the Dtr presentation of the king. Secondly, the inconsistencies
between the parable and the events do not follow the patterns of the
other narratives which utilized this technique of prophet/wise person
deceiving the king. Finally, the appeal to the Covenant Code, as
opposed to the Deuteronomic Code, is inconsistent with the

previously demonstrated redactional patterns ascribed to Dtr in 2 Samuel 10-12.

The compositional pattern observed in 11.1 + 12.26- 31, 11.6-13, and 11.14-25 is replicated in 12.5-15a. Immediately following the parable (12.1-4) there is a response of David to the situation, an announcement of punishment (12.5-6). This is followed by a pronouncement from Nathan, 'You are the man!' (12.7a). In 12.13a there is a second reaction of David, this time a confession, followed by a pronouncement of Nathan that the punishment for the sin will be paid by the next generation (13b-14).[145] Thus, there are two parallel units containing David's reactions and Nathan's responses to the reactions. In between these two parallel subunits there is a speech of Nathan which looks forward and backward (see Chart 7).

As in the other instances of this compositional pattern there are two parallel units which could both stand alone (vv. 5-7a, 13-14). In both of these David's reaction is followed by a response to that reaction by Nathan.

Chart 7. Compositional pattern in 12.5-14

Reaction of David	vv. 5-6
Response of Nathan	v. 7a
Speeches of Nathan	vv. 7b-12
Reaction of David	v. 13a
Response of Nathan	vv. 13b-14

As has been noted in some of the other instances of the pattern, the first unit is not very favorable to David, while the second shows him in a more 'appropriate' behavioral pattern to the situation. For example in 12.26 he is absent from the battle, while in 12.29-31 he is present and in charge. Similarly, in 11.17-18 he is totally absent from the scene, while in 11.25 he gives encouragement and direction to the war effort. In 12.5-6 he gives what turns out to be his own self-righteous indictment, while in 12.13a he offers a confession of his guilt.

A third way in which the unit is similar to the other examples of this compositional pattern is in its clarification of ambiguity. As noted above, the parable to which David reacts in 12.5-6 does not fit the situation described in 11.2-27a. In the speech of Nathan, however, there is mention of the wife of Uriah incidents (12.9, 10) which clarifies the issues.[146]

There is a significant difference, however, between the speech complex in 12.7b-12 and the speeches in 11.10b-11, 18-24, and 12.27-28. While these latter units used catchwords to hold together the parallel units surrounding them, in 12.7b-12 the speech intends to hold together not only 12.5-14 but also all of the David traditions from 1 Samuel 16 to 2 Samuel 20.

It has long been noted that 12.7bβ, *'nky mšḥtyk lmlk 'l yśr'l*, relates to the secret anointing of David by Samuel reported in 1 Samuel 16,[147] and that 12.10a, *l' tsr hḥrb mbytk 'd 'wlm*, and 12.11b, *wškb 'm nšyk*, relate to the events in 2 Samuel 13, 16, and 18; 1 Kings 1-2.[148] It has also been argued that part or parts of this speech are later redactions.[149] Similarly, there have been attempts to amend the text of 12.8a to read *bat* instead of *bēt*, so as to refer to Michal, the daughter of Saul.[150]

The genre of the unit begun in 12.7 a is a *rîb*[151] in which there is a recitation of the acts of Yahweh on behalf of David (12.7b-8).[152] This recitation parallels the narrative of David's rise to the throne. There is first the anointing to kingship over Israel (v. 7bα), which is related in 1 Samuel 16. Next there is mention of David's being saved from Saul (v. 7bβ), which is the thrust of the narrative in 1 Samuel 18-26.

There next follows a list of gifts which Yahweh has given to David which relate to the *bēt* and *nšy* of 'your master' (v. 8aα). While this is often described in terms of getting the 'harem' of his predecessor on the model of 2 Sam 16.22, there are other references to 'women' switching loyalty from their masters/husband to David in 1 Samuel. 1 Sam 18.7 speaks of women dancing and extolling David over Saul. Similarly, 1 Samuel 25 reports a marriage between David and Abigail after the death of her husband. Also 1 Samuel 18 and 2 Sam 3.14-16 speak to the marriage of David and Michal, the daughter of Saul. In addition, 2 Samuel 2-3 describes Abner switching his loyalty from Ishbosheth to David, from one *byt* to another.

2 Sam 5.1-3 describes the establishment of a covenant between David and the elders of Israel and Judah. This corresponds with the statement in 12.8aβ. Similarly, the remainder of the verse describes additions being made to these gifts (8b) which probably refers to the territorial expansions described in 2 Samuel 5 and 8, the consequence of Yahweh's giving David victory wherever he went (2 Sam 8.14b).[153]

Thus, 2 Sam 12.7b-8 provides a summary of the events described in 1 Samuel 16-2 Samuel 8. This summary suggests, therefore, that this block of material had already been arranged in its present order or was done simultaneously when the listing of the 'mighty acts of Yahweh on behalf of David' in 12.7b-8 was inserted into the speech of Nathan.

Following this listing of the 'mighty acts' there comes the specific charge about the Uriah and wife of Uriah incidents (12.9-10).[154] These verses function to tie the Nathan oracle to the events reported in 2 Sam 11.2-27a and thus to juxtapose them to the listing of the 'mighty acts'.

As has been noted, the announcements of punishment, the presence of the sword and the despoiling of the women are specifically carried out in the events of 2 Samuel 13–20. In this way the predictions and the events develop a prophecy-fulfillment schema as is so characteristic of the DtrH. Similarly, the close parallel between these events with the prophecies (e.g. wives despoiled in the sunlight [12.11] and Absalom's taking the concubines on the roof [16.22]) suggest that the compilation of 2 Samuel 13–20 also predates these oracles.

Thus, the Nathan oracle complex in 12.7b-12 has been shown to be either a later or simultaneous addition to the complex, since it presupposes both the collection in 1 Samuel 16–2 Samuel 8 as well as the complex in 2 Samuel 13–20. Similarly, its scant mentions of the Uriah, wife of Uriah incidents as a means of tying it to 2 Samuel 11 raises questions of the David–Bathsheba identification with the wife of Uriah complex.

Finally, traditionally the unit regarding Nathan and David in 2 Samuel 12 is concluded with the exit of Nathan in 12.15a, and 12.15b is taken as the beginning of a new unit on the death of the child conceived in adultery.[155] A variation on this theme is seen in those who argue that 12.15b-23 is a later addition to the story.[156] There are others who argue that 12.15b is the continuation of 11.27b, with the statement that Yahweh struck, *ngp*, the child being the consequence of his negative reaction, *wyr' hdbr*.[157]

There are several problems with viewing 12.15b as being separate from 12.15a and the subunit to which it belongs, namely 12.13-15a. The first problem with seeing 12.15b as starting a new unit is caused by the use of *ngp* in 12.15b. When *ngp* appears with Yahweh as the subject it most often refers to a battle situation in which the defeat of one of the parties is explained as the result of Yahweh performing a *ngp*.[158] There are, however, a few references in which Yahweh causes the illness of an individual as is the case in 12.15b. In these instances the verb *ngp* does not appear at the beginning of the unit. Rather it appears at the end of the unit. Thus to posit 12.15b as the beginning of a unit would be to suggest that the term functions radically differently here from the way it does in its corollary units.[159]

Another problem with seeing 12.15b as being the beginning of a new unit connected to v. 27b is the use of *'nš*. All other instances of the term are found in Micah, Isaiah and Jeremiah.[160] In these instances it is found in judgment speeches and is used as a metaphor for the surety of the judgment, by stating that Yahweh has afflicted the individual or group with an incurable disease. As long as 12.15b is considered to be part of the judgment speech begun in 12.13b, the usage of *'nwš* in 12.15b remains consistent with its appearance in other units. In other words, *'nwš* is used in 12.15b as confirmation that a prophetic judgement is assured.

Thirdly, in the announcement of punishment there is a general identification of *hbn hylwd lk* (12.14b). In 12.15b this identification is made specific as *hyld 'šr yldh 'št 'wryh*. Separating these phrases into different units would leave the first statement too general and might raise the question of the relationship of the eventts to follow in vv. 16f.

Finally, while the above argument regarding the phrase *wyr' hdbr b'yny yhwh* in 11.27b demonstrated that it was redactional, there was no way of tying it to a prophetic redaction. Thus, it appears that 12.15b is best seen as a continuation of the prophetic announcement of punishment in 12.13b-14.

The question remains, however: which verses were available to the Dtr as a source? As noted, given the lack of a concept of the juridical king in Dtr and given the quotation in 12.5 from the Covenant Code, 2 Sam 12.1-7a was probably received intact by Dtr.

Similarly, vv. 9 and 10 are repetitious in their usages of *bzh* and the mention of the marriage to Uriah's wife. Verse 9a also mentions the killing of Uriah in a war context, *bḥrb*. In addition, v. 9b, with its modification of how Uriah was killed and its specification that the Ammonite War was the context, suggests a redaction of a given text. Thus, we would conclude that v. 9a, with its specification of the charge in 7a, *'th h'yš*, was part of the original narrative.

Finally, in response to the question posed by v. 9a, the unit in vv. 13-15 was added. In this unit is found David's confession and Nathan's announcement of punishment on the child mentioned in 11.27a. In view of other cases of this compositional arrangement in similar units, it is not clear whether this unit in vv. 13-15 was part of the original prophetic response to the David–Bathsheba marriage or was a parallel tradition to the version in vv. 1-7a. Given its theological disjuncture with the theology of Dtr,[161] it was most probably already part of the pre-Dtr narrative and thus had to be worked around.

5. *The Redemption of David (2 Sam 12.16-23)*

The unit beginning in 12.16 focuses on the actions of David the penitent. The story line suggests that once the child born to David and the wife of Uriah had become ill, David began to enact what appeared to be mourning behaviors (vv. 16-17). He refused to eat with his servants. Once the child died the servants were afraid to tell him, fearing that he would do something rash (v. 18). Once David figured out that the child had died, he ceased his mourning activity and went to praise Yahweh (vv. 19-20). His servants questioned his reversal of the mourning behavior (v. 21), to which he responded that he was earlier trying to influence the deity, but since it didn't work, he has to go on with life (vv. 22-23).

The following is a structural outline for the unit.

A. Response of David to illness of child (16)
   1. General description
      a. David's behavior—*wybqš . . . h'lhym* (16aα)
      b. Beneficiary—*b'd hn'r* (16aβ)
   2. Specific behaviors
      a. *wyṣm . . . wb' wln wškb* (16b)
      b. Response of *zqny bytw—wyqmw . . . lhqymw* (17a)
      c. *wl' 'bh* (17b)
B. Report of death of child (18a)
   1. Temporal designation—*bywm hšby'y* (18aα)
   2. *wymt hyld* (18aβ)
C. Responses to death of child (18b-24a)
   1. Response of *'bdy dwd* (18b)
      a. Fear—*wyr'w*
      b. Motive clause
         (1) David's previous behavior—*l' šm' bqwlnw*
         (2) Question of anticipated response—*w'šh r'h*
   2. Response of David (19-20)
      a. Response to servants' behavior—*wyr' . . . wybn*
      b. Dialogue with servants
         (1) David's question—*hmt*
         (2) Response of servants—*mt*
      c. Resumption of life—*wyqm*

        (1) Restores self—*wyrḥṣ wysk wyḥlp*
        (2) Does obeisance—*wyb' . . . wyštḥw*
        (3) Resumes eating—*wyš'l wyśymw*
   3. Dialogue between David and his servants
     a. Response of servants to David's response (21)
        (1) Designation of speaker and addressee
        (2) Question of behavior—*mh hdbr hzh* // 12b, 14a
          (a) *ḥy ṣmt wtbk*
          (b) *mt . . . qmt wt'kl*
     b. Response of David to servants (22-23)
        (1) Description of previous behavior—*ṣmty w'bkh*
        (2) Motive clause—*yḥnny yhwh*
        (3) Question of continuation of behavior—*lmh zh*
        (4) Question of efficacy of continuation of behavior—
           h'wkl lhšybw
        (5) Statement of maxim—*hlk* vs *swb*

Würthwein has argued that this unit makes little sense following the Nathan prophecy.[162] Since Nathan has announced that the punishment will be diverted from David to the child, David's actions seeking to have the life of the child spared would be to deny the 'grace' which has been promised.[163]

The unit begins with the phrase *wybqš dwd 't h'lhym*. This is unusual wording for two reasons. First, the idiom for imploring the deity on the behalf of another normally uses *pll* in the *hithpa'el*[164] as opposed to *bqš*. Secondly, *bqš* is used very often in the sense of 'seeking' others in order to do them harm, which is not the case in 12.16-23.[165] Similarly, when it is used with the deity as the one being sought, *bqš* generally refers to a successful[166] or a desired[167] pursuit. In this instance, even though David approaches the deity with a 'pure and contrite heart', so to speak, the petitioning will be to no avail. Though *bqš* most often in such a context as 12.16-23 signals a positive or appropriate response, this is not the case in this unit. At this point, we merely note the unusual usage of the term and will return to re-examine it once we have reviewed the remainder of the unit.

12.16b-17 describes the behavior of David in his beseeching of the deity. As noted above these actions are generally taken to be mourning rituals.[168] This interpretation is reinforced by his washing, anointing, and changing his clothes after the child's death (12.20a).[169]

In other narratives which describe mourning rituals, there are both similarities and differences between the actions described here and those of mourning. For example, in passages which speak of the people in mourning there is weeping (*bkh*)[170] and a statement of mourning (*'bl*),[171] and at times mention of fasting (*ṣwm*).[172] There is not, however, any mention of the other behavior of David in 12.16b-17, namely lying on the ground and refusing to be raised up.

The behavior attributed to David in 12.16b-17 is reported in narratives describing repentance. Most notably these behaviors appear in 1 Kgs 21.27,[173] which describes Ahab's response to the prophecy of Elijah, and in Jonah 3.5, which describes the response of the people of Nineveh to Jonah's announcement of punishment. In both of these instances, the deity decided either to forestall or to abort punishment.

One might argue that, since in the incidents in 1 Kings 21 and Jonah 3 the response of the deity is positive, and in 2 Samuel 12 the response is negative, namely, the child dies (12.18a), there is no legitimate parallel between these units. It appears, however, that taken in full context, there is a very strong connection.

In 12.13a David confesses with the words, *ḥṭ't'y lyhwh*. This is followed by a statement of the transference of the punishment from David to the child (13b). This result is most surprising since the phrase, *ḥṭ' lyhwh* is most often used by the prophets as the reason for punishment, not for its aversion.[174] Similarly, in two other narratives when the phrase appears as a confession, Deut 1.41 and Josh 7.20,[175] it has no influence on averting the punishment. In the first instance, the Wilderness Wandering is enacted. In the second, Achan is stoned. Thus, the announcement in 2 Sam 12.13b is out of character with other instances of the phrase.

There are, however, two other narratives in which the phrase *ḥṭ'ty lyhwh* appears as a confession and in which the people are saved (Judg 10.15; 1 Sam 7.6).[176] In both of these instances, however, the confession is accompanied either by mention of ceasing apostasy and returning (*šwb*) to Yahweh (Judg 10.15) or by engaging in a covenant ceremony (1 Sam 7.6). It thus appears that, for the redactor of these units in addition to confession there are supplementary deeds which lead to the change of heart of the deity.

Confirmation that confession alone is not enough to avert the punishment is found in 1 Kgs 8.47-48, the seventh petition of Solomon in his prayer at the dedication of the temple. In these verses there is expressed the view that along with confession (8.47) there is also the requirement of returning to Yahweh (*šwb*)[177] in a complete manner (*bkl lbbm wbkl npšm*) (8.48). The means of this is *whthnnw 'lyk* (8.47).[178] This unit is universally ascribed to the DtrH, since it both presupposes the exile and quotes Deut 4.6-8.[179]

As argued above, 2 Sam 12.13-15 has been shown to be related to prophetic thought.[180] This subunit suggests that confession alone is necessary for the prophetic response of averting punishment. As Deut 1.41, Josh 7.20, 1 Kgs 8.47-48 demonstrate, for Dtr, confession alone is not enough. Similarly, 1 Kgs 21.27-29, the analogue to 2 Sam 12.13-23, demonstrates that the averting of the punishment is predicated upon both confession and supplication/repentance.

2 Sam 12.22 contains a clue that the behavior of David in 12.16-17 should be understood as supplication and not as mourning. As David argues, *my yd'*[181] *yhnny yhwh*. Similarly, once the child dies and the period of lament is over, the writer then has David go to the *byt yhwh* for worship (12.20).[182] Thus, David's actions are those of trying to influence the deity in a manner consistent with Israelite piety.[183]

We now return to the question of the usage of *bqš* in 12.16. As the Dtr received the tradition regarding David's responses, the pronouncement of the transference of punishment to the next generation was predicated solely on the confession, *ht'ty lyhwh* (12.13a). This was unacceptable theologically. Similarly, there was a concern of Dtr to argue for the continuance of the Davidic dynasty as long as the covenant was kept, as exemplified in 2 Sam 7.15-16 and 1 Kgs 8.25-26. Thus, 2 Sam 12.16-23 was constructed to present David as practicing appropriate repentance, while also arguing that the sin of 2 Samuel 11 was atoned for. The model of 1 Kgs 21.27 was utilized to construct the unit.

6. *The Birth of Solomon*

We come now to an examination of the unit which contains the third and completing verb of the birth narrative formula, *wy/tqr'*. The following is a structural outline of 2 Sam 12.24-25:

III. Birth of Solomon (2 Sam 12.24-25)

A. Spousal support—*wynhm*
   1. David
   2. Bathsheba—*'štw*
B. Birth of child
   1. Sexual relations—*wyb'* . . . *wyškb*

2. Birth—*wtld*
3. Naming of child—*wyqr'*
C. Divine Response
   1. Approval—*'hbw*
   2. Naming
      a. Messenger formula—*wyšlḥ*
      b. Naming—*wyqr'*
      c. Motive clause—*b'bwr*

The transition from the unit on the redemption of David (12.16-23) to the unit which narrates the birth and naming of Solomon (2 Sam 12.24-25) is not very smooth. While Ridout argues that the chiastic arrangement of balance between the accounts of Bathsheba's pregnancy in 11.2-5 and the birth of Solomon in 12.24-25 is obvious,[184] the first word of the unit, *wynḥm*, appears to be a continuation of the previous narrative. Thus, there is not a clear break between the unit in 12.16-23 and that in 12.24-25.

There are two problems, however, with associating 12.24aα, *wynḥm dwd 't bt-šb' 'štw*, with the previous narrative. The first is that throughout 12.16-23 the focus is solely on David and his exoneration and there is no consideration of Bathsheba at all. This is surprising, given the great attention directed towards 'the wife of Uriah' at his death through the use of *spd* and *'bl* in 11.26-27. Secondly, if this clause is removed from this unit, there would be no indication left as to who the actors are in the second part of the verse. The inclusion may best be explained, therefore, as another example of a transition between units which looks backward and forward.

The unit confronts us with an irregular birth formula. First 12.24aβ[185] contains a redundancy by the use of two sexual designations, *wyb'* and *wyškb*. Secondly, there is no reference to a pregnancy[186] in 12.24. These deviations in the birth formula first signal a stress on David as the primary actor in this drama, especially since the verbs are in the third-person masculine singular. Secondly, the deviations stress the understanding that it is the sexual act mentioned in this unit which leads to the birth. In other words, the narrator clearly signifies that it is this later sexual act that leads to the birth of Solomon, not the adultery.

As noted in the previous discussion of the birth formula, the naming of the child is missing in the first instance of *yld* in the narrative. In addressing the omission of the name for the child born in 11.27, Veijola has taken issue with the present structure in 11.27b-12.24a. He argues that there is an interpolation into the narrative[187] and that Solomon was the first-born child of Bathsheba.[188] He does this by first pointing out that the giving of the name is part of the narrative pattern.[189] He also notes that the name usually comes from the significance the birth has for the mother.[190] Similarly he argues that the siege at Rabbah could not have lasted for two years, which the current arrangement of a birth in 11.27 and another in 12.24 would suggest.[191]

The omission of the name of the child in 11.27a is a definite deviation from the genre of birth narratives. Similarly, it would appear that the closest parallel birth narrative in which the child is not named immediately is the birth of Moses, in Exodus 2, where because of the etiology, mention of the name is reserved for later in the narrative (Exod 2.10). In the case of Moses, the concern of the narrative is to explain how an Israelite leader could have an Egyptian name. Thus the name is withheld until two narratives can place him in the court of Pharaoh.

In the case of the relationship between 11.27 and 12.24, there is a need for narrative tension in delaying the name, so that it can be stressed that Solomon was not the child conceived in adultery. Therefore, the genre was not completed until the prophetic rebuke of David and the exoneration of the Davidic line through the death of the child of adultery had occurred. Then the narrator presents the birth of Solomon by means of an unusual birth formula, which contains the missing *naming* of the child from the overarching birth formula. Additionally, the narrator signals the completion of the exoneration of the Davidic line through the divine renaming in 12.25.[192]

Chart 8. Arrangement of blocks of narrative
in 2 Sam 11.2-12.25 around the birth formulae

wthr 2 Sam 11.2-5   (David–Bathsheba adultery)

2 Sam 11.6-25 (Death of Uriah)
2 Sam 11.26-27aα (Marriage of David and wife of Uriah)

wtld 2 Sam 11.27aβ

2 Sam 11.27b-12.15 (Prophetic judgment)
2 Sam 12.16-23 (Exoneration of David)

wtqr'[193] 2 Sam 12.24-25 (Birth and naming of Solomon)

Veijola is therefore correct in noting that the naming is missing from the first birth narrative, although it would appear that his claim that Solomon was the first-born child is without sufficient proof. In other words, the birth formula presented by Long constitutes an overarching schema which gives structure to the entire arrangement of the blocks of materials in 2 Sam 11.2–12.25. The present structuring of the material probably serves the function of both suggesting a political deal between David and Bathsheba (see 1 Kgs 1.13) and the exoneration of the Davidic line by presenting Solomon as the second son rather than as the offspring of an adulterous relationship. This arrangement is depicted in Chart 8.

This schema, however, leads to another problem for exegesis, namely resolving the conflict between the place of Solomon in the birth order as presented in 2 Sam 12.24 and 1 Chron 3.5. According to the latter, Bathshua gave birth to four children, the last of whom was named Solomon. This notation is part of a list of David's Jerusalem-born children. It is added to a list of David's sons born at Hebron (3.1-4), copied from 2 Sam 3.1-5.

1 Chron 14.3-7 replicates the list of sons in 1 Chron 3.5-9. There are some minor differences in the orthography of some of the names and there is no mention of Bathshua in 14.4. Even though this listing in 1 Chronicles 14 only includes the Jerusalem-born children, it presupposes the listing of the Hebron children in 2 Samuel 3, since it twice mentions 'wd in 14.3.[194] Thus, the question arises as to whether the Chronicler omitted the notation on Bathshua in 14.4, or whether the Chronicler added the notation of Bathshua's births in 3.5 to accomplish a particular purpose.

A further question arises, therefore, as to whether the notation of Bathshua in 1 Chron 3.5 is reliable, since, if it is, Solomon could not even be the child whose birth is noted in 2 Sam 12.24. In resolving this dilemma it is interesting to note first, that while the mother of each child is mentioned in the listing of the Hebron children (1 Chron 3.1-3), none but Bathshua is mentioned with regard to the Jerusalem children. Thus, while mention of her in 1 Chron 3.13 is in line with the structure of the listing in 2 Sam 3.1-5, it is out of line with the listing of the Jerusalem children (2 Sam 5.13-16). Thus, the reference to 'Bathshua the daughter of Ammiel' in 1 Chron 3.5 is probably a secondary addition by the Chronicler.

Secondly, it should be noted that the one aspect of the Hebron list of 1 Chron 3.1-4 that is most different from its parallel list in 2 Sam 3.1-5 is the notation about Abigail. In 2 Samuel 3 she is listed as the wife of Nabal. In the Chronicler's listing she is only listed as the Carmelite. It would thus appear that the Chronicler had a vested interest in disguising the notations of David's questionable dealings with the marriages both to Abigail and Bathsheba. The Chronicler dropped the mention of Abigail's former marriage, while changing Bathsheba's name to one which means simply, daughter of nobility, while at the same time reversing her father's name from '*ly'm* to '*my'l*[195] in order to eliminate the patronymic link to Ahithophel.

Therefore, it must be concluded that the note in 1 Chron 3.5 that Shimea, Shobab, Nathan, and Solomon (=Shummus, Shobob, Nathan, and Solomon in 1 Sam 5.14) were all children of Bathshua is not reliable. Rather it is the Chronicler's way of suggesting that Solomon was not the first child of David and Bathshua, and, therefore, not the product of adultery.

This conclusion is most important, for two reasons. First, it signals that the Chronicler had the materials as they appear in 2 Sam 10–12 and not only omitted the materials in 11.2–12.25, 27-28[196] but also altered the name and patronymic notation of Bathsheba to coincide with this exclusion. Secondly, it signals that the Chronicler attempted to protect the name and background of Solomon. While this is noticeable in having David claim that Yahweh has chosen Solomon as the successor to build the temple (1 Chron 28.5) and by the omission of the Dtr negative evaluation of Solomon in 1 Kgs 11.1-40, it also appears to be the operating principle at work in 1 Chron 3.5a.

The meaning of the name 'Solomon' has engendered considerable debate. Veijola disagrees with J.J. Stamm, who concluded that the name means 'complete',[197] and argues with Gerleman[198] that it means 'replacement'.[199] Unlike Gerleman, however, he argues that it is Uriah who is 'replaced' and not the child who died.[200]

Contrary to Veijola's suggestion that the meaning of the name *šlmh* is 'replacement', an alternative meaning can be given to the name. In light of the political dimension of the Bathsheba–David relationship, it would appear that the name means something like 'deal is accomplished'. Grammatically the name is an infinitive construct with an old third-person masculine singular pronominal suffix, 'his (or its) completion'. Thus, Solomon is the heir apparent, produced as the consummation of a deal between David and Bathsheba.

7. *Conclusions*

1. The argument has shown that on the compositional level two major schemata are in operation in the arrangement of the materials in 2 Sam 11.2–12.25. The first of these is the use of a birth narrative formula noted by both Neff and Long in which the three verbs *hrh*, *yld*, and *qr'* appear sequentially. We have argued that this formula provides an overarching organizing principle for the narrative, such that once the behavioral status of one of the verbs has been achieved, a narrative which depicts removal of impediments in the fulfillment of the next verb is presented. Thus, once Bathsheba is pregnant, *wthr*, Uriah is killed and she and David marry prior to the birth of the child. Similarly, once the child conceived in adultery is born, *wtld*, Nathan pronounces judgment on David and his house and then announces the diversion of the punishment to the child so conceived. Finally, once these acts have been performed, and a new child is born who is named, *wy/tqr'*, Solomon, the David-Bathsheba relationship has reached completion.

A second schema, namely two parallel units held together by a speech which uses catchwords from each unit to unite the two, to resolve ambivalent terms, and to give the appearance of one continuous and coherent unit, is employed three times in 2 Sam 11.2–12.25. It is employed twice in the Uriah murder complex (2 Sam 11.6-25). Both of these reflect DtrH interests and phraseology and in one case even quotes an earlier passage in the DtrH.

The third time the compositional technique is utilized (2 Sam 12.5-14), it performs a dual function. The first is to hold together the parallel units immediately surrounding the speech (2 Sam 12.5-7a, 13-14). The second is to summarize and hold together the entirety of the David traditions from 1 Samuel 16 through 2 Samuel 24. The speech offers a summary of previous events and through the use of a prophecy-fulfillment schema anticipates events to follow. The employment of this compositional technique encompassing so much of the Davidic material suggests that the hand of the final redactor, (Dtr) was heavily involved in the arrangement and composition all of the David traditions (see Chart 9 overleaf).

2. In line with this demonstration of the hand of the Dtr within the materials of 2 Sam 11.2–12.25, we have also uncovered something of the limits as well as some of the principles of this involvement. The Dtr may have had in written form a wife of Uriah narrative which

Chart 9. The David–Bathsheba Complex

Unit	Written by Dtr	Source material
David–Bathsheba adultery		11.2-5
Attempts to kill Uriah		11.6-10a
'Sex with wife'	10.10b-11	
		11.12-13
'Battle'		11.14-18
	11.19-22	
		11.23-25
Marriage of David & Bathsheba		11.26-27a
and birth of child		
Redactional Seam	11.27b	
Nathan–David confrontation		
Parable		12.1-4
Response of David		12.5-6
Judgment speeches		12.7a
	12.7b-8	12.9a
	12.9b-12	12.13-15
Exoneration of David	12.16-23	
Birth & naming of Solomon		12.24-25

involved David in a scheme to have a soldier killed and then marry his wife. Similarly, a prophetic redaction of this material, on the one hand, depicted the prophet-king struggle over adherence to the law but did not emphasize the the role of repentance. In addition the argument has noted that the Dtr may have overlaid these earlier materials with narratives about a David and Bathsheba marriage and about the death of the offspring/birth of Solomon. Similarly, the argument has reaffirmed the position taken in the previous chapter that Dtr did not so much alter received traditions, as rather supplement and build upon them in such a way as to reshape the overall narrative to fit Dtr theology.

3. The argument has shown that the David–Bathsheba narrative is better read as a tale of political deal-making and intrigue than one of mere lust having run awry. In so doing the argument was based upon the cues of the text, most particularly in the use of verbs and syntax, as well as comparisons to such usages in other contexts. Thus, the argument showed a close affinity between the David–Bathsheba affair with the Judah–Tamar narrative as well as to the David-Abigail–Nabal narrative. If the argument holds, then the marriage of David to Bathsheba should be viewed in the same light as the marriage to Michal, Abigail, and Maacah.

4. The argument has shown that the historical allusions in the narrative, most notably the patronymic genealogy for Bathsheba in 2 Sam 11.3, suggest that the David–Bathsheba narrative is placed in its current location within the Samuel corpus not for chronological but for theological reasons. In other words, the marriage to Bathsheba most probably took place after the Absalom revolt. The current location of the narrative within the text, however, is predicated on the summary and predictive functions of the Nathan speech in 12.7b-12.

5. The tradition about Solomon and Bathsheba in 1 Chron 3.5 when compared to 2 Sam 12.25 indicates that the Chronicler was aware of and had access to the David–Bathsheba tradition. The Chronicler was reacting to the political traditions in 1 Samuel 25 and 2 Samuel 11 and altered the genealogy in 2 Sam 3.1-5 to construct the genealogies in 1 Chronicles 3.

6. The argument has demonstrated that the arrangement of the material in 2 Samuel 10-12 is on the order of the Dtr dilemma over kingship as expressed in 1 Samuel 8. In other words, in foreign policy the king will be guilty of military excesses (2 Sam 10.1-11.1 + 12.26-31). With regard to domestic policy (2 Sam 11.2-12.25), it leads to abuses and oppression.

Chapter 5

SUMMARY AND CONCLUSIONS

In Chapter 1 we examined the main features of Rost's theory of a
TSN: a unified composition comprised of 2 Sam 6.16, 20-23; 7.13; 9-
20; and 1 Kings 1-2; a reliable historical narrative based on
eyewitness evidence; an apologetic document written during
Solomonic times to glorify the new monarch and explain how he
came to the throne. We then reviewed and analyzed the significant
research on the subject since the appearance of Rost's work.

Recent discussions concerning the boundaries of the TSN have
pointed to marked similarities between the Ishbosheth narratives in 2
Samuel 2-4 and narratives in 2 Samuel 15-20. As a consequence,
many scholars have argued for extending the beginning of the
narrative to include 2 Samuel 2-4. In addition, differences in
content, themes, and descriptions of events in 1 Kings 1-2 and 2
Samuel 9-20 have led to the hypothesis of literary dependence of the
former on the latter rather than the former as a narrative continuation
of the latter. In other words, 1 Kings 1-2 are seen as narratives
drawing on the content of 2 Samuel 9-20 at a secondary stage. Rost's
arguments concerning the beginning and ending of the TSN have
thus been seriously weakened by recent scholarship.

Similarly, analysis of his argument for unity has shown that this
concept, primarily predicated on the continuity of the story line,
cannot be substantiated in terms of a consistent and unified theme
running throughout all the chapters of the narrative. Instead, among
recent interpreters there are almost as many unifying themes posited
as there are theorists. Similarly, those advocating particular unifying
themes as the key to the nature and unity of the TSN often have to
gloss over differences and/or subsume under one of them such
disparate acts as consenting adultery and rape. Rost's argument of a

unified succession theme and recent modifications of his view on this issue have therefore become increasingly untenable.

Finally his arguments for a TSN as a reliable historical narrative written by an eyewitness during Solomonic times, predicated primarily on the inclusion of negative details about David, have been countered and explained in a variety of other ways, often leading to differing theories of authorship and date. The theory seemed to offer a comprehensive explanation of the evidence and satisfied a sense of justice in that the rich and powerful payed the price for their excesses. But this is hardly sufficient justification for it.

While part or parts of the material in 2 Samuel and 1 Kings could accommodate Rost's theory, the sharpest challenge to his views comes in trying to integrate the narratives of 2 Samuel 10–12 into the TSN.

In Chapter 2 we considered the ways in which 2 Samuel 10–12 have been related to the other chapters in the TSN. We reviewed previous arguments against the unity of the TSN based on difficulties in integrating these chapters. Dissimilarities between 2 Samuel 10–12 and the other narratives in the TSN were shown to be significant. In addition, a longstanding and major problem with regard to this material has been the recognition that the units within 2 Samuel 12 used for arguing for a continuously unified narrative and a prophecy-fulfillment schema are secondary. Similarly, historical illusions within chs. 10–12 seem to point backwards to personalities and events which in reality do not appear until chs. 15–20.

Such arguments and problems concerning the relationship of 2 Samuel 10–12 to the so-called TSN demonstrate that there is warrant for an in-depth investigation of these chapters both in terms of their internal structure and content and their relationship to the larger complex of material in the books of Samuel and 1 Kings 1–2.

The examination of 2 Samuel 10–12 began in Chapter 3 with exegetical reviews of the units in 2 Samuel 10.1–11.1 + 12.26-31, the so-called Ammonite War narratives, which Rost argued represented a historically reliable annalistic work into which the David–Bathsheba narratives were interpolated.

The Ammonite War narratives were shown not to be a unified, annalistic source deriving from the time of David. Such a conclusion is based on an analysis of both the structures of the various narratives and the terminology appearing in the text. Our analysis demonstrated that the war narratives in ch. 10 were originally separate from those in chs. 11 and 12. Secondly it showed that the war narratives in chs. 11–12 actually constitute two stories about battles at Rabbah, one fought by Joab (11.1 + 12.26) and the other by David (12.29-31). Both of these narratives, sharing many parallels, have been joined together by a speech of Joab using catchwords from both narratives and *Heilskrieg* motifs in order to give the impression of one continuous narrative. The speech is best understood as representing Dtr redactional work, while the parallel and originally independent narratives represent materials inherited by Dtr.

On the basis of word studies the analysis showed that the opening phrase of 10.1, *wyhy 'ḥry kn*, was a Dtr formula which functioned within the accounts about particular rulers to give the appearance of a continuous, chronological narrative. In addition it was shown that the term *ḥesed* was used in 10.2, as in certain other political narratives within the DtrH, as a means of presenting as acceptable behavior which ordinarily would be termed treasonable. Similarly we showed that v. 19 functioned to hold together the disparate narratives in vv. 6b-15 and 16-18 and that it used terminology derived from the 'war law' in Deuteronomy 20.

Our analysis showed that the historical allusion in 2 Sam 10.2 was most probably to the events described in 2 Sam 17.27-29. This would mean that the Ammonite War narratives have been edited out of chronological sequence. Similarly, the reference to Jericho in 10.5 is best understood as coming from a post-Davidic and Solomonic time when, archaeological evidence suggests, the site was inhabited.

The patterns of the Ammonite War narratives in 2 Samuel 10 are analogous to the Ammonite War narratives in Judges 11 and 1 Samuel 11. All of these Ammonite War narratives seem to function as authenticating the rule of the figures involved—Jephthah, Saul, and David. In the case of David, 2 Samuel 10–12 are placed early in his reign in the new capital of Jerusalem. The theme of *ḥesed* paid to the son of an ally of David in both 2 Samuel 9 and 10 helps explain the juxtaposition of these narratives and thus the present location of 2 Samuel 10.

The other Ammonite War complex in 2 Sam 11.1 + 12.26-31 serves as the framework for the David–Bathsheba marriage narrative. The use of the redactional seam in 11.1aα parallels a pattern found in 1 Kings 20 in which two originally unrelated war narratives are joined so as to make them appear to be part of a single complex and a single sequence. Thus, the hand of the final (Dtr) redactor can clearly be distinguished in the construction and arrangement of the Ammonite War narratives.

In Chapter 4 we analyzed the David–Bathsheba, David–Uriah, David–Nathan, and the birth of Solomon complexes in 2 Sam 11.2–12.25. Once again the analysis showed that the Dtr was involved in reshaping earlier traditions. Similarly the compositional pattern identified in 2 Sam 12.26-31 was shown to be replicated in three units in this material (11.6-13, 14-23; 12.5-14). In addition, the speech of Nathan in 12.7b-12 was shown to have been used to encompass and delineate the total David traditions from 1 Samuel 16 through 2 Samuel 24 summarizing the preceding material and anticipating the following chapters in a prophecy-fulfillment schema. Thus, the Nathan speech was edited as a central component in the total narrative complex beginning at 1 Samuel 16 and not merely as an element in a more limited TSN. The deuteronomistic character of the Nathan speech suggests that the entire David complex was edited and shaped by Dtr.

The analysis also showed that overarching birth narrative formulae, as identified by Neff and Long, gave structure to and provided narrative tension in the complex. The narrative formulae *wthr* (11.5), *wtld* (11.27a), *wt/yqr'* (12.25), concerned with conception, birth, and naming, normally appear sequentially in texts. Here, however, this is not the case. Thus, the *wthr*, first mentioned in 11.5, is left suspended until the death of Uriah and marraige of David and Bathsheba, at which point the *wtld* appears. Similarly, the concluding *wt/yqr'* does not appear until Nathan's pronouncement of judgment and the exoneration of David and the Davidic line through the death of the child conceived in adultery.

Thirdly, the analysis showed that the David–Bathsheba marriage is probably best understood as another example of a political marriage between David and a woman from an influential family, as a means of consolidating his power. The patronymic portion of the genealogy of Bathsheba in 11.3 suggests her prominent position. Similarly, the content and balanced structure in the units in 11.6-25 point to a dual attempt at bringing about the death of Uriah. Finally, the interpretation of the name *šelōmō* should be seen in terms of the 'completion' of a political strategy and this narrative should be taken as the antecedent to the reference to such an agreement in 1 Kgs 1.13, 17.

Fourthly, the analysis showed that the David–Bathsheba marriage has probably been presented out of its logical chronological sequence within the reign of David. The marriage most probably occurred after the Absalom revolt. The complex was placed in its current location in order to provide the setting for the prophecy in the prophecy-fulfillment schema operative in 2 Samuel 13–24. The Chronicler appears to be reacting to this questionable portrayal of David in the genealogy of the birth of Solomon in 1 Chron 3.5, and thus shows familiarity with the Samuel traditions about David and Bathsheba.

Thus, the analysis has shown that 2 Samuel 10–12 was given its present structure by DtrH composition using some traditional materials on the life and reign of David and joining them in a creative complex through the use of redactional seams and speeches to suggest a unified and coherent composition. Chart 10 depicts the nature of this complex.

Chart 10. Narrative blocks in 2 Samuel 10–12

10.1-19	11.2-27a	11.27b–12.15	11.1+12.26-31
Ammonite war narrative	David-Bathsheba political marriage	Prophetic judgment speech	Ammonite war narrative
		12.16-25 Reports on heirs to throne	

The David–Bathsheba marriage complex was given its pivotal location in the David narrative because of the importance of the summary and predictive nature of the Nathan speech in 12.7b-14. Similarly, the second Ammonite War narrative (11.1 + 12.26-31) was utilized to provide the context for the death of Uriah (11.17). The first Ammonite War narrative (10.1-19) was situated to give an introduction to the account of the siege of Rabbah and to conform to the Dtr schema in which early Israelite monarchs/leaders further establish their legitimacy to reign through a victory over the Ammonites (see Judg 11; 1 Sam 11). In addition the complex depicts the Dtr concept of the monarchial excesses in foreign and domestic policy as noted in the speech of Samuel in 1 Sam 8.11-18.

Prior to the final redactional shaping of the David narrative in light of 2 Samuel 10–12, the narrative as hypothesized in Rost's theory of the TSN did not exist. Since the material in 2 Samuel 10–12 has been shaped and redacted by the Dtr and given its present location, this means that Rost's theory of a pre-Dtr TSN must be abandoned. The present story line in the material is the product of Dtr redaction, not a reflection of actual events in their original sequence. For example, since the primary clues to locating these events chronologically in the reign of David were the veiled *ḥesed* in 10.2 and the patronymic portion of the Bathsheba genealogy in 11.3, the dislocation of these narratives was easily covered by the introductory copula, *wyhy 'ḥry kn*, in 10.1a. On the other hand, the coherence of the final form of the narrative still contains several inconsistencies and disjunctures.

There are some major implications of this study for further research. The first is the role and hand of the Dtr in the arrangement of the materials in the book of Samuel. The role of the Dtr was much more important in the treatment of this material than Noth and his followers suspected and delineated. Thus, the notion of early sources, such as a History of the Rise of David, like the TSN will also have to be rethought. Similarly, clues for uncovering DtrH's involvement have been shown to be the joining of parallel units by a redactional speech which uses catchwords from both as the means to resolve ambiguities and to give the impression of coherence. Other clues have been shown to be the joining of completely separate war narratives to give the impression of successive stages of a major campaign and the function of non-Israelites as literary foils to key Israelite characters allowing them to present 'orthodox Yahwistic dogma' as it relates to the situation in hand.

A second implication for further study is the chronology of events in the reign of David. This study would lend weight to the theories that the Absalom Revolt took place early in the days of David's reign in Jerusalem and that the David–Bathsheba marriage must be placed after the revolt.

A further implication has to do with the overall nature of the historical material about David. Given the hand of the Dtr in shaping these materials and the marked similarities between these war traditions and those of Saul, the assumption that once we reach the David traditions we have reached reliable 'historiography' may rest on less than solid ground. A theological emphasis may have overshadowed the historical traditions more heavily than is normally suspected.

NOTES

Notes to Chapter 1

1. (BWANT 6; Stuttgart: W. Kohlhammer). The work was reprinted with corrections in Rost's *Das kleine Credo und andere Studien zum Alten Testament* (Heidelberg: Quelle & Meyer, 1965), 119-253. The quotations from this work are taken from the English translation, *The Succession to the Throne of David*, trans. M.D. Rutter and D.M. Gunn, with an Introduction by Edward Ball (HTIBS, 1; Sheffield: Almond, 1982).

2. Ibid., 4.

3. Ibid.

4. Rost, *TSN*, 6-34. He states, 'V. 16 raises doubts on account of the rather awkward *whyh* which disturbs the flow of the narrative. It gives the impression of being an insertion. As will be shown later, we have here the beginning of the succession source which is dovetailed into the end of the ark narrative by means of the Michal scene and the preparatory statements in v. 16' (p. 13). See A. Campbell, 'The Ark Narrative (1 Sam 4-6: 2 Samuel 6): A Form-Critical and Traditio-Historical Study' (Ph.D. dissertation, Claremont Graduate School, 1974) 6-12 for a detailed summary of Rost on this block of material and P.D. Miller and J.J.M. Roberts, *The Hand of the Lord: A Reassessment of the 'Ark Narrative' of 1 Samuel* (Baltimore: Johns Hopkins University, 1977), 23 for a critique of Rost.

5. *Succession*, 33-34.

6. Ibid., 43-48. Rost contends that the writer of the succession story had in written form the Nathan prophecy, which was adapted to suit his purposes by adding the prophecies on the dynasty (*byt*).

7. Ibid., 57-62. The argument that the David-Bathsheba story is an interpolation in the Ammonite War accounts was previously made by B. Luther in his article, 'Die Novelle von Juda und Tamar und andere israelitische Novellen', *Die Israeliten und ihre Nachbarstämme* (ed. E. Meyer; AS; Halle: 1906), 184-85. Though Rost mentions the works of Winckler, Kittel, Cook and Gressmann (p. 57) (see note 4 above and E. Ball, 'Introduction to *The Succession to the Throne of David*', xliv n22 for specific

citations), he fails to give credit to Luther, whose arguments are very similar to and predate his own.

8. *Succession*, 62.

9. This is with the exception of the chapter on the Ammonite War, in which he pays very little attention to concerns other than content. We shall, therefore, have to review his work in this area much more closely.

10. In particular he reviews the work of K. Budde, *Die Bücher Samuel* (KHCAT 8; Leipzig: Mohr, 1902; S.A. Cook, 'Notes on the Composition of 2 Samuel', *AJSLL* 16 (1899/1900), 145-77; H. Gressmann, *Die älteste Geschichtsschreibung und Prophetie Israels von Samuel bis Amos und Hosea*, Die Schriften des Alten Testaments 2/1, 2nd revised edition, Göttingen: Vandenhoeck & Ruprecht, 1910; C.F. Keil, *Die Bücher Samuelis*, BCAT II/2, 2nd edition, Leipzig: Dörffling & Franke, 1875; R. Kittel, *Geschichte des Volkes Israel*, vol. 1, 5th/6th edition, Stuttgart: Friedrich Andreas, 1923; M. Lohr and O. Thenius, *Die Bücher Samuelis*, 3rd edition, revised by M. Lohr, Leipzig: Vandenhoeck & Ruprecht, 1898; W. Nowack, Richter, *Ruth und Bücher Samuelis übersetzt und erklärt*, HKAT I/4, Göttingen: Vandenhoeck & Ruprecht, 1902; C. Steuernagel, *Lehrbuch der Einleitung in das Alte Testament*, Tübingen: J.C.B. Mohr, 1912; J. Wellhausen and F. Beek, *Einleitung in das Alte Testament*, 4th edition, revised by J. Wellhausen, Berlin: Georg Reimer, 1878; H. Winckler, *Geschichte Israels in Einzeldarstellungen*, Völker und Staaten des alten Orients, 2-3, Leipzig: Pfeiffer, 1892-1900.

11. *Succession*, 66.

12. W. Caspari, 'The Opening Style of the Israelite Novelle', in *Narrative and Novelle in Samuel: Studies by Hugo Gressmann and Other Scholars 1906-1923*, ed. by D. Gunn, Sheffield: Almond, (forthcoming). We are indebted to D. Gunn for making available the manuscripts for this volume.

13. Rost, *Succession*, 67-68. It is Rost's use of content and 'working backwards' which provide the basis of the critiques of O. Eissfeldt; cf. especially his *The Old Testament: An Introduction* (New York: Harper & Row, 1965), 276, and D. Gunn, *The Story of King David: Genre and Interpretation* (JSOTS 6; Sheffield: JSOT, 1978), 15, where he argues Rost has 'put the cart before the horse.'

14. *Succession*, 68.

15. Ibid., 69.

16. Ibid., 71-72. He specifically cites 1 Kgs 2.1-4.

17. Ibid., 73.

18. Ibid.

19. Ibid., 74-77. The first one is eliminated, since it disagrees with the parable in 12.1-4 in terms of emphasis. The second is eliminated since it interrupts the flow between the identification of David as the guilty party and his confession in v. 13. Interestingly, though Rost's theory of a unified

narrative rests partially on the connection between these two speeches and the rest of the succession story in chs. 13ff., he does not see the designation of these two oracles as additions as subjecting his whole thesis to question.

20. Ibid., 81. For example, he cites 1 Kgs 1.5 as being parallel to 2 Sam 15.1 arguing for interrelation of theme and authorship.

21. Most notably Caspari, 'The Opening Style', and B. Luther 'Narrative in Genesis and Samuel: Judah and Tamar and other Israelite Novellen', in *Narrative and Novel*, ed. D. Gunn [forthcoming]. Again we are indebted to Dr. Gunn for making available the Luther article in its manuscript form.

22. Ibid., 81-83. For example, though 19.23 brings to a close the Absalom Revolt and seals the fate of Absalom, the same is not true for David. He thus argues that there is a need for continuation of the narrative, which is found in 1 Kings 1.

23. Ibid., 85-87. Needless to say, this is the weakest part of his argument and will be challenged by most scholars, who choose to begin with ch. 9. See below, § 2.

24. Ibid., 90.

25. Ibid., 94-98. We shall examine the various examples cited in this section, as well as the following sections, as they become relevant to our investigation in chapter 2 of this work.

26. Ibid., 99-104.

27. Ibid., 104-6.

28. Ibid., 106-8.

29. Most notably A. Weiser, *The Old Testament: Its Formation and Development* (New York: Associated Press, 1961), 162-65; G. Fohrer, *Introduction to the Old Testament* (Nashville: Abingdon 1968), 216-17; J.A. Soggin, *Introduction to the Old Testament* (rev. edn.; OTL, Philadelphia: Westminster, 1976), 189-94; O. Kaiser, *Introduction to the Old Testament: A Presentation of its Results and Problems* (Minneapolis: Augsburg, 1977), 154-60.

30. Cf. 'Nocheinmal: Text-, Stil- und Literarkritik in den Samuelisbüchern', *OLZ* 31 (1928), 8-1-12; *Die Komposition der Samuelisbücher* (Leipzig: J.C. Hinrichs, 1931); *Introduction*, 138. In all of these he fights to maintain his view that J is the author.

31. Cf. the reviews in R.G. Bowman, 'The Crises of King David: Narrative Structure, Compositional Technique, and the Interpretation of II Samuel 8.15–20.26' (PhD. dissertation, Union Theological Seminary in Richmond, 1981), 3-50, 166-170, 283-85; Gunn, *Story*, 19-34; G. Ridout, 'Prose Compositional Techniques in the Succession Narrative (2 Sam 7, 9-20; 1 Kings 1-2)' (PhD. dissertation, Graduate Theological Union, 1971), 1- 21; R. Whybray, *The Succession Narrative: A Study of II Sam 9-20 and I Kings 1 and 2* (SBT, 9; Naperville: Alec R. Allenson, 1968), 10-55. These are the most complete and thorough.

32. *Succession*, 86-87.

33. Ibid., 86.

34. Ibid., 66.

35. Ibid., 68, 71-72.

36. R.H. Pfeiffer and W.G. Pollard, *The Hebrew Iliad: The History of the Rise of Israel under Saul and David* (New York: Harper & Brothers, 1957), 80.

37. Gunn, *Story*, 67.

38. J. Van Seters, *In Search of History* (New Haven: Yale University, 1983), 280. In line with this argument of seeing 2 Sam 6.16, 20f. related to its context and not to the TSN, R.A. Carlson argues that this unit, with its use of *brk*, fits under the rubric of 'David under the Blessing' (*David the Chosen King: A Traditio-Historical Approach to the Second Book of Samuel* [Stockholm: Almquist & Wiksell, 1964], 94).

39. Gunn, *Story*, 66; S. Mowinckel, ('Israelite Historiography', *ASTI* 2 [1963], 10-11) and Van Seters (*Search*, 271-72) argue on form critical grounds that there was no pre-Dtr Nathan oracle to be found in 2 Samuel 7.

40. H.W. Hertzberg, *I and II Samuel* (OTL; Philadelphia: Westminster, 1976), 283, 286.

41. M. Noth, *The Deuteronomistic History* (Sheffield: JSOT, 1981), 55-56.

42. Ridout, 'Composition', 201-18.

43. *Succession*, 8.

44. *Story*, 66-67. This bespeaks the sentiments of W. Brueggemann, 'David and his Theologian', *CBQ* 30 (1968), 159n; J. P. Fokkelman, *King David (II Sam 9-20 & I Kings 1-2)*, vol. I, *Narrative Art and Poetry in the Books of Samuel* (Assen: Van Gorcum, 1981), 18.

45. P. Ackroyd, 'The Succession Narrative (So-called)', *Interp* 35 (1981), 384; R. Bowman, 'The Crisis of King David', 74.

46. H.M. Wiener, *The Composition of Judges II 11 to I Kings II 46* (Leipzig: J.C. Hinrichs, 1929), 5.

47. M. Smith, 'The So-called 'Biography of David' in the Books of Samuel and Kings', *HTR* 44 (1951), 169.

48. Hertzberg, *Samuel*, 295-96; T. Ishida, 'Solomon's Succession to the Throne of David—A Political Analysis', in *Studies in the Period of David and Solomon and Other Essays* (Winona Lake, IN: Eisenbrauns, 1982), 187; H. Schulte, *Die Entstehung der Geschichtsschreibung im Alten Israël* (BZAW, 128; Berlin: Walter de Gruyter, 1972), 140-41; T.C.G. Thornton, 'Solomonic Apologetic in Samuel and Kings', *ChQR* 149 (1968), 160.

49. *Search*, 282. Gunn notes that 2 Samuel 2.23; 3.27; 4.6; 20.10 are the only occurrences of the term *ḥmš* with *nkh* (*Story*, 80).

50. Van Seters, *Search*, 283. He cites 2 Sam 10.15-19a as an exception to this pattern, but he argues that this subunit belongs with 2 Sam 8. As will be shown below (see Chapter 3 §4 and Chapter 4 §2), David is in control

throughout the complex in 2 Sam 10-12.

51. *Story*, 52-53. It should also be pointed out that he also notes similarities with the war narratives of the Ark Narrative in 1 Sam 4, as well as with the death of Saul in 1 Sam 31.

52. Ibid., 67-68, 76-81; Van Seters, *Search*, 283.

53. Gunn, *Story*, 81-84.

54. Ackroyd, 'So-Called', 384; Fokkelman, *King David*, 18; Van Seters, *Search*, 283.

55. In the above analysis, however, it has been noted that there is a consistent difference between the elements which support the connection of 2-4 with the TSN as opposed to a connection with 2 Samuel 10-12. In other words, the very similarities between 2 Samuel 2-4 and the TSN point to a difference between 10-12 and the other sections.

56. 'Historiography', 11. (See discussion on these points in ch. 2 §1 below.)

57. 'Court History or Succession Document? A Study of 2 Samuel 9-20 and 1 Kings 1-2', *JBL* 91 (1972), 176-77.

58. 'Court History', 177. (See discussion on these points in ch. 2 §1 below.)

59. Ibid.

60. *Succession*, 80.

61. P.K. McCarter, Jr., *II Samuel* (AB; Garden City, NY: Doubleday, 1984), 13.

62. *David*, 140.

63. Ibid., 142. It is interesting that Carlson also appeals to the events in 1 Kings 1-2 as examples of the curse being carried out.

64. Ibid., 194.

65. Ibid., 198-203.

66. Ibid., 222.

67. *Succession*, 67.

68. Ibid., 68.

69. Ibid., 69-85.

70. Ibid., 94-96.

71. Ibid., 97-98.

72. Ibid., 99-104.

73. Ibid., 81-83.

74. *Composition of Judges*, 4. Since his work appeared three years after Rost's, it is interesting that Wiener makes no reference to Rost.

75. *DH*, 56-57. In this regard, Noth is followed by most scholars who undertake to refine his theory of the Deuteronomistic History, by positing more than one redaction. For example, see F.M. Cross, 'Themes of the Book of Kings and the Structure of the Deuteronomistic History', in *Canaanite Myth and Hebrew Epic: Essays in the History of the Religion of Israel*, 274-89 (Cambridge MA : Harvard University, 1973), esp. 275, where he discusses the use of the formula, 'to this day', *'d hywm hzh*, in etiologies as an indication of double redaction, but he does not deal with its occurrences as

such in 2 Sam 18.18. Similarly, R.D. Nelson, in his *The Double Redaction of the Deuteronomistic History* (JSOTS, 18; Sheffield: JSOT, 1981), cites the occurrence of the formula in 2 Sam 18.18 as an example which occurs in a source used by Dtr (p. 24), and never examines whether there is any other evidence in the unit for reexamining the 'Succession History' Theory. He also cites 2 Sam 14.16 as containing the Dtr concept of 'the people as Yahweh's inheritance' (68-69), but he notes it as an occurrence outside the DtrH. Cf. also P.R. Ackroyd, *Exile and Restoration* (OTL; Philadelphia: Westminster, 1968), 62 and A.D.H. Mayes, *The History of Israel Between Settlement and Exile: A Redactional Study of the Deuteronomistic History* (London: SCM, 1983), 83. In the same manner, works which deal with the Deuteronomistic History as a work reacting to the exile, such as R.W. Klein, *Israel in Exile: A Theological Interpretation* (OBT; Philadelphia: Fortress, 1979) and J.D. Newsome, Jr., *By the Waters of Babylon: An Introduction to the History and Theology of the Exile* (Atlanta: John Knox, 1979), do not even list this text in their scriptural index. The only exception to this are those scholars to be discussed later, who claim Dtr influence in the Nathan oracles in 2 Samuel 12.

76. *Search*, 278.

77. Interestingly, Carlson also connects the Cain/Abel incident with the Amnon/Absalom incident. He argues, however, that this connection is a demonstration of the D-group's editorial work of positing that the death of Uriah *bśdh* (11.23), like Abel's death, was avenged on a *šib'ātayim* scheme (Gen 4.14, 24; 2 Sam 12.6) (*David*, 166).

78. 'David and his Theologian', 158n. (See analysis of this position in Chapter 2 §2 below.)

79. J.A. Wharton, 'A Plausible Tale: Story and Theology in II Samuel 9–20, I Kings 1–2', *Interp* 35 (1981), 343-44.

80. Ibid., 347 and 346 respectively.

81. J. Blenkinsopp, 'Theme and Motif in the Succession History (2 Sam. XI 2ff) and the Yahwist Corpus', *VTSup* 15 (1965), 53-55.

82. Ibid., 52.

83. Ibid., 53. The theory of this motif appears to have one of its flaws here in that the sexual acts performed and/or desired in the remainder of the TSN are not by the children of the union of Bathsheba and David. Similarly, it is not the writer of the TSN but rather Dtr. who depicts Solomon as being guilty of sexual abuse leading himself astray, as Blenkinsopp notes with regard to 1 Kgs 11.1-3.

84. Ibid., 54. It is interesting that this motif blames the woman and her seduction of the man. As should be noted, 2 Sam 12.9a and 10b both charge David and not the 'woman' with the offensive behavior. Thus, to label the motif as 'the woman who brings death', makes a claim which the text does not support, while it does not hold the male accountable for his own actions.

85. He argues from the fact that Uriah is a Hittite, that Bathsheba must also be one (p. 62n). In so doing he ignores her patronymic designation in 2 Sam 11.3. Similarly, as noted above, his designation of motif places the blame at her 'feet', so to speak.

86. *King David*, 413.

87. Ibid.

88. It is interesting that Fokkelman focuses the question around illicit sex with women which leads to the death of a son. As one looks at each of the instances of 'illicit sex' of the sons, however, one immediately notes that what is at stake is the abuse/acquisition of power. Thus, the rape of Tamar is one of violence perpetrated by a more powerful individual upon a weaker one. On the other hand the portrayal of Absalom with the concubines in 2 Sam 16.20-23 is within the context of political maneuvering. In the same manner, Adonijah's request for Abishag is an attempt at accruing power in his struggle against Solomon. It would appear from this analysis, therefore, that Fokkelman is trying to argue that on the basis of the Absalom and Adonijah incidents, one way to accrue political power in ancient Israel is to be associated with particular women. On the other hand, David's sons were not the best political strategists. Though they knew how the game was played, they were poor players.

While the Amnon–Tamar rape has the political consequence of making her ineligible to live in the palace as a 'virgin daughter of the king' (2 Sam 13.19-20), this action was not taken to increase his power. Thus, there does not appear to be as clear a comparison of these sexual acts as Fokkelman would suggest.

Finally, this raises the issue as to whether the David-Bathsheba incident should be viewed in terms of the Amnon abuse of power model, the Absalom/Adonijah political dimension, or both. We shall examine these possibilities in Chapter 4 below.

89. *David*, 180. While he does not accept a TSN (cf. 1.2a), his treatment of this theme is applicable here.

90. Ibid, 181.

91. Ibid. Carlson's view that this arrangement is by coincidence is reinforced by the fact that none of the narratives in 2 Samuel 10-20 applies the casuistic prescriptions found in the analogous law recorded in the Deuteronomic Code. For example, David and Bathsheba are not stoned and Amnon is not forced to marry Tamar.

92. *Succession*, 84-85.

93. C. Fontaine, 'The Bearing of Wisdom on the Shape of 2 Samuel 11-12 and 1 Kings 3', *JSOT* 34 (1986), 62.

94. *Story*, 94.

95. Ibid.

96. Ibid., 94-108.

97. Ibid., 92.

98. H. Hagan, 'Deception as Motif and Theme in 2 Sam 9-20; 1 Kings 1-2', *Bib* 60 (1979), 302.

99. Ibid.

100. E.g. Judg 3.19; 4.21; 7.14ff.; 16.28ff., ibid., 325.

101. Ridout, 'Prose', 22-161.

102. K. Sacon, 'A Study of the Literary Structure of "The Succession Narrative"', in *Studies in the Period of David and Solomon and Other Essays*, ed. T. Ishida (Winona Lake, IN: Eisenbrauns, 1982), 31-38.

103. Ibid., 52.

104. Ibid., 38.

105. Alan J. Hauser, 'His Father's Son: Amnon's Rape of his Sister Tamar', unpublished paper presented at the International Meeting of the SBL, Copenhagen, August 1989. In fairness to Hauser, while he does equate the rape and murder, this is mainly on the level of 'plotting behaviour' of Amnon and David. He still, however, wants to connect the adultery and rape. We see this as a flaw in his argument. Secondly, since he equates David and Amnon and Tamar and Uriah, it appears that he should also equate Jonadab and Bathsheba. See Chapter 4 §1.

106. 'From Jerusalem to the Jordan and Back: Symmetry in 2 Samuel XV-XX', *VT* 30 (1980), 109-13. As will be shown below, there are various such schemes which do not agree on the balancing of the elements.

107. Gunn, *Story*, 65; McCarter, *II Samuel*, 275-76; Noth, *DH*, 56-57; *et al*.

108. Blenkinsopp, 'Theme and Motif', 47n2; L. Delekat, 'Tendenz und Theologie der David-Salomo Erzählung', in *Das ferne und nahe Wort* (BZAW, 105; Berlin: Töpelmann, 1967), 32-35; Whybray, *Succession*, 8.

109. *Story*, 65.

110. See Chapter 2 §4 for further discussion of this point.

111. *Introduction*, 50.

112. E. Würthwein, *Die Erzählung von der Thronfolge Davids—theologische oder politische Geschichtsschreibung?* (TS, 115; Zurich: Theologischer Verlag, 1974), 24. Fokkelman argues against this comparison of the roles of Nathan by noting that in 2 Sam 12.25 Yahweh sends him to rename Solomon. Thus, he claims, Nathan's actions in 1 Kings 1 are a continuation of his acting on behalf of 'Yahweh's anointed' (*King David*, 412). The problem with this line of argument, however, is that in 1 Kings 1 there is no claim that Nathan is acting under instructions from Yahweh. Rather he is presented as an initiator and as a partisan.

113. Ibid., 25.

114. W. Dietrich, *Prophetie und Geschichte: Eine redaktionsgeschichtliche Untersuchung zum deuteronomistischen Geschichtswerk* (Göttingen: Vandenhoeck & Ruprecht, 1972), 132.

115. Ibid., 131.

116. Ibid.

117. Ibid., 132. In this regard he is building upon the theory advanced by R. Smend, Jr. of there being a DtrG, analogous with DtrH, whose work was redacted by a DtrN concerned with legal matters (cf. his 'Das Gesetz und die Völker: Ein Beitrag zur deuteronomistischen Redaktionsgeschichte', 494-509, in *Probleme Biblischer Theologie*, Festschrift von Rad, ed. H.W. Wolff [Munich: C. Kaiser, 1971]).

118. T. Veijola, *Das Königtum in der Beurteilung der deuteronomistischen Historiographie: Eine redaktionsgeschichtliche Untersuchung* (AASF; Helsinki: Suomalainen Tiedekatemia, 1977), 112.

119. *Erzählung*, 46.

120. Ibid., 43.

121. Ibid., 36.

122. Ibid., 43.

123. Ibid., 41.

124. Ibid., 42.

125. Ibid., 44-45.

126. Ibid., 45-46.

127. Ibid., 16-17.

128. Ibid., 57-59.

129. *Die ewige Dynastie Davids und die Entstehung seiner Dynastie nach der deuteronomischen Darstellung* (AASF; Helsinki: Suomalainen Tiedeakatemia, 1975). His designation of redactional verses include 2 Sam 11.27b–12.15a, 12.15b-24a, 12.25; 15.25-26; 16.11-12; 19.22-23; 1 Kgs 1.30, 35-37, 46-48; 2.1-3, 4a, 5-12, 22b, 26b-27, 28a, 31b-33, 37b, 42a, 44-45.

130. He has argued his position successively in the following articles: 'Pour ou contre Salomon: La Rédaction prosalomonienne de I Rois, I-II', *RevBib* 83 (1976), 481-528; *idem*, 'Absalom et les concubines de son prère Recherches sur II Sam 16.21-22', *RevBib* 84 (1977), 161-209; *idem*, 'Affinités sacerdotales, deutéronomiques, élohistes dans l'Histoire de la succession (2 S 9-20; 1 R 1-2)', AOAT 212 (1981), 233-46.

131. 'Court History', 173.

132. Ibid.

133. Ibid., 177-80.

134. Ibid., 177.

135. Ibid., 175. See the argument in support of this thesis in Chapter 3 §1 below, most notably in the discussion on the meaning of *ḥesed*.

136. C. Conroy, *Absalom Absalom! Narrative and Language in 2 Sam 13-20* (Rome: Biblical Institute, 1978). See below the more detailed discussion of his points in Chapter 2 §1.

137. McCarter, *II Samuel*, 16. He has also followed Flanagan, but has rejected the positions of Würthwein, Veijola, and Langlamet, except in the instance of the materials in 2 Sam 12.

138. See above discussion of limits of the narrative in §2.

139. Cf. Gunn's extensive treatment in the Appendix of *Story* (115-18)

and Bowman ('Crisis', 19-20) for further bibliography.

140. *Succession*, 104.

141. Ibid., 105.

142. Brueggemann, 'David's Theologian', 158; Eissfeldt, *Introduction*, 138; J. Jackson, 'David's Throne: Patterns in the Succession Story', *CJT* 11 (1965), 183; R.H. Pfeiffer, *Introduction to the Old Testament* (New York: Harper & Brothers, 1941), 357; Sacon, 'Literary Structure', 54; *et al.*

143. Von Rad also relied on Myer, see 'Beginnings', 176.

144. *DH*, 55-56. In fairness to both Noth and von Rad, one must realize that both of their works appeared in Nazi Germany (1943 and 1944 respectively). It is interesting to note in this regard that Noth's theory of the Deuteronomistic Historian had the effect of arguing for the ordering of the Hebrew Canon for the books from Joshua onwards over the LXX ordering and that of Luther. Similarly, von Rad argues (incorrectly as most recently demonstrated by Van Seters [*Search*, 213-15]) that what is contained in the Hebrew Canon in the TSN is unique in terms of the ancient Near East and even superior to the Greeks in terms of historiography. The risks for both in their taking these positions at this time are obvious, since their positions argue for the intellectual 'superiority' of these non-Aryan precursors to the Jews of their day. It may just be, therefore, that their lack of critical examination in regard to the TSN may be more a function of subtle 'anti-Nazi propaganda and polemic' than an indication of questionable scholarship.

While one may be reticent to admit the role which politics may play in the pursuit of scholarship, one is familiar with the example of the use of the so-called 'Curse of Ham' as a major justification of slavery in the United States and of apartheid in South Africa. The above speculation, however, demonstrates how the technique was utilized as a combatant of oppression, as opposed to a facilitation of it.

145. 'Beginnings', 193-94. In this respect he is following a theory put forth by A. Alt ('The Formation of the Israelite State in Palestine', in *Essays on Old Testament History and Religion* [Oxford: Blackwell, 1966], 171-237). For a negative critique of this position see T.C.G. Thornton, 'Charismatic Kingship in Israel and Judah', *JTS* 14 (1963), 1-11, who argues that the fact that sons of deceased kings, from Saul on down, came to the throne, albeit for a short reign prior to coups in many instances, suggests that the principle of dynastic succession was operative in the north as well as in the south. See G. Bucellati, *Cities and Nations of Ancient Syria: An Essay on Political Institutions with Special Reference to the Israelite Kingdoms* (Rome: Institutio di Studi del Vicino Oriente, 1967), for an even more extensive critique of Alt.

146. So Hertzberg, *Samuel*, 376-77; Ishida, 'Solomonic Succession', 176; Ridout, 'Prose', 213; and Whybray, *Succession*, 50.

147. Delivered to the Society of Biblical Literature in December 1950, and

later published as 'Facts and Faith in Biblical History', *JBL* 70 (1951), 1-14. This position was an expansion of his treatment in his *Introduction*, 358-59.

Morton Smith differed with Pfeiffer and argued that the genre of the materials in the TSN was 'moral tractate' (cf. his 'So-Called "Biography"', 168).

148. 'Historiography', 7-12.
149. 'Tendenz', 26-36.
150. Ibid., 31.
151. 'Solomonic Apologetic', 160.
152. Ibid.
153. 'Tendenz', 27.
154. See above §2.
155. *Story*, 20.
156. *Succession*, 57.
157. Ibid., 50-55.
158. Ibid., 70-95.
159. Ibid., 96-116.
160. See above discussion in §2. Whybray also receives support from R.B.Y. Scott who states, 'the "Succession History" was produced by a writer of the wisdom school' (*The Way of Wisdom in the Old Testament* [New York: Macmillan, 1971], 105).
161. *Old Testament Wisdom: An Introduction* (Atlanta: John Knox, 1981), 41.
162. *Story*, 27. So also J.R. Porter, 'Old Testament Historiography', in *Tradition and Interpretation*, ed. G.W. Anderson (Oxford: Clarendon, 1979), 151.
163. *Story*, 38.
164. Cf. J. Van Seters, 'Problems in the Literary Analysis of the Court History of David', *JSOT* 1 (1976), 22-29.
165. *Story*, 38.
166. Ibid., 83. It is interesting, however, that he argues for the unity of the narrative inclusive of 1 Kings 1-2 (cf. *Story*, 91).
167. *Succession*, 73, 80.
168. *Absalom*, 102.
169. 'Court History', 175.
170. *II Samuel*, 15.
171. Ibid., 306.
172. Ibid., 307-08.
173. *Succession*, 104.
174. *Composition*, 4.
175. 'Solomon's Succession', 187.
176. M.H. Segal, 'The Composition of the Books of Samuel', in *The Pentateuch: Its Composition and its Authorship and Other Biblical Studies*

(Jerusalem: Magnes, 1967), 177.

177. *Iliad*, 16-17.

178. *Succession*, 105.

179. *Samuel*, 18-19.

180. 'Beginnings', 196-98.

181. For example Blenkinsopp, 'Theme', 56-57; Brueggemann, 'David', 157; Delekat, 'Tendenz', 31; Meadows, 'Study', 57; Noth, *The History of Israel* (Revised edn; New York: Harper & Row, 1960), 220; Ridout, 'Composition', 175-76; Thornton, 'Solomonic Apologetic', 161; Wharton, 'Plausible Tale', 351; Whybray, *Succession*, 54-55; Würthwein, *Die Erzählung*, 28.

182. *Introduction*, 276, 281.

183. *King David*, 139.

184. Ibid., 131.

185. Ibid., 266. Cf. above discussion in §2 in regards to the relationship between the arrangement of the materials in 2 Samuel 10-20 and the Deuteronomic Code according to Carlson.

186. *II Samuel*, 307.

187. Ibid., 15-16. This is in line with his theory of a prophetic redaction of the Samuel materials (p. 8).

188. Ibid., 13.

189. *Search*, 278. In support of his position he argues that the negative reference to David in 1 Kgs 15.5 is a gloss (290).

190. Ibid., 281-90.

191. Ibid., 291.

192. Cf. ch. 2 §2.

193. *Search*, 250-52.

Notes to Chapter 2

1. 'Historiography', 10. He also argued against the inclusion of 2 Sam 7.11b, 16 in the TSN, on the grounds that ch. 7 is an etiological legend whose intention is to provide a prose basis for the royal enthronement ritual within the New Year festival and to explain why it was Solomon and not David who built the temple, and that they were thus the 'prose historicization' of Pss. 89.20-38 and 132.11-12 (10-11). Thus, by implication, 2 Samuel 7 was written at a considerably later time than the events.

2. Ibid., 13.

3. Ibid., 7-8. He dates this composition on the acts of Solomon during the reign of Solomon, accepting von Rad's notion of a 'Solomonic period of enlightenment'.

4. Ibid., 13-14. He therefore referred to the Davidic materials as the

'history of David's family'.

5. As witnessed in the above quotation.

6. 'Court History', 172-81. Flanagan is vague on the subject of the date of this material.

7. He argues that since there is a connection between the Mephibosheth material in 9 with that in 16 and 19, as well as an interrelationship of the Ammonite campaigns with the mention of the refuge in Mahanaim in 17.27, then these materials belong with the 'Court history' and not with the Succession theme (p. 176). As we shall show below (cf. §4), though there is a connection between ch. 10 and 17.27, their chronological arrangement is most problematic in terms of historical reconstruction.

8. Ibid., 173-74. This is a restatement of Mowinckel's previous observation.

9. Ibid.

10. Ibid., 174-75.

11. Ibid., 175. Rost had argued that the marked similarities in the descriptions of the preparations for Absalom's revolt in 2 Samuel 15 and Adonijah's in 1 Kings 1 should be taken as evidence that there was a single author for the complex (*Succession*, 80). As will be seen below, McCarter argues that this could better be explained if the author of Kings copied from the pre-existent Absalom Revolt narrative (*II Samuel*, 12).

12. Ibid.

13. Ibid.

14. After the exclusion of the so-called 'succession materials'.

15. Once he went beyond the confines of the Absalom revolt, however, Flanagan had to admit: 'Beyond this point the balance in the narrative becomes less clear. Still, there are signs that the author may have been attempting to construct parallels but was not as successful as he had been in the central portion of his story' (ibid., 180). Similarly Flanagan's argument is 'not as successful' at this point.

It should also be noted that Gunn argues for such an interpretation of the structure of the flight from and return to Jerusalem, but for him the center is the crossing of the Jordan (cf. 'From Jerusalem to the Jordan', 112).

16. Ibid., 181.

17. Ibid.

18. *Absalom Absalom*. He did not assert that 2 Sam 13-20 had necessarily existed independently previously. Rather he stated, '2 Samuel 13-20 may well have existed from the start as part of a larger work (whatever that was) or these chapters may have reached their present form in several redactional phases. . . but the point is that even they have a relatively independent narrative identity and can therefore be legitimately studied on their own' (p. 6).

19. Ibid., 6. He admitted that the 'extent of the literary unity to which 2 Samuel 13-20 belongs is no longer clear, and the enormously complex

question of the composition of the books of Samuel would have to be faced before a satisfactory answer could be found' (pp. 5-6).

20. *Succession*, 81.

21. For example, in discussing the dissimilarities in the reactions of David to the death of the first child born to Bathsheba, and the death of Absalom, Conroy argued most emphatically that 'in 2 Samuel 12,19-24a David's attitude to the death of his son is detached and even coldly rational. There he radically contests the meaningfulness of mourning rites, while in 2 Samuel 19 he practices them to blind excess. . .[The] suspicion cannot be brushed aside that the difference in presentation may be due to two different hands' (*Absalom*, 75n-76n).

Brueggemann has tried to refocus this incongruity by suggesting that in both instances David acts contrary to the expectations of his servants (*David's Truth in Israel's Imagination and Memory* [Philadelphia: Fortress, 1985], 48). He misses the point, however, that the servant's reaction in 12.21 functions as a means to explain these actions while 19.5-7 functions to alter the behavior. Thus, the comparison breaks down.

22. Cf. ibid., ch. 4, 89-114.

23. Ibid., 101-103.

24. Ibid., 104.

25. Ibid., 103.

26. *II Samuel*, 15-16.

27. Ibid., 8.

28. Ibid., 306.

29. Ibid., 304-305.

30. Ibid., 290.

31. Ibid. Cf. his discussion of 1 Sam 15 in his *I Samuel* (AB; Garden City, NY: Doubleday, 1980), 260-71 where he argues for a pre-Deuteronomistic prophetic redaction of the earlier materials in Samuel.

32. Ibid., 308.

33. See above, Chapter 1 §2.

34. As we have noted, numerous organizing schema have been proposed as reflective of this unified story line. Blenkinsopp ('Theme and Motif') and Brueggemann ('David') argue for the interrelation of themes in the pentateuchal source J with those of the Succession Narrative; Whybray (*Succession*, 56-95) argues for sexual instruction as in Proverbs, most notably ch. 6, as the organizing principle; Hagan ('Deception as Motif') argues for a series of deceptions as the organizing motif; Gunn argues for an interplay between the themes of private and political life (*Story*, 88-94) and giving and grasping (94-108); while Fokkelman organizes all around the themes of sex and violence (*Narrative*, 411-30).

35. Brueggemann, 'David and his Theologian', 162.

36. 'Theme and Motif', 50-57.

37. We take issue with the designation 'the woman who brings death',

since it fails to capture the nuances of these situations. The narratives in Samuel used for this concept describe power relationships and power plays in which the woman becomes a confirmation of the power of the one to become associated with her (e.g. Abishag the Shunamite). Thus, it is not the woman who brings death in these narratives. Rather it is the male who dies by virtue of losing the power play.

38. See P. Trible, 'Depatriarchalizing in Biblical Interpretation', *JAAR* 41 (1973), 30-48, and her *God and the Rhetoric of Sexuality* (OBT; Philadelphia: Fortress, 1978), 105-15 on the behavior of the former and A. Berlin, 'Characterization in Biblical Narrative: David's Wives', *JSOT* 23 (1982), 69-85 for the latter.

39. *Succession*, 58.

40. Ibid., 59. He cited David's tricking Uriah in ch. 11, although there is no examination of specific terminology which designated this trick as grounded in wisdom. On the other hand he cited Jonadab's 'wise advice' in ch. 13; Joab's use of a 'wise woman' to trick David in ch. 14; David's sending Hushai to function as an advisor to foil Ahithophel in chs. 15-16. As noted, however, he ignored the dissimilarity between the first of these examples with the others. Similarly, it should be remembered that not all scholars accept the mention of the *yo'ês* as evidence of wisdom influence. For example J.L. Crenshaw argued that Hushai and Ahithophel are functioning more in political than sagacious roles (cf. *Old Testament Wisdom*, 53).

41. Ibid., 58-59. While Wolff and others have argued for wisdom influence upon the prophetic books, this has been based upon the use of formulaic expressions in particular speeches (cf. Wolff's discussion of the use of numerical sayings in the oracles against the foreign nations in Amos 1-2 in his *Joel and Amos* [Hermeneia; Philadelphia: Fortress, 1977], 138, 148); note also, his *Amos the Prophet: The Man and his Background* (Philadelphia: Fortress, 1973). Whybray's analysis, however, is the first instance of someone designating this particular unit as bearing 'wisdom' as opposed to 'prophetic' influence (see Fontaine, below).

42. Ibid., 57.

43. 'Bearing of Wisdom', 61-77.

44. Ibid., 61.

45. Ibid., 64.

46. Ibid., 70.

47. Ibid., 71.

48. This tradition can be seen as early as the Rabbinic period, as noted in *b. Yoma* 22b and *Midr. Ps.* 3.4, among others. Cf. J.M. Bassler, 'A Man for All Seasons: David in Rabbinic and New Testament Literature', *Interp* 40 (1986), 160-61 for further elaboration on this matter. Similarly, Gressmann described David's actions as traditional 'Oriental lust' (*Geschichtsschreibung*, 155).

49. *David*, 180-93. He treats this as a subtheme of his overall contention

that 2 Sam 13–24 is organized under the rubric of 'David under the curse'.

50. This is a term he adapted from Engnell's use of the term D-work (ibid., 22n). Given his recognition of various redactional and traditio-historical stages in the D-work's development, he argued, 'it would be justifiable to speak of a D-group instead of a single D-author' (ibid., 23).

51. Ibid., 181. A major basis for his contention that this is a D-group arrangement is the observation that other passages which speak of sexual concerns (e.g. Deut 27 and Lev 18 and 20) do not have the same listing and ordering of sexual offenses (p. 181n). He does not, however, address the fact that Deut 22.22–23.1 contains sexual laws which are not refuted in the TSN.

52. Ibid., 187. Interestingly he does note the existence of possible D-group or later additions to the text in 14.25-27 and 18.18 (p. 187n). It should also be noted that he is primarily arguing against Caspari's contention of separate 'Novellen' in 2 Sam 13–14 and 15–20 (cf. Caspari, 'Literarische Art und historischer Wert von 2 Sam. 15–20', *TSK* 82 [1909], 319, 333).

53. Ibid., 189.

54. Ibid. It is interesting that in this regard he does not see any difference between the nuances of these two incidents, the David–Bathsheba adultery and the rape of Tamar. Thus, he equates the *šākab* of adultery (11.4) with that of rape (13.14) and the divinely caused death of the child (12.14b) with fratricide (13.28-29), where in the former an innocent party is killed, while in the latter the guilty party is murdered without benefit of legal trial. Similarly, he ignores the fact that, though these laws appear to be side by side in the Deuteronomic code, their penalties are not equal, which would suggest that they should not be equated at the level at which Carlson is arguing.

55. Cf. the critique of Gunn on the relationship between the sexual scenes in chs. 11 and 13 in §2 below.

56. E.g. while Deut 22.22 requires death for *both* the man and the woman, the initial confrontation and pronouncement in 2 Samuel only involve David and not Bathsheba. Similarly, the penalty for rape is irrevocable marriage, according to Deut 22.29. Finally, though apodictically formulated, Deut 23.1 refers to a step-mother and not to concubines.

57. Thus, R. Alter argued, 'As a rule, when a narrative event in the Bible seems important, the writer will render it mainly through dialogue, so the transitions from narration to dialogue provide in themselves some implicit measure of what is deemed essential, what is conceived to be ancillary or secondary to the main action. Thus, David's committing adultery with Bathsheba is reported very rapidly through narration with brief elements of dialogue, while his elaborate scheme[s regarding]. . . Uriah are rendered at much greater length largely through dialogue. One may infer that the writer means to direct our attention to the murder rather than to the sexual

transgression as the essential crime' (*The Art of Biblical Narrative* [New York: Basic Books, 1981], 182).

58. See Chapter 1 §2 above.

59. *King David*, 413.

60. Ibid.

61. cf. M. Tsevat, 'Marriage and Monarchical Legitimacy in Ugarit and Israel', *JSS* 3 (1958), 237-43 in reference to 2 Sam 16.20.

62. Cf. note 37.

63. In the instance of the fratricide, Esther Fuchs argued that the vengeance motif in 2 Sam 13, as in the case of the rape of Dinah (Gen 34), is a political act of setting family lines straight. She argued her point from the wording of the text which does not concern setting things straight for the woman, but rather addressing the status of the men involved. Cf. her 'The Rhetoric of Rape in the Biblical Narrative', paper delivered at the 76th Annual Meeting of the Society of Biblical Literature, Anaheim, CA, Nov. 24, 1985.

64. Cf. Weiner, *Composition*, 5; Hertzberg, *Samuel*, 376; Thornton, 'Solomonic Apologetic', 160; Ishida, 'Solomon's Succession', 187; Schulte, *Die Entstehung*, 165; Sacon, 'Study', 45, 52; Van Seters, *Search*, 280-83; Gunn, *Story*, 67-68.

65. The exception is the war stories, which Sacon utilizes ('Study', 45) and which, as we shall show in the next chapter, follow certain conventions of structure and genre in war stories, and, thus, become weak links for connecting 2-4 with 10-12.

66. Cf. below note 89.

67. It is interesting that this theme of the 'sons of Zeruiah' is depicted by Gunn as a 'traditional motif' (*Story*, 39-40). However, he does not note the fact that this motif is different in 2 Sam 10-12, as exemplified by the way Joab assists David in the murder of Uriah in 11.17-24. Van Seters totally rejects Gunn's notion that this is a 'traditional motif' on the basis that the instances cited by Gunn of the motif appearing outside the 'Court History' (i.e. 2 Sam 2.8-4.12 + 9-20, as he calls it) are unfounded (cf. 'Problems', 23-25).

68. While Jackson has taken note of the difference in the portrayal of David and Joab's relationship in chs. 10-12, as opposed to that in 13-20, he argued that this is the conscious attempt of the writer to demonstrate that David has gone from being master to being servant (cf. 'David's Throne', 188). In so doing, however, he ignored the similarities in chs. 2-4 and 13-20, and thus, would have to explain why David went from servant to master to servant. Again, we see one who is trying to maintain the unity of the narrative and thereby being forced to posit intentional dissimilarities as the guiding principle of the writer.

69. *Search*, 283.

70. Ibid., 283n.

71. Ibid., 90.

72. Prior to Rost, W. Caspari had argued that the different portrayals of David in 10-12, 13-14, and 15-20 were argument for the existence of *Novellen* in these units ('Literarische Art', 318-22).

Carlson took issue with this by arguing that, 'Disparities in the description of the *personae* of the various stories are at most evidence of a lack of conceptional ability, but they by no means indicate that the units themselves cannot have originated with the same traditionalist or group of traditionalists' (*David*, 184). In support of his contention, he then argued that 'The best proof of this is the continuity, both psychological and religious, which characterizes the description of the main figure in the drama, king David' (ibid.). As has already been shown, however, such continuity is not evident even for David.

73. 'Beginnings', 190.

74. *Story*, 99.

75. Ibid., 100.

76. The argument is not that the 'narratives' found in these chapters do not read as a continuous 'story'. Rather the question is at what point in the transmission and development of the text is such a continuity to be posited.

77. *Art of Biblical Narrative*, 76.

78. Adele Berlin, *Poetics and Interpretation of Biblical Narrative* (BLS; Sheffield: Almond, 1983), 26-27.

79. With the exception of the 'indignation' in 2 Sam 12.5, none of these 'psychological motivations' are bespoken by the narrator. In fact all of David's 'ascribed' emotions are predicated on the verbs *šlḥ* and *'mr* in the Qal, neither of which can be accused of carrying 'great psychological baggage'. Similarly, the emotions of Bathsheba are predicated on wording which stresses the 'time of mourning' (11.27a) and David's comforting (12.24a), not her grieving.

80. L.G. Perdue, '"Is There Anyone Left of the House of Saul...?" Ambiguity and the Characterization of David in the Succession Narrative', *JSOT* 30 (1984), 69-71.

81. Ibid., 74. He has been followed in this track by Gail A. Yee, 'Literary Ambiguity and 2 Sam 11: The David and Bathsheba Story', paper presented at the 76th Annual Meeting of the Society for Biblical Literature, Anaheim, CA, November 24, 1985. Sternberg (*The Poetics of Biblical Narrative: Ideological Literature and the Drama of Reading* [Bloomington: Indiana University, 1985]) offers another twist on this theme of ambiguity. He argues that the intention of the narrator is to present the details of the story in such a way that one can argue either of two conflicting hypotheses. For example one could build a case that Uriah does not know about the David-Bathsheba adultery. Similarly one can build a case that he knows and is playing the deceived but powerless husband (pp. 201-209). Similarly one can build a

case that David thinks Uriah knows or that David thinks Uriah doesn't know (pp. 209-213). In order to argue one view over the other, however, decisions must be made as to whether the words and actions of each character are to be understood as genuine or as subterfuge. Thus, he argues the narrator has consciously structured the narrative to command both conflicting ideas and the reader must fluctuate between both positions.

82. Solomon is listed here as a main character in this section since Rost argues that the whole intention of chs. 10–12 is to introduce the successor to the throne (*Succession*, 62). Similarly, Blenkinsopp argued that the theme of 'sin externalized in a sexual form which leads to death' is possible because of the 'inclusion of Solomon and his mother at the beginning and end' ('Theme and Motif', 48).

83. Mowinckel argued that the existence of both of these almost identical lists suggests that the materials in 1 Kgs 1–2 are separate from 2 Sam 9–20, since they seem to function as concluding segments to a block of narrative ('Israelite Historiography', 12). Hertzberg argued that the 'reason for the further introduction of the list of David's officials here in 2 Sam 20.23-26. . . can be found in the restitution of Joab to his old position. It is as though the sentence began 'so once again. . . '. The problem is thus not why the list occurs here a second time. . '. (*Samuel*, 374).

McCarter offered a less convincing alternative solution to the duplication in speculating that, since 21.1-14 originally preceded ch. 9, when the Dtr editor moved it to its current location, he replicated the list (*II Samuel*, 435). Thus, he posited that the original order was an officials list, the story of the famine (now 21.1-14) and then the Mephibosheth story (9.1-13). Once the famine story was relocated along with its accompanying 'officials list' (since he held the list in 20.23-26 to be the more original, 435), a second officer's list was drawn up to precede the Mephibosheth story.

The problem with this line of argument is that it does not clearly speak to the function of the 'officials lists' in their contexts nor offer an explanation of the differences between them. No reason is offered for the duplication in the first place. The question is still raised why the editor did not merely relocate the officers list *and* the famine story. Rather McCarter's theory implies that these lists function as introductions to the 'House of Saul–House of David' tension–reconciliation motif being tied to both the famine and Mephibosheth narratives.

We would suggest that both lists function as interludes and were so placed by the final redactor. In other words, they conclude major segments of the narrative, 2 Sam 1–8 and 9–20. Their concluding function is seen in the similarity between their locations in the overall narrative. Both of them appear after major events in the reign of David, the consolidation of the empire in ch. 8 and the close of the Absalom and Sheba civil rebellions in ch. 20.

Secondly, one notes that the difference in 8.16, employing the patronymnic of Joab, and 20.23, which omits it, could best be explained by the unit's conclusive function. In other words the fact that he is not mentioned in the war stories of ch. 8, while he is a major character in the events narrated in ch. 20, establishes the need, or lack of need, for the patronymic in each respective listing.

84. J. Bright, *A History of Israel* (3rd edn, Philadelphia: Westminster, 1981), 202; S. Hermann, *A History of Israel in Old Testament Times* (2nd edn, Philadelphia: Fortress, 1981), 161; H. Jagersma, *A History of Israel in the Old Testament Period* (Philadelphia: Fortress, 1983), 111, and Noth, *History*, 210 argue for the authenticity of these lists. The shared view is that the first describes conditions at the beginning of David's reign, while the second describes those at the end.

85. By the same token one wonders what happened to Bathsheba and Solomon during this time. In attempting to address this concern Whybray speculates, '[Solomon] thus remains an unknown mysterious figure during the period when his brothers are attempting to usurp the throne. This impersonal treatment is perhaps intended to emphasize that he stood aloof from the conflict' (*Succession*, 52). Conroy disagreed with this, arguing: 'A simpler explanation might be that the narrator was not concerned with Solomon or his succession in chs. 13–20' (*Absalom*, 78n).

86. 2 Sam 16.23; 17.7, 11, 15, 21. As Whybray noted, 'It then becomes apparent that... wisdom and counsel are present as fundamental concepts throughout the book' (*Succession*, 58). As noted above, he ignores the absence of these concepts in chs. 10–12.

87. 2 Sam 13.3; 14.2, 20; 20.16 (cf. ibid., 45).

88. Flanagan noted this as 'the only case of such mediation within the Court History where it is customary for historical events to communicate divine will' ('Court History', 176).

89. Würthwein correctly noted that this makes little sense given the third announcement of punishment as grace from the deity (*Tendenz*, 24–25). In other words, since the punishment has been moved (*h'byr*) from David to the child (2 Sam 12.13b), the removal of the punishment from the child would mean its reimposition upon him. Thus, one would have to understand David's actions as requesting his own death. If, however, 12.1-15a is an interpolation, David's behavior, beseeching the deity to spare the child 'afflicted' (*wygp*) by Yahweh (12.15b) because of his displeasure (*wyr'*) (11.27b) would make sense. See 4§4 on our treatment of 12.15b following 11.27b and 4§5 for our explanation of David's behavior.

90. 2 Sam 15.31; 16.11, 12, 18; 17.14; 18.19, 28, 31.

91. Conroy (p. 93), in arguing that 13–20 is a coherent unit separate from 10–12, stated that 'the "departure/return" pattern is the dominant narrative pattern of 2 Samuel 15–20; it plays a secondary but not unimportant role in chh. 13–14; and it *affects the reader by gaining his sympathy to some extent for Absalom in chh. 13–14 and to a much greater extent for David in chh. 15–20'*

(emphasis added).

92. As noted above, Van Seters refers to this behavior as characteristic weakness (*Search*, 283). However, this appears to be a modern-day interpretation of 'inappropriate executive behaviors'. One must, however, hear the 'strength of ultimate trust' in the words 'It may be that the LORD will look upon my affliction and that the LORD will repay me with good for this cursing' (2 Sam 16.12), which is David's response to Abishai, who wishes to punish Shimei for cursing David.

93. Rost argued that 2 Sam 12.7b-12 was secondary but not Deuteronomic (*Succession*, 73-77); von Rad, 'Beginning', 180; Hertzberg, *Samuel*, 314; Thornton, 'Solomonic Apologetic', 161; McCarter, *II Samuel*, 306-7; Delekat, 'Tendenz', 32; Whybray, *Succession*, 8; Carlson, *David*, 159; Blenkinsopp, 'Theme and Motif', 47n2; C. Conroy, *1-2 Samuel 1-2 Kings* (OTM; Wilmington, DL: Michael Glazier, 1983), 116-17; A.F. Campbell, *Of Prophets and Kings: A Late Ninth-Century Document (1 Sam 1-2 Kings 10)* (CBQMS 17; Washington: CBAA, 1986), 82; Gunn, *Story*, 65; *et al.* follow him in this respect. We must recall, however, that prior to Rost, Gressmann had argued that these verses were later additions (*Geschichtsschreibung*, 156).

It is interesting that on the one hand von Rad argues that the David–Bathsheba story 'never had an independent existence outside its present setting', while on the next page arguing that ch. 13 is 'apparently without any connection with what has gone before. . . ' (pp. 180-81).

94. Cf. Chapter 1 §2 above.

95. *Samuel*, 314.

96. *Story*, 65.

97. *Die Entstehung*, 122.

98. *Prophetie und Geschichte*, 127.

99. *Die ewige Dynastie*, 155n.

100. 'A Traditio-Historical Study of II Samuel 9-20, I Kings 1,2' (Ph.D. dissertation, Southern Baptist Theological Seminary, 1975) 155-68.

101. *Of Prophets and Kings*, 82.

102. Cf. Chapter 1 §2 above.

103. *Succession*, 57-62.

104. Noth, *Deuteronomistic History*, 56-57; Gunn, *Story*, 65; McCarter, *II Samuel*, 275-76; Hertzberg, *Samuel*, 303, *et al.*

105. Flanagan, 'Court History', 176; Pfeiffer, *Hebrew Iliad*, 88-89; Jackson, 'David's Throne', 188; Fokkelman, *King David*, 41.

106. In terms of historical allusions within the text we are in accord with McCarter's comments to the effect that, 'The working assumption in the following sketch of David's life, therefore, is that there is much material of Davidic and Solomonic date embedded within the stories about David in Samuel and Kings. This material can be utilized as a principal resource for David's biography, provided that we remain sensitive to the apologetic

character of the early narrative. The purposes for which these early documents were produced was not to record historical data but to defend and justify David's behavior. Thus, while we can probably rely on the general accuracy of reports of events that were publicly known, we must be cautious in evaluating accounts of private events...' (cf. 'The Historical David', *Interp* 40 [1986], 119).

107. For example see H. Ewald, 'The Rise and Splendor of the Hebrew Monarchy', vol. III of *The History of Israel* (London: Longmans, Green, and Co., 1871), 151; Gressmann, *Geschichtsschreibung*, 153; H. Tadmor, '"The People" and the Kingship in Ancient Israel: The Role of Political Institutions in the Biblical Period', *JWH* 11 (1968), 14; Hertzberg, *I & II Samuel*, 303; H.P. Smith, *Samuel*, 313; Ackroyd, *Second Book of Samuel* (New York: Cambridge University, 1977), 97; *et al.* As McCarter argued, 'Hanun's father, Nahash, was an enemy of Saul (I Samuel 11) and may have regarded himself *ipso facto* an ally of David' (*II Samuel*, 270).

108. For example, Ackroyd, 'Succession Narrative', 386 and J. Wellhausen, *Sketch of the History of Israel and Judah* (3rd edn; London: A. & C. Black, 1981), 49-50; Smith, *Samuel*, 307; H. Graetz, *Volkstümliche Geschichte der Juden* (3 vols.; Leipzig: Oscar Leiner, 1888), I, 54; G. Weber, *Das Volk Israel in der alttestamentlichen Zeit* (Leipzig: Wilhelm Engelmann, 1867), 171; D.S. Oettli, *Geschichte Israels bis auf Alexander den Grossen* (Stuttgart: Vereinsbuchhandlung, 1905), 291; A. & R. Neher, *Histoire biblique du peuple d'Israël* (Paris: Adrien-Maisonneuve, 1962), 308; J.A. Soggin, 'The Davidic-Solomonic Kingdom', in J.H. Hayes and J.M. Miller (eds.), *Israelite and Judaean History* (OTL; Philadelphia: Westminster, 1977), 351; *idem*, *A History of Ancient Israel from Beginning to the Bar Kochba Revolt, A.D. 135* (Philadelphia: Westminster, 1984), 58; Noth, *History*, 194; F. Castel, *Histoire d'Israël et de Judah: Des origines au IIme siècle après Jésus-Christ* (Paris: Centurion, 1983), 89.

109. For example Gressmann, *Geschichtsschreibung*, 154; Bright, *History*, 202n; Pitard, *Ancient Damascus: A Historical Study of the Syrian City-State from Earliest Times Until Its Fall to the Assyrians in 732 B.C.E.* (Winona Lake, IN: Eisenbrauns, 1986), 89-95; L. Wood, *A Survey of Israel's History* (Grand Rapids, MI: Zondervan, 1970) 270-71.

110. For example H.H. Milman, *The History of the Jews from the Earliest Period down to Modern Times* (3 vols.; New York: W.J. Widdleton, 1874), 340-42; Campbell, *Of Prophets and Kings*, 80.

111. 2 Sam 17.27. Langlamet views this incident as redactional since it disrupts the flow between 17.24-26 and 18.1. He argued that this incident serves the purpose of setting the stage for the events described in 19.32-40 ('Pour ou contre Salomon?', 355).

112. 2 Sam 12.26-31. So G. B. Caird, 'Exegesis of II Samuel', *IB*, 1136; Bright, *History*, 209; H. P. Smith, *Old Testament History* (New York: Charles Scribner's Sons, 1903), 146n; Gressmann, *Geschichtsschreibung*, 158;

Hertzberg, *Samuel*, 357; Ackroyd, *Second Book of Samuel*, 164.

113. 2 Sam 12.26-31.

114. *II Samuel*, 394. As will be argued below, we accept this interpretation.

115. Cf. 2 Sam 16.23 and 17.1-14. For this reason Caird dismissed the possibility that the two references to Eliam are to the same individual ('Exegesis', 1099), while J.A. Wharton argued, 'Does the storyteller expect his listeners to know that Eliam was one of the David's heroes and the son of David's trusted Ahithophel. . .? If so, is David's act of treachery still reverberating in his life when Ahithophel defects to Absalom at the most critical juncture?' ('A Plausible Tale', 343).

116. Interestingly McCarter did not entertain this possibility. Instead he noted, 'This suggests that the identity of Bathsheba's father was significant, although I cannot discover why' (*II Samuel*, 285).

117. G. Ricciotti, 'From the Beginning to the Exile', vol. I of *The History of Israel* (Milwaukee: Bruce, 1958), 289.

118. Wood, *Survey*, 278.

Notes to Chapter 3

1. *Geschichtsschreibung*, 153.

2. Ibid., 153-54.

3. See above Chapter 1 §2 and Chapter 2 §5.

4. H.P. Smith, *Samuel* (ICC; Edinburgh: T. & T. Clark, 1977), 316.

5. *Geschichte Israels in Einzeldarstellung* (2 vols.; Völker und Staaten des alten Orients, 2-3; Leipzig: Pfeiffer, 1895), 139.

6. *Search*, 286.

7. *Succession*, 60.

8. 'Court History', 176.

9. *Succession*, 62.

10. *Search*, 286.

11. *II Samuel*, 275-76.

12. B. Peckham notes that the word *wyhy* itself is a 'disjunctive opening formula' which signals a new unit. *The Composition of the Deuteronomistic History* (HSM, 35; Atlanta: Scholars Press, 1985), 76n16.

13. 2 Sam 9.12-13 is generally taken as a redactional summary bringing to a close this segment of the David–Mephibosheth cycle. Cf. Ackroyd, *The Second Book of Samuel* (CBC; New York: Cambridge University, 1977), 94; P. Dhorme, *Les Livres de Samuel* (Etudes Bibliques, Paris: Librairie Victor LeCoffre, 1910), 345-46; R.D. Gehrke, *1 and 2 Samuel* (St. Louis: Concordia, 1968), 283; Gunn, *Story*, 69; McCarter, *II Samuel*, 264; H. Smith, *Samuel*, 312.

14. As will be demonstrated in the examination of the next unit, it is the Aramean muster (v. 6b) which prompts David's subsequent dispatch of the

army, not Hanun's actions. Were this not the case, the actions described in v. 7aβf. would follow immediately upon the end of v. 5.

Interestingly, J.M. Myers recognized the problem when he stated, 'The insult administered to David's ambassadors of good will by the suspicious Hanun drew no immediate reprisal from David'. He then ignored the signals this makes for a break in the units and continued, 'The Ammonites may have regarded that fact as a sign of weakness on his part, though according to both Samuel and Chronicles they must have anticipated trouble eventually for they called upon their Northern neighbors for assistance' (*I Chronicles* [AB; Garden City, NY: Doubleday, 1979], 138).

15. Most probably in response to this awkward construction and its implications for suggesting a separation between these units, the Chronicler preceded the second *bny 'mwn* with the name Hanun and altered the tense of the third verb from imperfect with *waw*-consecutive to the infinitive construct with *lamed* designating purpose (1 Chron 19.6b). While scholars have long recognized this reworking of the tradition, they have ignored the structural problems resolved by this syntactical rearrangement. Therefore, H.G.M. Williamson suggested the changes were made with the purpose of 'making it more intelligible to later readers' (*I and II Chronicles* [NCBC; Grand Rapids, MI: Wm.B. Eerdmans, 1982], 140). Similarly E.L. Curtis stated, 'The sources or the motives of the changes introduced in the text by the Chronicler are mostly obscure' (*The Books of Chronicles* [ICC; Edinburgh: T. & T. Clark, 1910], 238).

It should also be noted that this addition of Hanun to v. 6 responds to the fact that his name only appears in this first unit in 2 Sam 10. Such an omission in the other units in the 'Ammonite War narratives', especially when the Syrian king is mentioned by name in the second battle narrative (vv. 16 and 19), is peculiar, to say the least.

16. As noted above, Rost has advocated the position that 10.1-6a is from a different author than 10.6b-19, because of differences in style (*Succession*, 59-61). In this regard he is followed by Gunn (*Story*, 65, 70). Similarly Flanagan ('Court History', 176) argues that the presence of David in the Aramean conflict suggests a difference in the 'siege at Rabbah', which he states starts in 10.1. As will be argued below, Rabbah is not mentioned at all in ch. 10 and thus cannot be taken for granted as the location of the battles and events described.

17. It should also be noted that a variation of the formula appears in 15.1, *wyhy m'hry kn*.

18. Ackroyd, *Second Samuel*, 28, 86, 96, 102, and 137; Dhorme, *Les Livres de Samuel*, 279, 335, 347; Karl Gutbrod, *Das zweite Buch Samuel* (BDAT; Stuttgart: Calwer, 1958), 27; Hertzberg, *I & II Samuel*, 290. Interestingly, as can be seen from this listing, not all commentators raise the issue, and those who do give no consideration to the formula in all its appearances.

19. *Succession*, 60.

20. Cf. Ackroyd, *Second Samuel*, 102; Blenkinsopp, 'Theme', 46n; Conroy, *Absalom*, 42; and Meadows, 'Study', 177-78 argue that it is not Dtr, while Carlson (*David*, 47) maintains that it is. While Ridout notes the occurrences of the formula within the TSN as marking off 'major divisions of the TSN', he ignores the occurrences outside the TSN and dismisses the possibility that it is redactional ('Composition', 79).

21. 2 Chron 20.1 and 24.4. Blenkinsopp has argued that it also appears in Gen 15.14 and 25.26. However, in both instances the formula does not appear at the beginning of a unit and the wording is *w'ḥry kn*.

22. 1 Chron 18.1//2 Sam 8.1; 1 Chron 19.1//2 Sam 10.1; 1 Chron 20.4//2 Sam 21.18.

23. *David*, 41.

24. 'Study', 177.

25. *Succession*, 58.

26. *David*, 42. One does have to wonder, however, why there would be the need to interpolate an introductory connective copula into an already existing unified narrative. Carlson does not suggest that it replaced an existing formula, nor does he examine how the narratives would hold together as a continuous composition without the copula. It would appear that his argument is predicated more on his attempt to hold together his thesis of *qllh* as a D-group organizing principle as well as a thesis of a preexistent unified TSN, than allowing the data to lead him.

27. *Story*, 70.

28. *Absalom*, 42.

29. Ibid., 43.

30. Technically 2.1 is not 'during' the reign. However, it opens the unit in which David is made king of Judah at Hebron. In the same manner, it would appear that the phrase 'during the reign' is a better formulation of the nature of the occurrences of the formula than Conroy's designation of the joining of 'separate episodes' (*Absalom*, 42).

31. See above Chapter 2 §5

32. Caird, 'Exegesis', 1157; Carlson, *King David*, 221-22; Hertzberg, *Samuel*, 381; McCarter, *II Samuel*, 443.

33. Cf. J. Flanagan, 'The Relocation of the Davidic Capital', *JAAR* 47 (1979), 237; N.L. Tidwell, 'The Philistine Incursions into the Valley of Rephaim (2 Samuel v 17ff.)', *VTSup* 30 (1979), 200.

34. Cf. Noth, *DH*, 18-25; Nelson, *The Double Redaction of the Deuteronomistic History* (Sheffield: JSOT, 1981), 29-42; J. A. Soggin, *Judges* (OTL; Philadelphia: Westminster, 1981), 7-12; Gray, *I and II Kings* (2nd edn; OTL; Philadelphia: Westminster, 1970), 55-58; Weippert, 'Die "deuteronomistischen" Beurteilungen der Könige von Israel und Juda und das Problem der Redaktion der Königsbücher', *BIB* 53 (1972), 301-39.

35. Cf. McCarter, *I Samuel*, 383-87 and Ralph W. Klein, *1 Samuel* (WBC; Waco, TX: Word Books, 1983), 237-39 for the history of debate on this verse.

Also, since it is not at the beginning of the unit, we would disregard its relevance for the present discussion.

36. Soggin (*Judges*, 255) states, 'Chapter 16 is composed of at least two episodes joined together only in a very precarious way'. Similarly the discontinuity between the 'miracle story' which features Elisha and the 'historical narrative' of Aramean-Israelite conflict in 2 Kings 6 is discussed by J. Gray, *Kings*, 468, and G.H. Jones, *1 and 2 Kings* (2 vols.; NCBC; Grand Rapids, MI: Wm. B. Eerdmans, 1984), 429-32, in which the formula is noted as a 'redactional seam'. Similarly, the question of chronological rearrangement of these traditions was raised by R. Kittel, *A History of the Hebrews*, vol. II, *Sources of Information and History of the Period down to the Babylonian Exile* (London: Williams Norgate, 1909), 292; Bright, *A History of Israel* (3rd edn; Philadelphia: Westminster, 1981), 254n; H. Donner, 'The Separate States of Israel and Judah', in Hayes and Miller (eds.), *Israelite and Judaean History*, 400.

37. Cf. J.M. Myers, *II Chronicles* (AB; Garden City, NY: Doubleday, 1965), 114 and 136-37 respectively and H.G.M. Williamson, *1 and 2 Chronicles*, 292 and 319 respectively.

38. Thus, Conroy's objection that like materials are not joined by the formula in each instance has been addressed. Conroy's question why the formula does not also appear in 1 Samuel still remains.

39. It should be noted that the Chronicler attempts to solve this problem by mentioning Nahash and omitting mention of Hanun in v. 1 (cf. Curtis, *Chronicles*, 238).

40. He is generally assumed to be the same Nahash mentioned in 1 Sam 11.1-2 and 12.12//1 Chron 19.1. Cf. Ackroyd, *I Samuel*, 96; D.K. Budde, *Die Bücher Samuel erklärt* (Tübingen: J.C.B. Mohr [Paul Siebeck], 1902), 247; Caird, 'Samuel', II, 1094; Dhorme, *Samuel*, 347; Driver, *Notes on the Hebrew Text and the Topography of the Books of Samuel* (2nd edn.; Oxford: Clarendon, 1913), 287; K. Gutbrod, *Das Buch vom Reich: Das Zweite Buch Samuel* (Stuttgart: Calwer, 1958), 135; Hertzberg, *Samuel*, 303; McCarter, *II Samuel*, 270; Smith, *Samuel*, 313; Van Seters, *Search*, 281n.

Interestingly in 1 Samuel he is referred to as 'the Ammonite' without any further title. Similarly, F. Cross dates him to the 10th century and adds him and Hanun to the list of Ammonite kings (cf. 'Notes on the Ammonite Inscription from Tell Sîrān', *BASOR* 212 [1973], 14).

41. Num 21.26; Judg 11.17; 1 Sam 22.3; 2 Kgs 3.7f.; etc.

42. Judg 11.17; 2 Kgs 3.26.

43. 2 Kgs 5.1, 5, 6.

44. 1 Kgs 20; 2 Kgs 3; 5; 6 etc.

45. Judg 11.12, 14.

46. Cf. e.g. S.J. DeVries, *1 Kings* (WBC; Waco, TX: Word Books, 1985), 248; J. Gray, *Joshua, Judges and Ruth* (NCBC; Grand Rapids: Eerdmans, 1986), 178; Jones, *Kings*, II, 337; J.M. Miller, *The Old Testament and the*

Historian (Philadelphia: Fortress, 1976), 32-33; J.A. Soggin, *Judges*, 211-12.

47. Boling, *Joshua*, 322.

48. Cf. 1 Kgs 11.43//2 Chron 9.31; 14.20, 31//2 Chron 12.16; 15.8//2 Chron 13.23; 15.24//2 Chron 17.1; 16.6, 28;22.40, 51//2 Chron 21.1; 2 Kgs 8.24//2 Chron 22.1; 10.35; 12.22//2 Chron 24.27; 13.9; 14.16, 29; 15.17//2 Chron 26.33; 15.22, 38//2 Chron 27.9; 16.20//28.27; 20.1//2 Chron 32.33; 21.18//2 Chron 33.20; 21.26; 24.6//2 Chron 36.8.

49. See above note 34.

50. Ben Hadad (2 Kgs 13.24) and Esarhaddon (2 Kgs 19.37).

51. On the hand of the Dtr in these units and the relevant research into the questions of specific identifications see Gray, *Kings*, 592; Jones, *Kings*, II, 497; and Noth, *DH*, 72; on 2 Kgs 13.24-5 and 19.37 see Gray, *Kings*, 695-96 and Jones, *Kings*, II, 582-83.

52. The authorship of this listing is in much dispute. Noth designates it as an addition to P (*A History of Pentateuchal Traditions* [Chico, CA: Scholars Press, 1981], 266). He is followed by Bruce Vawter (*On Genesis: A New Reading* [Garden City, NY: Doubleday, 1977], 373), Van Seters (*Search*, 51), and Norman K. Gottwald (*The Tribes of Yahweh: A Sociology of the Religion of Liberated Israel, 1250-1050 B.C.E.* [Maryknoll, NY: Orbis, 1979], 511). Von Rad, on the other hand, designates it as J (*Genesis* [OTL; rev. edn.; Philadelphia: Westminster, 1972], 346), while Peckham designates it Dtr2 (*Composition*, Fig. 7)

53. The fact that this listing is not one of dynastic succession does not account for the alteration, since both formulae include a name and genealogical data, which could be included in the same position.

54. S. Bin-Nun notes that the formula, *wymlk* ... occurs in Kings as well as in 2 Sam 10.1. While she views it as coming from the author of Kings in that book, she does not speculate on the implications of its use in 2 Sam 10.1 (cf. 'Formulas from Royal Records of Israel and Judah', *VT* 18 [1968], 427).

55. G. Tucker sees Josh 2.9-14 as part of the pre-Dtr redaction of the Rahab-spy saga, but only the verses which precede it (9b, 10b, 11b) derive from the Dtr ('The Rahab Saga [Joshua 2]: Some Form-Critical and Traditio-Historical Observations', in J.M. Efird [ed.], *The Use of the Old Testament in the New and Other Essays: Studies in Honor of William Franklin Stinespring* [Durham, NC: Duke University, 1972], 73). While he notes 'Some of the inconsistencies in the story, then, turn around the relationship of the speeches to the narrative framework' (p. 76), he does not, designate the whole unit 9-14 as Dtr. He is followed in this by T.C. Butler (*Joshua* [WBC; Waco, TX: Word Books, 1983], 31).

Soggin on the other hand not only argues that 'This first speech [vv. 9-14] is full of elements borrowed from the ancient confession of faith which an Israelite might put into the mouth of a stranger whom he was trying to describe as sympathetic to his compatriots', but he follows Noth in arguing that it is 'composed of Deuteronomic fragments and comments by the ancient "compiler"' (*Joshua* [OTL; Philadelphia: Westminster, 1972], 41).

R.C. Boling, who argues that the 'Rahab story was only incorporated into the final edition of the book' by Dtr2 (pp. 146-47), notes a textual problem in v. 12 with the omission of 'and give me a sign', the result of haplography (p. 142). T. Butler also notes this textual problem but points out that this clause serves to 'connect the saving of Rahab's family with the red thread and not with an oath' (*Joshua*, 54). Sakenfeld omits the phrase, and concentrates on superior/inferior social status for the explanation of the use of the term in the unit, which ignores the political import of the actions and the broader context (*The Meaning of Hesed in the Hebrew Bible: A New Inquiry* [HSM, 17; Missoula, MT: Scholars, 1978], 62-68).

Rather than seeing the textual problem as the result of haplography, it might be better to explain the phrase 'and give me a sign' as an interpolation which connects the saving, which is here attributed to her *ḥesed*, to another tradition which connected her saving to the use of a red thread. This interpretation would suggest, therefore, that the whole unit struggles with why the *ḥerem* was not totally carried out by elevating Rahab's treachery to a theologically acceptable negotiation. In this way, treason is sanctified as *ḥesed* and the abrogation of the laws of *ḥerem* are excused as the result of reciprocal *ḥesed*. It would, therefore, appear that such concerns would fit into the scope of Dtr, to whom we should attribute the whole unit.

56. Gray dates the unit to the last years of the Hittite empire (*Joshua*, 198), while Soggin argues that the expression 'land of the Hittites' (v. 26) is the Dtr way of referring to greater Syria (*Judges*, 29). Albright has argued that the narrative on the destruction of Ai in Joshua 7-8 is a reworking of this older tradition on Bethel ('The Israelite Conquest of Canaan in the Light of Archaeology', *BASOR* 74 [1939], 74-76). In addition to this is the confusion of location of Bethel and Luz (cf. Josh 18.22) and the use of the closing etiological formula '*d hywm hzh*. Thus, even though only the tribe's action toward the man (not the traitor's action) is called *ḥsd*, we would suggest that the use of *ḥesed* in this unit is additional evidence of Dtr attempts to reshape this tale about the House of Joseph by using a term which theologically renames treason.

57. Attention has been focused on 1 Sam 15.6 in terms of the location of the Kenites on the edge of Amalekite territory by appealing to Budde's reading of *h'm* in Judg 1.16 as *h'mlky* ('Richter und Joshua', *ZAW* 7 [1887], 101); cf. Dhorme, *Samuel*, 131; Driver, *Notes*, 122; Hertzberg, *Samuel*, 125; Klein, *I Samuel*, 150; McCarter, *I Samuel*, 266; and Smith, *Samuel*, 132; and on speculating about a possible treaty between the Kenites and Israel cf. Gottwald, *Tribes*, 578. The specific reference to *ḥesed* in 1 Sam 15.6 is assumed to be related to the action of the Kenites in Num 10.29-32.

Most recently F. Foresti has argued that v. 6 is secondary on the basis of its interruption of the flow of the narrative (v. 5 *wyb'* and v. 7a *wyk*), inconsistencies of singular and plural verbs in the verse, and the use of the term *bny yśr'l* (*The Rejection of Saul in the Perspective of the Deuteronomistic School: A Study of 1 Sam 15 and Related Texts* [STT; Rome: Edizioni del Teresianum, 1984], 46-47). In this respect, J.H. Grønbaek argues that the exodus tradition mentioned in v. 6b is deuteronomistic (*Die Geschichte vom Aufstieg Davids (1. Sam. 15-2 Sam. 5): Tradition und Komposition* [Copenhagen: Munksgaard, 1971], 51-52).

58. Gunn designates this a shift of loyalty from Saul to David by Jonathan (cf. *The Fate of King Saul: An Interpretation of a Biblical Story* [Sheffield: JSOT, 1980], 81).

59. While there is general agreement that the reference to *ḥesed* in v. 14 relates to the events described in 2 Sam 9 (cf. Dhorme, *Samuel*, 182; Grønbaek, *Die Geschichte*, 125; Hertzberg, *Samuel*, 174; Klein, *I Samuel*, 207; and Smith, *Samuel*, 188), lately, McCarter has argued that not only are these verses editorial' but also that they come from the hand of the 'Josianic historian himself' (*I Samuel*, 344).

60. In fact this is Saul's charge against Jonathan in 1 Sam 20.30. While Sakenfeld attempts strenuously to argue that Jonathan is not placed into this position by the request for *ḥesed* (*Faithfulness*, 11) her argument is not convincing.

61. This could also explain why there is no object mentioned as having been sent by David. The text reads 'and he sent *lnḥmw byd 'bdyw*', which 1 Chron 19.2 emends to read 'he sent *ml'kym lnḥmw*'. In spite of this the various commentaries suggest that a 'gift was sent' (cf. the opening statement by Gressmann at the beginning of the chapter).

62. It is interesting to note that in four of our texts in which *ḥesed* is rendered and repaid by humans, spies and/or ambush situations are involved: Rahab and the spies; House of Joseph in ambush on Bethel; Saul in ambush on Amalekites; and Jonathan is to *ḥqr* Saul's intentions.

63. Cf. De Vries, *1 Kings*, 36; Jones, *Kings*, I, 108; Long, *1 Kings*, 44; Montgomery, *Kings*, 89; and E. Würthwein, *Die Bücher der Könige: 1. Könige 1-16* (ATD; Göttingen: Vandenhoeck & Ruprecht, 1977), 20. Note also that one of Nahash's sons, Shobi, was present in that delegation.

64. In this respect, commentators follow M. Noth, *Die israelitischen Personennamen in Rahmen der gemeinsemitischen Namengebung* (BWANT 3.10; Stuttgart: W. Kohlhammer, 1928), 225.

65. While Veijola designates 1 Kgs 2.7 as Dtr (*Das Königtum*, 19n), no others do. It is interesting in this regard that Long observes that the arrangement of the instructions to Solomon in vv. 5-9 is not uniform in that the first and third set of instructions give the charges against the party and then the instructions to punish them, while in v. 7 the order is reversed with the instructions to do *ḥesed* followed by the reasons (*1 Kings*, 44). Given the unusual nature of these references and the use of this term, and argument

could be made that 1 Kgs 2.7 is an interpolation by Dtr.

66. While Soggin notes the fact that the double naming of the protagonist is one of the complexities of the Gideon cycle, he does not resolve the problem with any satisfactory explanation (*Judges*, 103-104). Noting that grammatically the name suggests one who strives for Baal, Burney argues that Baal in this context should be understood as Yahweh (*Judges*, 201), while Gray rejects this explanation in favor of an interpretation of the name being anti-Baal worship (*Judges*, 172). The use of the dual name, both in this complex and outside it in the DtrH, does seem to suggest that several traditions have been combined.

If our analysis of the reference to *ḥesed* is correct, the etiology given in Judg 6.32, would suggest that in tearing down the altar of Baal, he had broken his allegiance with his townspeople and thus put his life in jeopardy. This could also be the basis of the expectation of reciprocity, which was not honored.

67. C.F. Burney, *The Book of Judges with Introduction and Notes on the Hebrew Text of the Book of Kings* (New York: Ktav, 1970), 266; Gray, *Judges*, 242; Veijola, *Das Königtum*, 107. Soggin is more cautious in his designation (*Judges*, 161).

68. In 2 Sam 2.6 David tells the men of Jabesh that Yahweh will repay them for burying Saul and Jonathan. On the basis of this incident, Sakenfeld argues that either Yahweh or the person can repay this act of loyalty ('Meaning of *Ḥesed*', 40-42). One must note, however, that Sakenfeld groups all political occurrences of *ḥesed* together under the title 'secular' and does not differentiate whether treason is part of the action. It is our contention that this political motivation of the actor is essential in differentiating the basis of the loyalty, as well as in assessing the intention of the writer in the use of the term *ḥsd*.

69. 1 Sam 13.4 and 2 Sam 16.21.

70. 1 Sam 13.4.

71. Exod 7.18, 21; 8.10; 16.20; Isa 50.2.

72. Gen 34.30; Exod 5.21; 1 Sam 27.12. In Exod 16.24 the context is to show divine causation, and thus the *hiph'il* is used, while Prov 13.5 and Eccl 10.1 stress the consequences of negative behavior for the individual.

73. Cf. Dhorme, *Samuel*, 109; McKane, *1 Samuel*, 126; Smith, *Samuel*, 95.

74. 1 Chron 19.6 recognizes this and changes it to a *hithpa'el* to conform to the usual use of the *hiph'il* to suggest conflictive relations among parties, while maintaining the sense that the *bny 'mwn* brought this conflict upon themselves.

75. Smith notes, 'it is probably not hypercritical to see in the change from Jonathan to Saul an evidence of change of author' (*Samuel*, 95).

76. *I Samuel*, 230. Cf. Foresti, *Rejection*, 160n15 for extensive bibliography on this point.

77. As we shall note below, there are marked similarities between the use

of Ammonite War traditions in this and other units. At this point we can note that the beginning of our unit (*wyšlḥw . . . wyśkrw*, v. 6b), though seeming abrupt, is no more so than the opening of the account of the Ammonite war with Jephthah (*wyṣ'qw bny 'mwn*, Judg 10.17a) and that with Saul (*wy'l nḥš*, 1 Sam 11.1a). In all three there is a statement of unprovoked Ammonite aggression.

78. Though he does not argue for a separation between 10.6a & b, Richard Bowman also notes that it is Ammonite aggression which starts the war ('The Crisis of King David: Narrative Structure, Compositional Technique, and the Interpretation of II Samuel 8.15-20.26', [Ph.D. dissertation, Union Theological Seminary in Virginia, 1981], 189.)

79. See above discussion of *b'š*.

80. While Fokkelman calls David's response the 'lull before the storm' (*Narrative Art*, 45), Deist correctly notes that 'there is no indication whatsoever that David considers revenge' ('David: A Man after God's Own Heart? An Investigation into the David Character in the So-called Succession Narrative', *OTWSA* 27/28 [1984-85], 102).

The tendency to bring David's response to the act of Hanun in line with Joab's hyperbolic speech in v. 12 is seen in Josephus, who writes, 'When the king of Israel saw this, he had indignation at it, and shewed openly that he would not overlook this injurious and contumelious treatment, but would make war with the Ammonites, and would avenge this wicked treatment of his ambassadors on their king' (*Ant*, 7. 6, 154).

81. Cf. Ackroyd, *Second*, 96; Caird, 'Exegesis', 1096-97; Dhorme, *Les Livres*, 350-51; Hertzberg, *Samuel*, 305; McCarter, *II Samuel*, 272; Ridout, 'Prose', 56-57.

82. Ibid.

83. Verses 6a, 15a, and 19a.

84. The Chronicler omits this notation of regrouping found in v. 15b. In addressing this omission Curtis claims that 'The Chronicler has abridged and simplified the narrative' (*Chronicles*, 241). He is right to do so since the omission does make for a smoother transition to the muster mentioned next. He does not, however, note that this omission leaves their location uncertain. Thus, he has to speculate that 'The Arameans had *apparently* returned to the north, where they rallied. . '. (ibid., 240) [emphasis added]. Thus, we note that the function we attribute to v. 15b is confirmed by this speculation.

85. While a specific location is not presented, the notation does describe what happened to the Syrians.

86. Gen 19.30-38 is a 'pejorative ethnological saga' which presents them as the product of the incestuous union of Lot and one of his daughters (cf. Bruce Vawter, *On Genesis*, 242-43). This tradition of kinship is stressed in an interpolation to the introduction to the DH in Deut. 2.19 (cf. A.D.H. Mayes, *Deuteronomy* [NCB; Greenwood, SC: Attic Press, 1979] 136, 139; Gerhard von Rad, *Deuteronomy* [OTL; Philadelphia: Westminster, 1966] 42).

Interestingly, it is often noted that there is a loose connection between the Lot saga and the birth/incest narratives in Gen 19 (Walter Brueggemann, *Genesis* [Atlanta: John Knox 1982], 176-77; Gerhard von Rad, *Genesis* [OTL; Philadelphia: Westminster, 1972], 223). Thus, both of these Pentateuchal references to the kinship between Israel and Ammon can possibly be credited to redactors.

87. Cf. Jer 49.1-6; Ezek 21.28-32; 25.1-10; Amos 1.13; Zeph 2.8.

88. Cf. Isa 11.14; Jer 9.26; 25.21; 27.5; 40.11, 14.

89. See below, for a discussion of 1 Sam 11.47 and 2 Sam 8.12. Dtr's negative view of Ammon is also seen in 1 Kgs 11 where Solomon not only marries an Ammonite princess, but also builds a temple to Milcom, the Ammonite God (cf. De Vries, *1 Kings*, 142; Gray, *Kings*, 271; Jones, *Kings*, I, 232).

90. Cf. Num 21.24; Deut 2.37; 3.16; Josh 12.2; 13.10, 25; Judg 11.12-15). Instead there are the conflicting traditions of Deut 2.19 and Josh 13.25.

91. Given the depiction of Saul in 1 Sam 11 as a charismatic leader, especially in his cutting up the oxen (v. 6), this narrative is most often compared with Judg 19, as opposed to the Jepthah–Ammonite War tradition in Judg 11, as we are proposing. For bibliography on the former points of comparison see Lyle M. Eslinger, *Kingship of God in Crisis: A Close Reading of 1 Samuel 1–12* (Sheffield: Almond, 1985), 367.

In addition to the six similarities cited here, there is the added similarity that in both of these narratives (Judg 11; 1 Sam 11) a conflict arises over Ammonite and Gileadite territory. We would suggest that from the standpoint of tradition history, these two narratives are better compared with each other than Judg 19 and 1 Sam 11.

The importance of the observation that 1 Sam 11 should be understood in the light of Judg 11 instead of Judg 19 is seen in the actions of Saul in cutting up the ox as a means of summoning 'all Israel' with the threat of a curse (1 Sam 11.7). This action is generally contrasted with the Levite dismembering the concubine in Judg 19 (cf. Hertzberg, *Samuel*, 93; McCarter, *I Samuel*, 203). The above analysis would suggest that Saul's actions are better understood as his attempt to keep from falling victim to the trouble faced by Jephthah, who 'went it alone' (Judg 12.1-6). Thus, Saul's cutting the ox and issuing a curse is best seen as an 'insurance policy'.

92. Though the claim of the Ammonite king that Israel has taken their land (Judg 11.13) is refuted, he refuses to negotiate and 'listen to reason' (v. 28); the king desires to disfigure the people of Jabesh-Gilead (1 Sam 11.2b); and Hanun disgraces David's messengers (2 Sam 10.4).

93. In this instance we are in agreement with McCarter (*1 Samuel*, 199-200) in his argument for emending *wyhy kmḥryš* of MT in line with 4QSam^a. This is further supported by LXX's *kai egenēthē hōs meta mēna*. This is preferable to Driver's *kmhdš* (*Notes*, 85)

94. See above §1.

95. The result of battle is presented as the basis for Jephthah's claim to leadership (Judg 11.9), while there is the call to renewal of the kingship of Saul after the defeat (1 Sam 11.14). In regard to the latter Birch has argued that a prophetic redactor has placed this narrative in its present location 'to serve a definite purpose in the later prophetic editor's treatment of Saul's career as God's anointed' ('The Rise of the Israelite Monarchy: The Growth and Development of I Sam. 7-15' [Ph. D. dissertation, Yale University, 1970], 105-107). J.M. Miller has argued that this narrative is interpolated into the story of Saul's rise to kingship as a young man, and probably concerns an event which took place later in Saul's reign (cf. 'Saul's Rise to Power: Some Observations Concerning 1 Sam 9.1-10.16; 10.26-11.15 and 13.2-14.46', *CBQ* 36 [1974], 167-68, and more recently Miller and Hayes, *History*, 136-38).

Similarly, as our discussion of *ḥesed* above noted, the war of 2 Sam 10 most probably took place late in David's reign, and, thus, it is out of chronological sequence. Its location in the narrative, however, suggests that it took place early in the Jerusalem phase of his reign, when he was consolidating his power, having conquered other territories in ch. 8 and having brought Saul's only surviving heir to the palace (ch. 9).

96. Judg 11.33 labels the result of Jephthah's war with the Ammonites, in which over twenty cities were conquered, a *mkh gdwlh m'd*, and makes the claim that *wykn'w bny 'mwn mpny yśr'l*, the Ammonites were subdued by Israel. Similarly Saul's battle bespeaks defeat using *hkh* such that *wl' nš'rw bm šnym yḥd* (1 Sam 11.11b), while David's defeat bespeaks ritual humiliation.

97. It is interesting to note that while there are narratives in 2 Kings which speak of rebellions of Edom and Moab, there is no such record of Ammonite rebellion. Thus, the question of subjugation under either Jephthah, Saul or David becomes equally suspect.

98. See above §1.

99. While *nḥš* means snake, *ḥnwn* can be taken to be from the root *ḥnn*, loathsome (as opposed to BDB's suggestion that it comes from *ḥnn*, favored [337]).

In describing the Tell Sīrān text, which lists kings of Ammon, from the mid-seventh to sixth centuries, Cross reconstructs a listing of kings and adds the names Nahash and Hanun, who, he states, are listed in Deir 'Alla' texts ('Notes on the Ammonite Inscription from Tell Sīra-0', *BASOR*, 212 [1973], 14n). They are not, however, listed in the Tell Sīrān inscription.

100. See Veijola, *Das Königtum*, 79-80 and Klein, *I Samuel*, 133-34 for comparisons of these units and their redactional character.

101. The listing follows MT.

102. LXX's addition of Beth-Rehob to 1 Sam 14.47 is probably to be understood as harmonization of these two lists.

103. See below for discussion of the comparison between 2 Sam 8 and 10.

104. On the first problem see McCarter, *II Samuel*, 251. On the second see Klein, *I Samuel*, 141.

105. It appears to be an attempt to rectify this and specifically to tie the events described in vv. 1-6a to those in vv. 6bf., that the Chronicler adds the name of *ḥnwn* (1 Chron 19.6b).

106. Just as in our previous unit, David's emissaries arrive in *'rṣ bny 'mwn* (v. 2).

107. Cf. Noth, *History*, 195; Bright, *History*, 202; Hertzberg, *Samuel*, 304; McCarter, *Samuel*, 272 et al.

108. It could be in recognition of this omission that the Chronicler again adds a notation that the battle was arrayed at Madeba (1 Chron 19.7b). We would argue that this is a more probable explanation than the elaborate reconstruction offered by McCarter on the basis of 4QSam[a] (*II Samuel*, 268). While this location is rejected by most commentators and historians as being too southerly (cf. Bright, *History*, 202n40; Y. Aharoni, *Land of the Bible: A Historical Geography* [Philadelphia: Westminster, 1967], 263), it could be that the Chronicler wanted to locate the battle far enough south to demonstrate a threat to David, as well as to reserve the battle at Rabbah for later.

109. E.g. 1 Sam 26.6-9; 2 Sam 3.30f.; 16.9-11; 18.12f.

110. See above Chapter 2 §3

111. Contrary to Van Seters' objections ('Problems', 24-25) Gunn has made a good case for the existence of a David versus the 'Sons of Zeruiah' tradition (*Story*, 39-40). Our argument is that here the tradition is presented in reverse.

112. Cf. Exod 12.37; Num 11.21; Judg 20.2; 1 Sam 4.10; 15.4; 2 Kgs 13.7.

113. When used of non-Israelite nations, the term always refers to Arameans. It should be noted that the only other times we find such, however, are in the parallel passages to our unit in 1 Chron 19, as well as in 2 Sam 8.4//1 Chron 18.4, which is viewed as parallel to our unit, and in 1 Kgs 20.29, where the results of the war is an example of Yahweh's 'reversing the outcome'.

114. See below for a discussion of the Aramean traditions.

115. Gerhard von Rad, 'Deuteronomy and the Holy War', in *Studies in Deuteronomy* (London: SCM, 1953), 47-48. Unlike many war stories, however, there is no mention of the ark, the shout, or the trembling. Interestingly, von Rad notes the similarities to the Holy War Motif in 2 Sam 11.11, but does not recognize the motif in Joab's speech in 2 Sam 10.

116. This term, when used by itself in narratives, as it is in this unit (as opposed to *gbry ḥyl*), refers to professional soldiers. (Cf. Josh 8.3; 1 Sam 17.51; 2 Sam 16.6; 12.8, 10; 20.7; 1 Kgs 1.8, and the extensive listing in 2 Sam 23.) In the poetic passages found within the DtrH such as the Songs of

Deborah and Hannah, we find mention of them as enemy foils for Yahweh, since his victory over them is a demonstration of his might and power (cf. Judg 5.13, 23; 1 Sam 2.4). Thus, the *gbrym* must be viewed as formidable powers in both traditions.

117. H. Kosmala, '*gbr*', in *TDOT* II, 374.

118. McCarter, *II Samuel*, 269.

119. It may be in recognition of this change that Josephus puts these words into the mouth of David, and not Joab (*Ant.* 7. 6).

120. Cf. 2 Sam 2.1.

121. See discussion below on this verse.

122. Beth-Rehob is also mentioned in Judg 18.28, however, in this unit the place mentioned is geographically too far south to be identified with the same location as the one mentioned in 2 Sam 10.8 (cf. Soggin, *Judges*, 276).

123. Num 13.21 mentions that the spies went from the Wilderness of Zin to Rehob, near the entrance of Hamath, while 2 Sam 8.3 mentions Hadadezer the '*son of Rehob* king of Zobah', which is generally taken to be a reference to the same geographical location as our Beth Rehob (cf. Malamat, 'Aspects', 4). Neither of these notations, however, uses the specific terminology in our text.

124. As will be shown below, this narrative seems to have the one in 2 Sam 10 as its basis.

125. Cf. Pitard, *Ancient Damascus*, 88-89, for bibliography on these archaeological attempts to locate these cities.

126. There appears to be no satisfactory explanation of the Chronicler's use of *šwpk* for the name of the general (1 Chron 19.16, 18). In the present case the function of Shobach being mentioned in 2 Sam 10.16 and 18 as both general of the army and as one whom David himself wounded and killed, is to demonstrate the military prowess of David. Since the tradition did not record the death of Hadadezer in an Israelite-Aramean war (see discussion of the comparison between the wars in 2 Sam 8 and 10, below), the introduction of Shobach into the second narrative suits the purpose of building the status of David by having him get close enough to the leader to inflict upon him a mortal wound.

127. There have been attempts to identify this Helam with *Hliam*, which LXX inserts in Ezek 47.16 after *sbrym* (cf. Driver, *Notes*, 288), while others attempt to locate the site with the reference to *Alema* (1 Macc 5.26) in the Transjordan (cf. R. Smend, 'Beiträge zur Geschichte und Topographie des Ostjordanlandes', *ZAW* 22 [1902], 137; Dhorme, *Livres*, 351; and most recently McCarter, *II Samuel*, 273). It must be noted that in these instances the names are not identical and cannot be further corroborated. Thus, these identifications are not convincing. It would appear that the impetus for identification is the presupposition that we are here dealing with an accurate historical narrative and, thus, the geographical location must be ascertainable.

128. Cf. McCarter, *II Samuel*, 272 for the history of the debate on the exact geographical location of this reference.

129. Interestingly, Josephus takes this to be the name of the general, and follows the Chronicler in omitting the name of the geographical location (cf. *Ant*. 7. 6).

130. The *gbrym* and *bḥwry yśr'l* of vv. 7 and 9 above.

131. Cf. Ackroyd, *Second Samuel*, 98; Budde, *Samuel*, 249; Caird, 'Samuel', II, 196-97; Smith, *Samuel*, 316.

132. Cf. Chapter 2 §5 for a brief summary of these similarities.

133. Cf. Chapter 2, note 109.

134. Cf. Chapter 2, note 108.

135. This is generally assumed not to be a reference to the Euphrates, because of geographical considerations (McCarter, *II Samuel*, 272).

136. Cf. McCarter, Ibid., 248.

137. In this regard we would note that there is a pattern of anonymity with regard to the characters in vv. 6b-15.

138. In this regard we note that it uses *'rk*, which also occurs in 10.8, 9, and 10.

139. The accounts are similar in that David appears as the primary force in the battles and all the verbs are in the 3ms.

140. Interestingly, we do get a corollary to this type of report in 12.26-31.

141. This conclusion is only in regard to the individual narratives. It does not preclude the possibility that both 2 Samuel 8 and 10 were compiled by Dtr.

142. In vv. 6b-15, the numbers of the opposing army were given, while in vv. 16-19 it is the casualty report which is numbered.

143. Although in Deuteronomy 20 the process is the outcome for cities which initially offer peace in place of war, and in 2 Sam 10.19 it happens after the war, the connection is still valid.

144. Josephus states, '. . . he determined to make war with them no longer by his generals, but he passed over the river Jordan himself' (*Ant.* VII 6).

145. (Cf. Gray, *Kings*, 369, Jones, *Kings*, 300, and W. Richter, *Traditionsgeschichtliche Untersuchungen zum Richterbuch* [BBB; Bonn: Peter Hanstein Verlag, 1966] 9). It must be noted that their intention in appealing to this passage in this way is to argue for the historicity of the building notice in 1 Kgs 16.34, which is in conflict with the archaeological data and which all admit is a secondary notice added to the Dtr closing formula on the reign of Ahab. They argue that it comes from the archives of Ahab's reign and that it is placed there by Dtr to further demonstrate the negative assessment on the Omride dynasty. They also note that it fits the prophecy fulfillment motif of Dtr, given its relationship to Josh 6.26, which all argue postdates this notice.

In this regard we would propose that the function of this building notice in

1 Kgs 16.34 is to pave the way for the mention of Jericho in the 'Ascension of Elijah' unit in 2 Kgs 2, where there is mention of a band of prophets living and operating at Jericho. In this regard it is interesting to note that the route followed by Elijah and Elisha mentions some of the same geographical locations as the Dtr 'all Israel conquest traditions' in Josh 2-9, inclusive of the splitting and crossing of the River Jordan, albeit in reverse order. Thus, just as Dtr used the destruction etiology during a historical time which is chronologically improbable for the Jericho destruction to explain ruins at Jericho, Dtr also speaks of its rebuilding in a similar manner to suit the purpose noted above.

146. We assume that the choice of this verse by other scholars is predicated on the designation of the genre of the unit as 'historical narrative'.

147. Kathleen M. Kenyon, *Archaeology in the Holy Land* (4th edn; New York: W.W. Norton, 1979), 208. For a more extensive treatment of this subject see her *Digging Up Jericho: The Results of the Jericho Excavations* (New York: F.A. Praeger, 1952-1956), 259-63. These findings have recently been reconfirmed by K. Prag (cf. 'The Intermediate Early Bronze-Middle Bronze Age Sequences at Jericho and Tell Iktanu Reviewed', *BASOR* 264 [1986], 70-71).

148. Commentaries on 2 Samuel do not raise the issue of the archaeological evidence (cf. Ackroyd, *2 Samuel*, 96; Hertzberg, *Samuel*, 304; McCarter, *II Samuel*, 270). This is most surprising given the hornets' nest the archaeological findings create with the reference to Jericho in the conquest narratives of Joshua (cf. Trent C. Butler, *Joshua* [WBC; Waco, TX: Word Books, 1983], 32-33 for a summary and bibliography on this subject).

149. *Notes*, 287.

150. This is also the orthography used in P passages in Num (22.1; 26.3, 63; 31.12; 33.48, 50; 34.15; 35.1; 36.13) and Deut (32.49; 34.1, 3), which Noth designates as P or additions to P (cf. *A History of Pentateuchal Traditions* [Chico, CA: Scholars Press, 1981], 274-76), and in Ezra 3.2; Neh 3.2; 7.36; 1 Chron 6.63; 19.5; 2 Chron 28.15.

151. Jericho is mentioned in Josh 2; 4; 5; 6; 8.2; 10.28, 30; 12.9; 13.32; 16.1, 7; 18.12, 21; 20.8; 24.11; 1 Kgs 16.34; 2 Kgs 2.4, 5, 15, 18. In most of these units it is mentioned in reference to the destruction etiology of Joshua chs. 2-6, and in both chs. 2 and 6 it only appears in the introductory and closing seams of the narratives. This may suggest that the whole Jericho tradition is based in Dtr traditions.

152. According to Cross, 'Themes', 174-89, and Nelson, *Double Redaction*, 2 Kgs 25 stems from Dtr 2.

153. Peckham, *Composition*, 76n16.

154. Cf. Dhorme, *Samuel*, 362; Gunn, *Story*, 65; Hertzberg, *Samuel*, 303; McCarter, *II Samuel*, 275-76; Smith, *Samuel*, 317.

155. So Dhorme, *Samuel*, 352.

156. Ridout ('Prose', 63-64) misses this difference in his theory of chiastic structure, when he argues that 12.26-31 balances 11.1, where first David (11.1a), and then Joab (12.28), send for each other, and *both* return to Jerusalem in the end. As the structural outline demonstrates, v. 31 only speaks of David and his muster, *h'm*, returning to Jerusalem. There is no mention of the return of Joab, his servants, and 'all Israel' (11.1). Thus, the chiasm of David-Joab as the beginning and end is not upheld.

157. Cf. Dhorme, *Samuel*, 362; Hertzberg, *Samuel*, 318 and McCarter, *II Samuel*, 312 *et al*. Josephus appears to sidestep the issue by writing of Joab 'cutting off the water supply' as a tactical maneuver which leads to the worsening of the conditions in the besieged city (*Ant.* 7.7).

158. This may be what lies behind Josephus's reference to Joab's capture of the Metropolis (*Ant.* 7.7). In addition to this is the fact that *zr' hmlwkh* (2 Kgs 25.25) is the only instance of *mlwkh* being used where it refers to the royal family. In all other instances of the term, either in construct—*dbr hmlwkh* (1 Sam 10.16), *mšpṭ hmlwkh* (1 Sam 10.25), and *ks' hmlwkh* (1 Kgs 1.46)—or as the object of the verb (1 Sam 11.14; 14.47; 18.8; 2 Sam 16.8; 1 Kgs 2.15, 22; 11.35; 12.21; 21.7; 1 Chron 10.14) it refers to a vast geographic area, a kingdom. Thus, in the phrase *'yr hmlwkh, hmlwkh* most probably relates more to the city's significance for the kingdom (capital), than to the royal family.

159. Frank S. Frick, *The City in Ancient Israel* (SBLDS, 36; Missoula: Scholars, 1977), 80.

160. It is probably in an attempt to avoid this awkwardness and confusion of terminology that the Chronicler leaves out all references to these other locations and merely sticks with Joab sacking Rabbah (1 Chr 20.1b), and then has David just appear on the scene for the ritual humiliation (v. 2f).

While all commentators stress the omission of the David-Bathsheba-Uriah-Nathan materials from the Chronicler's account, they all but ignore the omission of the materials in 2 Sam 12.27-28. For example Braun cites the omission as the Chronicler's 'rather mechanical method of extracting from the text of 2 Samuel' (*I Chronicles*, 210).

161. We choose this terminology to describe David taking the crown, which may have been Milcom's or their king's, depending on the interpretation of the ambiguous term in v. 30, *mlkm*. See McCarter, *II Samuel*, 311 for a discussion of the textual problems in this verse.

S. Horn has argued for an interpretation of *mlkm* being 'their king' ('The Crown of the King of the Ammonites', *BASOR* 193 [1969], 180). He states, however, that this is in spite of the archaeological evidence.

162. It should be noted that there is no mention of an Ammonite conquest in 2 Sam 8.

163. This must be what lies behind the Chronicler's addition of the word *'rṣ* preceding *bny 'mwn*.

164. While Bowman cites this difference, he does not entertain the

possibility of different authorship ('Crises', 193).

165. Note the use of *šlḥ* in each instance.

166. Cf. Deut 28.10; 2 Sam 6.2; 1 Kgs 8.43; Jer 7.10, 11, 14, 32, 34; Amos 9.12. While McCarter points out this characteristic use of the phrase, he chooses to explain its current nuance as solely political (*II Samuel*, 312).

167. Cf. Gray, *Kings*, 414-18, for a review of the history of scholarship on this unit. While the issue of chronology will not be raised at this time, it is also significant to see that 1 Kgs 20 has also been shown to be out of chronological sequence with the events described in 1 Kgs 22.

168. This excludes mention of the parallel passage found in 1 Chron 20.1.

169. Cf. Long, *I Kings*, 212.

170. De Vries, *1 Kings*, 247, 249.

171. Long, *1 Kings*, 212, 219.

172. Cf. Hermann, *History*, 279-80, for a review of the problems created by the Chronicler's abbreviated report of the events described in 2 Kgs 24.10-17, and the various attempts at resolving the conflicts.

173. Myers, *II Chronicles*, 218.

174. Noth (*History*, 177) argues that the spring time was the usual time for large-scale military campaigns. Given the usage of this introductory formula in all three of its contexts, it is probably best to amend the MT *hml'kym* (2 Sam 11.1a) to the Chronicler's *mlkym* (1 Chr 20.1). This generic explanation is more probable than McCarter's attempt to tie it to the reference to *hmlkym* in 10.19. In addition, since the argument has already demonstrated that the siege report in 11.1aβ suggests an earlier separation of the war narratives in 10.19 and 11.1, the link between 10 and 11 has been broken.

175. By implication we are arguing that like the theological evaluations in 11.27b and 12.25, 12.1-24 has been interpolated between 11.27a and 12.26.

176. Hertzberg, *Samuel*, 292.

177. McCarter, *II Samuel*, 252.

Notes to Chapter 4

1. McCarter states, 'In desperation. . .', *II Samuel*, 288.

2. This summary follows Smith's division of 'the adultery, the attempt at concealment, the murder of Uriah' (*History*, 148). Ackroyd refers to this division as 'scenes' (*Second*, 101).

3. Interestingly, Hertzberg states that in so doing, David achieves his objective (*Samuel*, 312).

4. This is in contrast to the sexually suggestive descriptions in passages such as 2 Sam 13.1-2, 8, etc. As David Gunn notes, 'It is striking how the emotions and actions of chapter 13 are heightened compared with those of

chapters 11 and 12. *David's dealings with Bathsheba have a curiously matter-of-fact character'* (*Story*, 99) (emphasis added).

5. For a complete bibliographic review of this line of argumentation cf. Gale A. Yee, "Fraught with Background': Literary Ambiguity in II Samuel 11', *Interp* 42 (1988), 242n10. This paper was originally delivered at the 1985 Annual Meeting of the Society of Biblical Literature, held in Anaheim, CA. I am indebted to Dr. Yee for sharing a copy of the unpublished manuscript with me.

6. Ibid.

7. Driver (*Notes*, 289) argues that the text should be amended to *h'mr*, the participle preceded by *h*, on the basis of his reading of 1 Sam 16.4, which he similarly reconstructs (ibid., 132). In this regard most other commentators follow him in his rendition of 2 Sam 11.3 but not in his reading of 1 Sam 16.4, where they follow LXX in reading *wy'mr* as *wy'mrw* in the plural (e.g. Klein, *Samuel*, 157; McCarter, *I Samuel*, 274).

8. It is interesting to note that there is no speculation about another speaker as subject of the verb *'mr* in this verse.

9. Rost made note of this cluster when he discussed verbs being heaped upon each other which strive 'toward richer expressiveness' (*Succession*, 91). He also cited examples in 2 Sam 13.14; 14.2; 1 Kgs 1.49, all of which contain emotion-laden verbs, such as *ḥzq*, and *'nh* (13.14). He failed to note, however, the lack of such emotion-filled verbs in this constellation.

10. Deut 23.15; 2 Sam 7.6.

11. Enoch (Gen 5.22); the priest to replace the Elide line (1 Sam 2.35); Samuel (1 Sam 12.2); Hezekiah (2 Kgs 20.3).

12. 1 Sam 23.13; 25.15; 30.31.

13. Cf. J.M. Miller and John H. Hayes, *A History of Ancient Israel and Judah* (Philadelphia: Westminster, 1986), 162-68.

14. This may suggest editorial work on the part of the final redactor of the Samuel materials. It is highly unlikely that all four of these instances with this alteration of the usual connotation of *hthlk* were part of the material in its earliest stage of transmission.

15. 'Crises', 99-100.

16. The verb occurs 27 times in these three chapters. As Bowman correctly notes, both Uriel Simon ('The Poor Man's Ewe-Lamb: An Example of a Juridical Parable', *Bib* 48 [1967], 209) and Ridout ('Prose', 144-45) also note the high incidence of the term *šlḥ* in this complex. However, they fail to interpret its significance in the narrative.

17. 'A Personal and Political Crisis of King David: Narrative Structure, Compositional Technique, and the Interpretation of II Samuel 10-12', unpublished paper presented at the 1986 Annual Meeting of the Society of Biblical Literature, Atlanta, Georgia. Bowman argues in this context that Bathsheba has 'accrued power' by virtue of her liaison with David. As will be

argued below, however, it is her familial association that gives her power. See the following discussion on the identification of Bathsheba in 11.3.

18. Cf. D.L. Christensen, 'Huldah and the Men of Anathoth', in *Society of Biblical Literature 1984 Seminar Papers* (ed. K.H. Richards; Chico, CA: Scholars, 1984), 399-404, who argues that the DtrH is arranged around women strategically placed within the narrative, namely on the ends Deborah//Huldah as positive characters—and in the center—Jezebel//Athaliah as negative characters. This unit might suggest that there were complementary patterns to this utilization of politically significant women at pivotal points in the narrative in addition to the ones that Christensen notes.

Similarly Carole Fontaine has suggested that the Samuel sources' preference for Bathsheba and her connection to Eliam has other semantic advantages. First it connects her to the Sheba revolt in 2 Sam 20 and the 'seven-fold' restitution in 12.5 (so LXX). In this way she argues that according to the Samuel tradition she is the occupant of a 'high role' ('The Shape of 2 Samuel 11-12', 75). In this she is taking issue with the view of Whybray (*Succession*, 40) that Bathsheba is just a 'good natured, rather stupid woman'.

19. This aspect of her identifying information is almost universally ignored. For example, though Meadows notes that 'Genealogical and patronymic notations are often significant' he then goes on to speak only of the marital relationship and the adultery ('Study', 128). The tendency to ignore the patronymic reference is reinforced by the other references to her in 11.27 and 12.9 where she is only referred to as the wife of Uriah, a point which will be explored later.

20. *The Purpose of the Biblical Genealogies* (Cambridge: Cambridge University Press, 1969), 79-80.

21. While Phillis Bird argues that, 'The two most common images of woman in the historical writings are those of wife and mother frequently combined when the woman is portrayed as a historical individual' ('Images of Women in the Old Testament', in *The Bible and Liberation: Political and Social Hermeneutics*, ed. N.K. Gottwald [Maryknoll, NY: Orbis Books, 1983], 268), here we have Bathsheba portrayed as *daughter* and wife.

22. The name *bt šb'* is unusual, in that there is only one other woman identified with a name which translates as 'daughter of X'. The LXX consistently refers to her as *Bersabee* both here and in 1 Kgs 1-2 and 1 Chron 3.5b. The Chronicler, however, refers to her as *bt šw'*. Most exegetes suggest that the *waw* in the latter should be pronounced just like the *vet* (and not as a *shuruq* as MT points it), as a way of resolving this problem in the two MT designations (so Driver, *Notes*, 289 and Budde, *Samuel*, 251). Carlson notes that the name given by the Chronicler means 'daughter of nobility' and should be given priority over that of the Dtr (*Chosen*, 161).

It would appear, however, that since her genealogy connects her family to the Absalom Revolt, which is omitted from the Chronicler's account, there was probably a tendency for the Chronicler to alter her name to the latter designation, along with its connotation. Thus, the Chronicler attests to Solomon's mother being an aristocrat.

23. The Chronicler records the name of Bathshua's father as Ammiel. It would appear that this may have been a desire to sever once again the connection to Ahithophel. Interestingly *'my'l* is the inverse of *'ly'm*.

24. Interestingly, while Bright makes note of the Eliam-Ahithophel connection in 16.23 and 23.34 when he discusses David's military men, he does not raise this in his discussion of the David–Bathsheba relationship (*History*, 209).

25. R. Wilson states, 'The biblical genealogies may be used as sources for historical research, but they cannot be used uncritically. Each individual genealogy must be examined, as an attempt made to assess the reliability of each of the components. As a part of this process, the peculiar nature of genealogy must be taken into account, and in particular the function of any given genealogy must be determined. Only in this way can genealogies be safely used in historical research' (*Genealogy and History in the Biblical World* [New Haven: Yale University, 1977], 246).

26. A. Malamat evidently ignores these genealogical data, since he claims that Bathsheba is a foreigner from the 'local aristocracy of Jerusalem' ('Aspects', 9). So also O.J. Baab, 'Marriage', in *IDB*, III, 287.

27. Several commentators have pointed to this connection in the genealogy. Dhorme simply takes note of the fact (*Samuel*, 352). Caird cites this incident of David 'bringing shame on his granddaughter' as the motivating factor behind Ahithophel's switch to support Absalom ('Exegesis', 1099) as does Budde (*Samuel*, 251). As previously noted McCarter notes its implied significance, but confesses, 'I don't know why'. Similarly Fokkelman takes note of the information provided in 11.3, but he appears to miss the significance of the genealogical statements by stating that David 'ignores the information' and sees nothing more than a beautiful woman (*King David*, 52). As the above analysis has demonstrated, David definitely does not 'ignore the information'. Finally, Deist cites this identification as support that even though David knows her and her connections, his lust overcomes him (106).

28. Cf. J.D. Levenson and B. Halpern, 'The Political Import of David's Marriages', *JBL* 99 (1980), 507-18 for a discussion of the Abigail marriage in this context.

29. The parenthetic nature of the phrase *why' mtqdšt mṭm'th* as a later interpolation has long been attested and will be dealt with below.

30. Cf. the above discussion of the tripartite formulation in v. 5. One could also note that this designation of 'partnership' is less emotionally charged than some of the more male-centered disparaging interpretations of her behavior, most notably those of Delekat ('Tendenz', 29) and Ewald (*History*, III, 105).

31. So G. Andr, '*ṭm*", *TDOT*, V (1986), 337. Cf. McCarter, *II Samuel*, 286 for the history of the interpretation of this phrase referring to her cleansing herself after menstrual uncleanness, which would put her close to the point of ovulation.

32. Lev 15 is appealed to in explicating the sense of Ps 51.7.

33. *Geschichtsschreibung*, 155. Sternberg adds a subtle twist on this and argues that the phrase *why' mtqdšt mṭm'th* functions to eliminate Uriah as the father of the child (*Poetics*, 198).

34. Hertzberg states that such knowledge was common 'even in antiquity' (*Samuel*, 310).

35. James G. Williams argues for the 'wife-sister' and the 'barren woman' motifs (*Women Recounted: Narrative Thinking and the God of Israel* [BLS; Sheffield: Almond, 1982], 46-53). The former is better termed the 'jeopardizing of the matriarch'.

36. E.g. Samson's *nzr* status (Judg 13.5, 7) and Hannah's vow for Samuel (1 Sam 1.11).

37. Given the etiologies in vv. 37-38, it appears that this narrative is an ethnological etiology attesting to tribal relationship between Israel and Ammon and Moab, while utilizing sex as a means of discrediting the latter two.

38. Recently Rendsburg has argued for a relationship between the narrative in Gen 38 with that of the TSN. He equates David with Judah, Bathsheba with Bathshua, the wife of Judah, and Tamar, the daughter of David (2 Sam 13) with Tamar, the daughter-in-law of Judah ('David and his Circle in Genesis xxxviii', *VT* 36 [1986], 441). Thus, he misses the nuance that the illicit sex between Judah and Tamar is the parallel of the illicit sex between David and Bathsheba.

39. Thus, Lot's daughters get him drunk and Tamar dresses as a *znh* as opposed to a widow. One may argue that the analogy of these narratives with the narrative in 2 Sam 11 is inconsistent, since, as argued above, David knows the identity of Bathsheba, *hl' z't*, while Lot does not know he is being used, nor does Judah recognize Tamar. This difference is minimized by two factors. First is the fact that Judah's lack of recognition of Tamar is part of the literary device of the narrative, which is demonstrated by the event taking place in a locality called *'ynym*, 'Eyes'. Thus, there appears to be a pun in operation in his inability to recognize her. Secondly, in both narratives the women are attempting to reconcile their having been 'wronged' by the male, Lot having moved to Zoar and Judah refusing to give Tamar to Shelah. Thus, the lack of complicity of the male is understood and expected.

40. See above discussion in note 22.

41. Just as it is important for Judah not to recognize Tamar, so too it is important for David to recognize Bathsheba in order for the liaison to occur.

42. 2 Sam 15.10 has the Absalom revolt beginning in Hebron, which would suggest southern dissatisfaction with David and his reign. Since Giloh, the home of Ahithophel, is close to the Hebronite territory (cf. V.R. Gold, 'Giloh', *IDB*, II, 399), such a familial alliance could only benefit him. While 2 Sam 19.41-43 suggests both tensions between Israel and Judah regarding David, it would also point to his need to re-cement his ties and loyalties within the region. It is this need which the Bathsheba marriage alliance would help address.

43. 'Crisis', 194-98.

44. *Story*, 88-94.

45. We are indebted to Professor Don C. Benjamin of Rice University for pointing us in the direction of this categorization.

46. In this regard there is rejection of Stoebe's thesis that the David–Bathsheba narrative was originally separate from the David–Uriah complex and that they have been joined at a later stage by a 'compiler' ('David und Uria', *Bib* 67 [1986], 388-90).

47. David greets Uriah with a threefold *šalōm*, in which he inquires about Joab, the army, and the war. This is unusual for two reasons. First, as was seen in the previous chapter the army, *h'm*, was a term used in connection with David and not Joab during the Ammonite War narratives. This might suggest a redactor's attempt at conflating traditions. Similarly, there are only two other passages in the canon in which one finds a threefold *šalōm*. Interestingly, one is in 1 Sam 25.6, when David sends his 'band of men' to Nabal. The other is when the Shunamite woman's son dies and she goes to see *'yš h'lhym* (2 Kgs 4.26).

48. Cf. Stoebe, 'David und Uria', 391.

49. While this reaction is duplicated in LXX, as McCarter correctly points out, it precedes the report of the *ml'k* and, thus, is still problematic (*II Samuel*, 284). As will be pointed out below, his elaborate theory of haplography in both MT and LXX is unnecessary in resolving this textual problem.

50. It should be noted that such an 'open battle' is not in line with the picture in 11.1, where Joab, his servants and all Israel are depicted besieging Rabbah.

51. As noted in our discussion of 12.26-31, the first unit in 12.26 bespeaks the second attack authorized on Rabbah.

52. In this regard we note another word play similar to those found in the David–Nabal–Abigail narrative in 1 Sam 25. While David tries to get Uriah drunk, *wyškrhw* (v. 13), at the palace, when Abigail returns from her successful attempt at stopping David from attacking Nabal, she finds him drunk (*škr m'd*) at a feast *kmšth hmlk* (25.36).

53. Smith (*Samuel*, 318) and Herzberg (*Samuel*, 310) claim this phrase means 'refresh thyself after thy journey'. Gutbrod (*Das zweite*, 140) and

McCarter (*II Samuel*, 286) take the phrase to be a euphemism for sexual intercourse, primarily on the basis of the use of *rgl* in Ruth 3.4, 7 and Ezek 16.25. Similarly, Simon appeals to Abravanel in his claim of a sexual meaning ('The Poor Man's Ewe-Lamb', 214).

Since Uriah's speech in 11.11 refers to *škb* one might have additional evidence for interpreting *rgl* in this way. As regards the phrase *rḥṣ rglk* as a euphemism for sexual intercourse, in Deut 23.9-11 there is a law which speaks about a ritual bath, *rḥṣ*, for a soldier who becomes unclean due to a *mqrh lylh*. Thus, it would appear that such a euphemism is based in ancient war practices, which conforms to our narrative context.

There is an interesting twist on the phrase *rḥṣ rglk*, in that when David sends his men to propose to Abigail on his behalf after the death of her husband, Nabal, she accepts with the promise that she will perform this act for *'bdy 'dny* (1 Sam 25.41). It is not clear how one should interpret this phrase in that context. It does, however, raise the question of literary interrelationship between 2 Sam 11 and 1 Sam 25.

54. Y. Yadin has argued that this is a reference to the city, Succoth, in the Transjordan. However, given the other *Heilskrieg* references in this speech, this interpretation appears to be unacceptable. See his article, 'Some Aspects of the Strategy of Ahab and David', *Bib* 38 (1955), 341-43.

55. The wording of 11.12b is ambiguous, since it mentions that Uriah stayed 'that day and on the next day'. Since v. 13 speaks of Uriah being summoned and then spending the night, this could suggest that he was not sent back the 'next day' as v. 12 promised. McCarter argued that the day was calculated beginning at sundown and that this is therefore a reference to evening/morning reckoning.

56. S. Bar-Efrat argues that the major point is the contrast in characters between the adulterer David and the loyal Uriah ('Literary Modes and Methods in the Biblical Narrative in View of 2 Samuel 10-20 and 1 Kings 1-2', *Immanuel* 8 [1978], 24).

57. So Gutbrod (*Das zweite*, 140); Smith (*Samuel*, 318); McCarter (*II Samuel*, 286); *et al.*

58. Cf. Driver, *Notes*, 290. Abigail uses a variation on this oath in attempting to dissuade David from acting violently against her husband (1 Sam 25.26).

59. The mention of *skwt* and the ark noted above.

60. Deist raises this as a possibility for 'speculation' on the motivation of David, but then only wonders 'am I over-suspicious?' ('David', 106).

61. So Smith, *Samuel*, 318; Hertzberg, *Samuel*, 310; Ackroyd, *Second*, 101-2.

62. *Samuel*, 251. Rashi was apparently the first to make this connection.

63. So George W. Coats, *Genesis* (FOTL, 1; Grand Rapids, MI: Eerdmans, 1983), 289.

64. Were *mś'h* to be taken as 'a gift', one would expect the use of the *hiph'il* in this clause.

65. The appearance of this term in such a context is most interesting. While Boling (*Judges* [AB; Garden City, NY: Doubleday, 1975] 288) assigns this chapter to the exilic Deuteronomist, Soggin states, 'The chief difficulty in this narrative is presented by the now generally accepted fact that *here we have two accounts of the same event somewhat crudely combined into an apparently unitary narrative*' (*Judges*, 293-94) (emphasis added).

66. Interestingly, R.P. Carroll notes that the fleeing, trumpet, and signal combine to bespeak a threat and are reversals on a *Heilskrieg* motif (cf. *Jeremiah* [OTL; Philadelphia: Westminster, 1986], 191).

As D. W. Thomas notes, 'The occurrence in the letters of some words which are rarely used in Biblical Hebrew serves as a reminder that these words must have been in commoner use than their rare appearance in the Old Testament would suggest' (cf. 'The Lachish Letters', *JTS* 40 [1939], 11).

67. While the consonantal text suggests that *mś'h* is a participle, the Massoretic pointing is for a *hiph'il* III *h* as opposed to a III ' participle. There also appears to be textual evidence for rendering *mś'h* as a participle, since, as McCarter notes, LXXL 'points to a different reading' than MT by the use of the term *ton parestekoton*, which he translates as 'those who stand by' (*II Samuel*, 280). While this is one of the meanings of *paristēmi*, it can also have a legal connotation of defendant (cf. H.G. Liddel and R. Scott, *A Greek and English Lexicon* [Revised edn; 2 vols.; Oxford: Clarendon, 1948], 1340). Similarly, LXXB uses the term *arsis*, which can be translated as burden, but also has the meaning of 'witness' (ibid., 248). Thus, it would appear that LXXL and LXXB had taken the sense of the one who would testify in the king's behalf.

McCarter, on the other hand, rejects the readings of LXX and on the basis of 4QSam[a] and Josephus (*Ant.* 7.132) emends the text to read 'he marched out with the weapons bearers [*n'y hklym*] of the king (ibid). In arriving at this reconstruction, however, he is relying more on Josephus for his interpretation than on either of the received texts.

68. Cf. Smith, *Samuel*, 318; McCarter, *II Samuel*, 285.

69. Note the previously observed connections between his speech in 11.11 with the *Heilskrieg* motif, as well as a connection with the war law in Deut 23.9-12.

70. See above Chapter 3 §1.

71. It is interesting that in this section of the narrative the woman is referred to in terms of her position, *'št 'wryh*, and not in terms of her name, Bathsheba. In fact, within 2 Sam 10–12 the name Bathsheba only occurs in 11.3 and 12.24. All other references to her are either in terms of the impersonal *'šh* or the 'wife of Uriah' designation (11.5; 12.10). Ridout argues that the function of this framing of the name is to return at the end of the narrative to the beginning point ('Prose', 65). On the other hand, it could

possibly be explained by the attempt to present the woman as object (so Williams, *Women Recounted*, 46-47 in his treatment of the 'she's my sister' motif re: Sarai/h).

Given the above-noted argument on the use of the *qal* to describe the actions of the woman as a free agent who is working in cooperation with David, this may not be the best explanation. Instead the inclusio may signal that there was originally a 'wife of Uriah' tale concerning an unnamed woman taken by David which has been secondarily adapted by the addition of the name Bathsheba the daughter of Eliam in 11.3 and Bathsheba the wife of David in 12.24.

72. Cf. §1 above.

73. As is the case in the closing unit, 12.24-25.

74. 'Prose', 67.

75. BDB, 704. In addition to this unit the use of this verb with the proposition *l* only occurs in 2 Sam 1.12 in the account of the death of Saul and Jonathan, and 1 Kgs 13.30 in the account of the death of the anonymous Man of God.

76. A. Baumann, "*bl*', in *TDOT*, I (Grand Rapids, MI: Eerdmans, 1974), 45.

77. Cf. Gen 50.10, which suggests seven days for this period. Deut 34.8, which suggests a month, should thus be interpreted as hyperbolic.

78. As noted above (note 71) there may have been a 'wife of Uriah' tale and a David–Bathsheba tale which have been combined. If so, it is possible that the *spd* went with the former and the *wy'br h'bl* went with the latter.

79. This is in contrast to the other verbs suggesting a time dimension, which accompany *'bl*, namely *wy'š* (Gen 50.10), *wytmw* (Deut 34.8), and *wšlmw* (Isa 60.20). In these instances the verbs suggest completeness and/or action, while the use of *'br* in 11.27 suggests a more passive 'fulfilling of the requirements'.

80. The primary meaning is 'to muster an army' or 'to gather a harvest'. Interestingly there are the references to David's musters in chs. 10 and 12. In this sense there may be the double play on words with David's 'in-gathering' of women, whose familial connections could be 'mustered' in time of trouble.

81. Driver, *Notes*, 291; BDB, 62.

82. Cf. Gen 38 and Ruth 2. Also see Roland de Vaux, *Ancient Israel*, I (New York: McGraw-Hill, 1961), 40.

83. Along with these thematic similarities, one must also note the word-play convergence between the Abigail and Bathsheba marriage narratives. (Cf. the various notes above in which these similarities have been pointed out.) The question as to whether there is any literary dependence of one on the other is not, however, easily discerned, though these parallels seem to be more than just happenstance.

84. Robert W. Neff, 'The Announcement in Old Testament Birth Stories'

(Ph.D. dissertation, Yale University, 1969), 55.

85. Though the preceding phrase *wthy lw l'šh*, 'and she became his wife', is a marriage formula, it does not have sexual overtones. This is seen in the fact that in all other units which use this as the marriage formula within a birth narrative (cf. Gen 20.12; 24.67; 1 Sam 25.42; Ruth 4.13), there are other verbs which allude to the sexual act.

86. This also adds weight to our earlier argument that the intention in sending Uriah to have sex with Bathsheba was not to cover up the adultery but rather to move him out of the way.

87. *The Problem of the Etiological Narrative in the Old Testament* (Berlin: Alfred Töpelmann, 1968), 50.

88. Gen 4.25; 16.15; 19.37, 38; 21.2-3; 29.32, 33, 34, 35; 30.5, 7, 10, 12, 17, 19, 23; 35.16-18; 38.3, 4, 5; 46.18, 25; Exod 2.22; 1 Sam 1.20; 4.19; 2 Sam 12.24; Isa 8.3; Hos 1.3, 6, 8; 1 Chron 7.16, 23.

89. Gen 4.1, 17, 20; 22.24; 25.2; Exod 6.20, 25; Num 26.59; 1 Kgs 11.20; 1 Chron 2.19, 21, 24, 29, 35, 49; 4.6; 2 Chron 11.19, 20.

90. Moses in Exod 2.2.

91. Jephthah's half brothers (Judg 11.2) and Hannah's other children (1 Sam 2.21).

92. The prostitutes before Solomon (1 Kgs 3.18) and the Shunamite woman (2 Kgs 4.17).

93. See Chapter 2§4.

94. 'Beginnings', 198-99. It is most interesting that there is no outcry from him, or any of the other scholars who follow him, over the lack of such a divine 'comment' after the rape of Tamar in 2 Sam 13. The closest that one comes to suggesting such an omission is Phyllis Trible, who ends her treatment of 2 Sam 13 with the words, 'Who will preserve sister wisdom from the adventurer, the rapist with his smooth words, lecherous eyes, and grasping hands? In answering the question, Israel is found wanting—*and so are we*' ('Tamar: The Royal Rape of Wisdom', in *Texts of Terror: Literary-Feminist Readings of Biblical Narratives* [Philadelphia: Fortress, 1984], 57).

95. *Samuel*, 312.

96. *Samuel*, 357.

97. 'Samuel', II, 1102.

98. 'Poor Man's', 212n.

99. *Story*, 108.

100. *Truth*, 50.

101. *Samuel*, 254.

102. 'Prose', 64.

103. 'Crises', 125-26.

104. *Samuel*, 321.

105. *II Samuel*, 298.

106. *David*, 139.

107. *Prophetie*, 132.

108. H. Weippert, 'Die "deuteronomistischen" Beurteilungen', 309-10.

109. T.N.D. Mettinger, *King and Messiah: The Civil and Sacral Legitimation of the Israelite Monarchy* (Coniectanea Biblica Old Testament Series, 8; Lund: Gleerup, 1976), 30.

110. It is interesting that this is another link between the narratives in 2 Sam 11 and Gen 38. Here the linkage is not to the illicit sexual act of Judah/Tamar however, as are the other linkages noted above. Rather this linkage is to the Onan-Tamar incident where the sexual act of only the man is deemed unpleasing to the deity. Another significant difference between the Gen 38 and 2 Sam 11-12 narratives in regard to this theological evaluation is that in Gen 38 it is the man who dies, while in 2 Sam 12.14 the punishment is said to 'pass' on to the next generation.

111. *King and Messiah*, 30n17.

112. Abraham-Hagar-Sarah; Onan-Tamar-Er; Saul-David-dancers.

113. See above Chapter 3§3.

114. See above Chapter 4§3.

115. W. Roth argues that this is the 'apex' of the complex in 2 Sam 10-12, since in it 'the knot is tied and its solution initiated' ('You Are the Man! Structural Interaction in 2 Samuel 10-12', *Semeia* 8 [1977], 5).

116. D. Daube, 'Nathan's Parable', *NT* 24 (1982), 276. Cf. also H. Seebass, 'Nathan und David in II Samuel 12', *ZAW* 86 (1974), 203-11.

117. Daube, 276-77.

118. Ibid., 277. Also P. W. Coxon argues that the ewe-lamb is to be identified with Bathsheba on the basis of the parallel usages of *'kl . . . šth . . .* and *škb* in 11.11-12 and in 12.3, and on the basis of the pun of her name using *šb'*, which he suggests should be the reading (so LXX) in place of *'rb'tym* (so MT) in 12.6 ('A Note on "Bathsheba" in 2 Samuel 12,1-6', *Bib* 62 [1981], 17).

As a way of resolving this particular incongruity Delekat argues that the ewe-lamb stands for Uriah, with Yahweh being the rich man and David the poor ('Tendenz', 30). Such an interpretation is clearly unsuitable, since, as Bowman correctly notes, the response in 12.6-7a assumes David to be the culprit, not Yahweh ('Crisis', 128).

119. He defines this genre as a narrative which 'constitutes a realistic story about a violation of the law, related to someone who had committed a similar offense with the purpose of leading the unsuspecting hearer to pass judgement on himself' ('Poor Man's Ewe-lamb', 220-21).

120. Ibid., 221.

121. 'David and the Tekoite Woman', *VT* 20 (1970), 421.

122. *The Just King: Monarchical Authority in Ancient Israel* (JSOTS, 12; Sheffield: JSOT, 1979), 128.

123. *Story*, 47.

124. Whitelam, *Just King*, 128-29.

125. 'The Wise Women of 2 Samuel: A Role Model for Women in Early Israel?', *CBQ* 43 (1981), 21.

126. *Kingship and the Gods: A Study of Ancient Near Eastern Religion as the Integration of Society and Nature* (Chicago: University of Chicago, 1978), 342.

127. 'King, Kingship', *IDB*, III (1962), 12-13. So also G. von Rad, *Deuteronomy* (OTL; Philadelphia: Westminster, 1966), 138 and A.D.H. Mayes, *Deuteronomy* (NCB; Greenwood, SC: Attic, 1979), 288.

128. Even though Deut 17.9 mentions *špṭ*, most commentators agree this is not a reference to the *mlk* (cf. Mayes, *Deuteronomy*, 268 and von Rad, *Deuteronomy*, 118.

129. Mayes, *Deuteronomy*, 271; von Rad, *Deuteronomy*, 119.

130. While 1 Sam 8.11 mentions *mšpṭ hmlk*, this seems to refer to a 'law for the king' and not a 'function of the king'. Similarly, the narrative in 1 Sam 30.21-24 is used by Dtr as an etiology for the war practice of division of the spoils (cf. 30.25). One notes that, as opposed to the narrative in 2 Samuel, in 1 Sam 30 David is not a king and the text concerns a legislative and not a juridical function.

By the same token the argument being made is not that the king in ancient Israel had no juridical function, since this is the underlying assumption of many narratives (see below). Rather the argument is that in the above-cited legislation, it appears that the Dtr is trying to alter this tradition by proposing alternative modes for resolution of appellate cases.

131. So Whitelam, *Just King*, 140.

132. See above Chapter 2 note 83 for a discussion of these lists.

133. *Of Prophets and Kings*, 83.

134. Jer 22.3; 23.5; 33.15.

135. Carroll, *Jeremiah*, 417. This is also confirmed by the use of *mšpṭ* in Ps 72.1. As Mowinckel notes, 'In the enthronement psalms the sense of (re-) establishment of the right order and the right relation between the nations is generally included in the word'. (*The Psalms in Israel's Worship* [2 vols.; Nashville: Abingdon, 1962], I, 146). Similarly, it should be noted, that though there is mention of judging in this psalm, it is the root *dyn* which is utilized in this capacity. (Cf. G. J. Botterweck, *dyn*, *TDOT*, II, 188 for a discussion of the differences in this term and *špṭ*.)

136. This speech holds together the reaction of the Queen to Solomon's passing her test (10.4-5) and the report of her giving him gifts (10.10), which parallels the gifts mentioned in 10.2. This structure parallels the compositional pattern noted in 2 Sam 12.26-31. Similarly, as in the cases of Rahab (Josh 2) and Uriah (2 Sam 11), a non-Israelite speaks the will of Yahweh for the people/king. See above comparison of Uriah and Rahab in §4.2. This would suggest that the Dtr is also involved in the shaping of these units.

137. Similarly the phrase is used of Yahweh in Deut 10.18, in regard to divine provision of protection for the oppressed.

138. G. Macholz has argued that the term *šm'* in this unit refers to a particular office of an arbiter, and thus, this unit does not speak about a juridical function for the king himself ('Die Stellung des Königs in der israelitischen Gerichtsverfassung', *ZAW* 84 [1972], 314-16). Since there is no such listing of an office like this in the 'officials list' in either 2 Sam 8.16-18 or 20.18-20, Whitelam rejects this notion (*Just King*, 140).

139. While all commentators agree that the story itself is a legend (Noth, *Könige* [BKAT; Neukirchen-Vluyn: Neukirchener Verlag, 1968], 48; E. Würthwein, *Die Bücher der Könige*, 37; Gray, *Kings*, 116), Long argues that its current function is to demonstrate Solomon's wisdom (*1 Kings*, 70). De Vries adds the note that the introduction of the unit in 3.16-28 by the particle *'z* suggests that it is Dtr who has incorporated this narrative in its current location (*1 Kings*, 57). In this designation he is following Montgomery ('Archival Data in the Book of Kings', *JBL* 53 [1934], 46-52).

140. As noted above, this unit is one of the examples of Simon's 'juridical parable'. 2 Sam 14 and 2 Sam 13, to which it relates, both concern the crime of fratricide. Thus, some of the problems raised between the parable in 2 Sam 12.1-4 with the events in 11.2-27a do not appear in 2 Sam 13-14.

141. Camp suggests that there is no real difference between these narratives in which a prophet vs. a wise person is the protagonist ('Wise Women', 21).

142. So Simon, 'Poor Man's', 221, *et al.*

143. *1 Kings*, 222.

144. It should be noted that in the situation of Uriah, David does the opposite of Saul and Ahab in the war situation, in that while they did not kill their opponent in the battle as directed, David has his innocent 'opponent' put to death in battle.

145. This scene of confession by the king and transference of the punishment to the next generation is similar to the confrontation between Elijah and Ahab after the killing of Naboth and the seizing of his land by Ahab (1 Kgs 21.27-29). It should be noted that these verses have been argued to be from the hand of the Dtr (cf. Jones, *Kings*, II, 360; Long, *Kings*, 228). What is also interesting is that both of these authors note the similarity between the 1 Kgs 21 unit and the 2 Sam 12.13f. unit, but do not raise the possibility of a common of redactor.

Finally, it is interesting that the first unit of the compositional pattern (12.5-7a) is similar to the narrative in 1 Kgs 20.35-43, while the second unit (12.13-15) is similar to the narrative in 1 Kgs 21.20-29.

146. It should be noted that in this indictment there is only mention of the murder and subsequent marriage and no use of the name Bathsheba. There is not, however, any mention of adultery as part of the crime (so Hertzberg, *Samuel*, 314). Similarly, in the regnal formula on the reign of Abijam (1 Kgs 15.1-8), within the DtrH's theological evaluation, there is a negative note on David, which mentions *bdbr 'wryh hhty* (15.5bβ). These notations could add

weight to the suggestion that there was originally an independent 'wife of Uriah tradition', which has been overlaid with the David–Bathsheba story (see above note 71).

147. Budde, *Samuel*, 255; Dhorme, *Samuel*, 359; Hertzberg, *Samuel*, 313; McCarter, *II Samuel*, 300.

148. Ackroyd, *Second Samuel*, 111; Budde, *Samuel*, 256; Dhorme, *Samuel*, 359; Hertzberg, *Samuel*, 314; McCarter, *II Samuel*, 300.

149. See above Chapter 2 n. 93 for a summary of the positions taken on this issue.

150. As McCarter points out, this reconstruction is based on the Syriac reading, as opposed to MT or LXX (*II Samuel*, 295). So also Ackroyd, *Second Samuel*, 110; Budde, *Samuel*, 256; Dhorme, *Samuel*, 359; Driver, *Notes*, 291; Smith, *Samuel*, 324.

151. In this regard we are following M. de Roche in speaking of a dispute between two aggrieved parties in which the 'harmed party seeds restitution for his grievance by his own means, according to his own concept of justice' ('Yahweh's *rîb* against Israel: A Reassessment of the So-Called 'Prophetic Lawsuit' in the Preexilic Prophets', *JBL* 102 [1983], 570).

152. It is interesting that this genre, which is generally used for indicting and resolving conflicts with the collective, is used for a dispute with an individual. E. Wilson correctly identifies this as the meaning of *Rîb* in 2 Sam 15.2 and 4 ('*Rîb* in Israel's Historical and Legal Traditions: A Study of the Israelite Setting of *Rîb*-Form' [Ph.D. dissertation, Drew University, 1970] 223-24).

153. It is interesting that 2 Sam 12.8b, which follows the reference to the establishment of the united kingdom is so often interpreted in terms of the acquisition of women (cf. Smith, *Samuel*, 323; *et al.*).

154. These verses are difficult because of the repetition of the *bzh* and the wife of Uriah reference. Similarly there are two references to the killing of Uriah in v. 9, the second of which adds mention of the Ammonite Wars. Thus, it appears that v. 9a was in tack and the addition in 9b is redactional. Similarly, since 9a begins with a question, *mdw'*, it most probably followed the announcement in v. 7a, *'th h'yš*.

155. Ackroyd, *Second Samuel*, 107, 112; Dhorme, *Samuel*, 360; Hertzberg, *Samuel*, 308; McCarter, *II Samuel*, 293.

156. Cf. T. Veijola, 'Salomo—Der Erstgeborene Bathsebas', *VT* 30 (1979), 233-34.

157. Ackroyd, *Second Samuel*, 112; Dietrich, *Prophetie*, 127-29; Würthwein, *Erzählung*, 24.

158. E.g., Judg 20.35; 1 Sam 4.3; 2 Chron 14.11.

159. Cf. 1 Sam 25.35; Isa 19.22; 2 Chron 13.20.

160. Mic 1.9; Isa 17.11; Jer 15.15; 30.12, 15.

161. See discussion of vv. 16-23 below.

162. *Erzählung*, 24-25.

163. See above §4 regarding this point (i.e. 12.13-15).

164. Cf. Gen 20.7; Num 21.7; Deut 9.20; 1 Sam 7.5; 12.19; 2 Kgs 19.4; Isa 37.4; Jer 29.7; 42.2, 20; Ps 72.15.

165. Cf. Exod 2.15; 4.24; 1 Sam 19.10; 2 Sam 21.2; 1 Kgs 11.40; Jer 26.21; Pss 54.5; 86.14; Esth 3.6; 2 Chron 22.9. It should be noted that in these instances the search is shown to be unsuccessful. Similarly it is also very interesting to note that this list crosses most parts of the canon and a variety of literary types.

166. Cf. Exod 33.7f.; Deut 4.29; Jer 29.13; Hos 3.5; Ps 105.3; Prov 28.5. It should be noted that at times the announcement of punishment in prophetic passages is that the search will be unsuccessful (e.g. Amos 8.12).

167. Cf. Jer 50.4; Hos 5.15 7.10; Zeph 1.6; 2.3; Zech 8.22; Ps 27.4, 8.

168. See Chapter 2 note 21.

169. Interestingly this is the behavior forbidden to the Wise Woman of Tekoa, so as to appear to be in mourning (2 Sam 14.2). Conversely, this is the behavior of Ruth prior to her attempt to seduce Boaz (Ruth 3.3).

170. Cf. Gen 23.2; Deut 34.8; 1 Sam 30.4; 2 Sam 1.24; 3.32; 19.2, etc.

171. Cf. Gen 37.34; 2 Sam 13.37; 14.2; 19.2; 1 Chron 7.22; 2 Chron 35.24.

172. Cf. 1 Sam 31.13; 2 Sam 1.12.

173. See above note 145 on the relationship between 2 Sam 12.13-26 and 1 Kgs 21.27.

174. Cf. Isa 42.24; Jer 40.3; 44.23; 50.7, 14; Zeph 1.17.

175. Butler notes that because of its general nature, Achan's confession is often viewed as a later addition to the text (*Joshua*, 85-86). This would not alter our contention that the confession does not avert the punishment in the final form of the narrative.

176. The appearance of Holy War motifs suggests a Dtr origin to these narratives.

177. There is an interesting play on this verb in 12.23.

178. Interestingly, this is also David's object, as stated in 2 Sam 12.22b.

179. Cf. De Vries, *Kings*, 127; Gray, *Kings*, 226; Jones, *Kings*, I, 204; Long, *Kings*, 104; Nelson, *Double Redaction*, 71-72; Noth, *DH*, 97; Würthwein, *Könige*, 95-96.

180. See discussion of *ngp* and *'nwš* in §4.

181. This is also the wording which introduces the rationale for the repentance behavior of the people of Nineveh in Jonah 3.9.

182. This term has been noted to be anachronistic. McCarter argues that, since it occurs also in 1 Sam 1.24 and 3.15, this could lend credence to a prophetic origin for this unit (*II Samuel*, 302). One problem with this conclusion is that in 1 Sam 1.24 Samuel is deposited in the *byt yhwh* not as a prophet but as a priest. Similarly, while there is a 'call motif' in 1 Sam 3, the structure of the chapter is to demonstrate the incompetence of Eli as a priest

and the competence of Samuel in receiving and interpreting oracles in the *byt yhwh*.

In addition to the above references to a *byt yhwh* in narratives which describe events in pre-Solomonic times, the phrase also appears in Deut 23.19, Josh 6.24, and Judg 19.18, none of which could be argued to be prophetic in origin. In all of these narratives *byt yhwh* refers to a 'temple'. Thus, it appears that Dtr used the term in reference to the 'Temple' prior to its construction.

183. *ḥnn* is one of the verbs used in the plea for redemption in individual laments which speak to medical problems (cf. Pss 6.3; 31.10; 41.5, 11).

184. 'Prose', 65.

185. The way in which this verse is cantonated is most interesting, in that the *atnach* does not come until after the double designation of the sexual act, as though this were the form of the *nḥmh*.

186. The LXX adds the words *kai synelaben* at this point.

187. *Die ewige Dynastie*, 155n.

188. 'Salomo', 248. In this regard he is following Würthwein, who claims the omission of the name makes the narrative in 11.27 incomplete (*Die Erzählung*, 32).

189. Ibid., 235.

190. Ibid.

191. Ibid., 238. So also McCarter, *II Samuel*, 303.

192. Cf. McCarter (*II Samuel*, 303-304) for a review of research on the meaning of *ydydyh*.

193. Following the Qere of 12.24b.

194. Braun, 179; Curtis, 208; Myers, *I Chronicles*, 106-107.

195. See above §1.

196. See above Chapter 3§4.

197. 'Der Name des Königs Salomo', *ThZ* 16 (1960) 297.

198. 'Die Wurzel *šlm*', *ZAW* 85 (1973) 13.

199. Veijola, 'Salomo', 235.

200. Ibid., 248.

BIBLIOGRAPHY

Ackroyd, P.R. *Exile and Restoration*. OTL. Philadelphia: Westminster, 1968.
—*The First Book of Samuel*. CBC. New York: Cambridge University, 1971.
—'The Hebrew Root *b'š*', *JTS* 2 (1951): 31-36.
—'Kings, I and II'. In *IDBS*. Edited by George A. Buttrick. Nashville: Abingdon, 1975,
    V: 516-519.
—*The Second Book of Samuel*. New York: Cambridge University, 1977.
—'The Succession Narrative (So-called)'. *Interp* 35 (1981): 383-397.
Achtemeier, E. *The Old Testament and the Proclamation of the Gospel*. Philadelphia:
    Westminster, 1973.
Aharoni, Y. *The Land of the Bible: A Historical Geography*. Philadelphia: Westminster,
    1967.
Ahlström, G.W. *Aspects of Syncretism in Israelite Religion*. Lund: Gleerup, 1963.
—*Royal Administration and National Religion in Ancient Palestine*. Leiden: E.J. Brill,
    1982.
Albright, W.F. *From the Stone Age to Christianity*. 2nd edition. Garden City:
    Doubleday, 1957.
—'The Israelite Conquest of Canaan in the Light of Archaeology'. *BASOR* 74 (1939):
    74-76.
—*Yahweh and the Gods of Canaan*. Garden City: Doubleday, 1968.
Allen, Leslie C. *The Greek Chronicles*. 2 vols. Leiden: E.J. Brill, 1974.
Alt, A. 'The Formation of the Israelite State in Palestine'. In *Essays on Old Testament
    History and Religion*, pp. 171-237. Translated by R.A. Wilson. Oxford: Blackwell,
    1966.
Alter, R. *The Art of Biblical Narrative*. New York: Basic Books, 1981.
Anderson, A.A. *Psalms (1-72)*. NCBC. Grand Rapids: Eerdmans, 1972.
—*Psalms (73-150)*. NCBC. Grand Rapids: Eerdmans, 1972.
Anderson, G.W. *The History and Religion of Israel*. The New Clarendon Bible. Vol. 1.
    London: Oxford University, 1966.
Andre, G. *'ṭm''*. In *TDOT*, vol. V, pp. 332-342. Edited by Helmer Ringgren. Grand
    Rapids: Eerdmans, 1986.
Andreason, Niels-Erik A. 'The Role of the Queen-Mother in Israelite Society'. *CBQ* 49
    (1983): 179-194.
Auerbach, E. *Wüste und gelobtes Land*. Berlin: Wolff, 1932.
Baab, O.J. 'Marriage'. *IDB* III: 278-87. Edited by G.A. Buttrick, Nashville: Abingdon,
    1962.
Ball, E. 'Introduction to Rost's Work'. In L. Rost. *The Succession to the Throne of*

David, pp. xv-l. HTIBS 1. Translated by M.D. Rutter and D.M. Gunn. Sheffield: Almond, 1982.

Bardtke, H. 'Erwägungen zur Rolle Judas im Aufstand des Absolom'. In *Wort und Geschichte*, pp. 1-8. AOAT, 18. Edited by H. Gese & P. Ruger. Neukirchen-Vluyn: Kevalaer, 1973.

Bar-Efrat, S. 'Literary Modes and Methods in the Biblical Narrative in View of 2 Samuel 10-20 and 1 Kings 1-2'. *Immanuel* 8 (1978): 19-31.

—'Some Observations on the Analysis of Structure in Biblical Narrative'. *VT* 30 (1980): 154-73.

Bassler, J.M. 'A Man for All Seasons: David in Rabbinic and New Testament Literature'. *Interp* 40 (1986): 156-169.

Baumann, A. *"bl'*. In *TDOT*. Edited by G. Botterweck and H. Ringgren. I:44-48. Grand Rapids, Eerdmans, 1974.

Begrich, J. *Die Chronologie der Könige von Israel und Juda und die Quellen des Rahmens der Königsbücher*. Beiträge zur Historichen Theologie, 3. Tübingen: J.C.B. Mohr, 1929.

Benzinger, I. *Javist und Elohist in den Königsbüchern*. BWANT 27. Berlin: W. Kohlhammer, 1921.

Berlin, Adele. 'Characterization in Biblical Narrative: David's Wives'. *JSOT* 23 (1982): 69-85.

—*Poetics and Interpretation of Biblical Narrative*. Sheffield: Almond, 1983.

Bin-Nun, S.R. 'Formulas from Royal Records of Israel and Judah'. *VT* 18 (1968): 414-432.

Birch, B.C. 'The Rise of The Israelite Monarchy: The Growth and Development of I Sam. 7-15'. Ph.D. dissertation, Yale University, 1970.

Bird, Phyllis A. 'Images of Women in the Old Testament'. In *The Bible and Liberation: Political and Social Hermeneutics*. Edited by Norman K. Gottwald. Maryknoll, NY: Orbis, 1983, 252-288.

Blenkinsopp, J. *A History of Prophecy in Israel*. Philadelphia: Westminster, 1983.

—*Prophecy and Canon: A Contribution to the Study of Jewish Origins*. University of Notre Dame Center for the Study of Judaism and Christianity in Antiquity, 3. Notre Dame: University of Notre Dame, 1977.

—'Theme and Motif in the Succession History (2 Sam. XI 2ff) and the Yahwist Corpus'. *VTSup* 15 (1965): 44-57.

Boling, Robert G. *Joshua*. AB. Garden City: Doubleday, 1982.

—*Judges*. AB. Garden City: Doubleday, 1975.

Botterweck, G.J. *'dyn'*. In *TDOT*, III: 187-194.

Bowman, R.G. 'The Crises of King David: Narrative Structure, Compositional Technique and the Interpretation of II Samuel 8:15-20:26'. Ph.D. dissertation, Union Theological Seminary in Virginia, 1981.

—'A Personal and Political Crisis of King David: Narrative Structure, Compositional Technique, and the Interpretation of II Samuel 10-12' [Unpublished paper presented at the 1986 Annual Meeting of the Society of Biblical Literature, Atlanta, Georgia].

Braun, Roddy. *I Chronicles*. WBC. Waco, TX: Word Books, 1986.

Bright, John. *A History of Israel*. 3rd edition. Philadelphia: Westminster, 1981.

Brueggemann, W. 'David and his Theologian'. *CBQ* 30 (1968): 156-181.

—*David's Truth in Israel's Imagination and Memory*. Philadelphia: Fortress, 1985.

—*Genesis*. Atlanta: John Knox, 1982.

—'Life and Death in Tenth Century Israel (Gen. 37, 39-48, 50; II Sam. 9-20, I K. 1-2)'. *JAAR* 40 (1972): 96-109.

—'On Coping with Curse: A Study of 2 Sam 16:5-14'. *CBQ* 36 (1974): 175-192.

Bucellati, G. *Cities and Nations of Ancient Syria. An Essay on Political Institutions with special reference to the Israelite Kingdoms*, Rome: Instituto di studi del Vicino Oriente, 1967.

Budd, Philip J. *Numbers*. WBC. Waco, TX: Word Books, 1984.

Budde, K. *Die Bucher Samuel*. KHCAT, 8. Leipzig: Muhr, 1902.

—*Geschichte der althebräischen Literatur*. Die Litteraturen des Ostens 7. Leipzig: C.F. Amelangs, 1906.

—'Richter und Josua'. *ZAW* 7 (1887): 93-166.

Burney, C.F. *The Book of Judges with Introduction and Notes on the Hebrew Text of the Book of Kings*. New York: Ktav, 1970.

Butler, Trent C. *Joshua*. WBC. Waco, TX: Word Books, 1983.

Caird, G.B. '*Exegesis of I Samuel*'. *IB*. 12 vols. Nashville: Abingdon, 1953, II: 876-1040.

—'Exegesis of II Samuel'. *IB*. 12 vols. Nashville: Abingdon, 1953, II: 1041-1176.

Camp, Claudia V. 'The Wise Woman of 2 Samuel: A Role Model for Women in Early Israel'. *CBQ* 43 (1981): 14-29.

Campbell, A.F. *The Ark Narrative (I Sam 4–6; 2 Sam 6): A Form-Critical and Traditio-Historical Study*. SBLDS 16. Missoula: Scholars, 1975.

—*Of Prophets and Kings: A Late Ninth-Century Document (1 Sam 1–2 Kings 10)*. CBQMS 17. Washington: CBA, 1986 .

Campbell, K.M. 'Rehab's Covenant'. *VT* 22 (1972): 243-244.

Carlson, R.A. *David, the Chosen King. A Traditio-Historical Approach to the Second Book of Samuel*. Translated by Eric J. Sharpe and S. Rudman. Stockholm: Almquist & Wiksell, 1964.

Carrol, R.P. *Jeremiah*. OTL. Philadelphia: Westminster, 1986.

Caspari, W. 'The Opening Style of the Israelite Novelle'. Translated by D.E. Orton. In *Narrative and Novelle in Samuel. Studies by Hugo Gressmann and Other Scholars 1906-1923*. Edited by D. Gunn. Sheffield: Almond (forthcoming).

—'Literarische Art und historischer Wert von 2 Sam. 15-20,' *TSK* 82 (1909): 317-48.

Castel, F. *Histoire-d'Israël et de Juda: Des origines au IIème siècle après Jésus-Christ*. Paris: Le Centurion, 1983.

Childs, Brevard. *Introduction to the Old Testament as Scripture*. Philadelphia: Fortress, 1979.

Christensen, D.L. 'Huldah and the Men of Anathoth'. In *Society of Biblical Literature 1984 Seminar Papers*. Edited by K.H. Richards. Chico, California: Scholars, 1984, 399-404.

Clements, R.E. 'The Deuteronomistic Interpretation of the Founding of the Monarchy in I Sam 8'. *VT* 24 (1974): 378-410.

Clines, D.J.A. *Theme of the Pentateuch*. JSOTS, 10. Sheffield, England: JSOT, 1978.

Coats, G.W. *Genesis*. FOTL, 1. Grand Rapids: Eerdmans, 1983.

Cohen, M.A. 'The Rebellions During the Reign of David. An Inquiry Into Social Dynamics in Ancient Israel'. In *Studies in Jewish Bibliography, History, and Literature in Honor of I. Edward Kiev*. Edited by C. Berlin. New York: Ktav, 1971, 91-112.

Conroy, Charles, M.S.C. *Absalom Absalom! Narrative and Language in 2 Sam 13-20*. Rome: Biblical Institute, 1978.

—*1-2 Samuel 1-2 Kings*, Wilmington: Michael Glazier, 1983.

'The Contendings of Horus and Seth'. Translated by E.F. Wente. In *The Literature of*

Ancient Egypt, pp. 108-126. Edited by W.K. Simpson. New Haven: Yale University, 1973.

Cook, S.A. 'Notes on the Composition of 2 Samuel'. *AJSLL* 16 (1899/1900): 144-177.

Cornill, C.H. *Introduction to the Canonical Books of the Old Testament*. New York: Putnam's Sons, 1907.

Coxon, P.W. 'A Note on Bathsheba in 2 Samuel 12:1-6'. *Bib* 62 (1981): 247-250.

Crenshaw, J.L. *Old Testament Wisdom: An Introduction*. Atlanta: John Knox, 1981.

Crim, Keith R. *The Royal Psalms*. Richmond, Virginia: John Knox, 1962.

Cross, F.M. 'Ideologies of Kingship in the Era of the Empire: Conditional Covenant and Eternal Decree'. In *Canaanite Myth and Hebrew Epic: Essays in the History of the Religion of Israel*. Cambridge: Harvard University, 1973, 219-273.

—'Notes on the Ammonite Inscription from Tell Sîrân'. *BASOR* 212 (1973): 12-15.

—'The Themes of the Book of Kings and the Structure of the Deuteronomistic History'. In *Canaanite Myth and Hebrew Epic: Essays in the History of the Religion of Israel*, pp. 274-289. Cambridge: Harvard University, 1973.

Curtis, Edward L. *Chronicles*. ICC. New York: Charles Scribner's Sons, 1910.

Dahood, Mitchell, *Psalms I: 1-50*. Anchor Bible. Garden City: Doubleday, 1965.

Daube, D. 'Nathan's Parable'. *NT* 24 (1982): 275-288.

Davis, J.J. *The Birth of a Kingdom: Studies in I-II Samuel and I Kings 1-11*. Grand Rapids: Baker Book House, 1970.

Deist, F.E. 'David: A Man After God's Heart? An Investigation into the David Character in the So-called Succession Narrative'. In *Studies in the Succession Narrative*. Edited by W.C. van Wyk. Pretoria, South Africa: OTWSA 27 (1984) and OTWSA 28 (1985) Old Testament Essays, 99-129.

Delekat, L. 'Tendenz und Theologie der David-Salomo Erzählung'. In *Das ferne und nahe Wort*. BZAW 105. Berlin: Töpelmann, 1967, 26-36.

De Roche, M. 'Yahweh's *rîb* against Israel: A Reassessment of the So-Called 'Prophetic Lawsuit' in the Preexilic Prophets'. *JBL* 102 (1983): 563-574.

DeVries, S.J. *I Kings*. WBC. Waco, TX: Word Books, 1985.

Dhorme, Le P.P. *Les Livres de Samuel*. Paris: J. Gabalda, 1910.

Dietrich, W. *Prophetie und Geschichte. Eine redaktionsgeschichtliche Untersuchung zum deuteronomistischen Geschichtswerk*. FRLANT 108. Göttigen: Vandenhoeck & Ruprecht, 1972.

Donner, Herbert. 'The Separate States of Israel and Judah'. In *Israelite and Judean History*. OTL. Edited by John H. Hayes and J. Maxwell Miller. Philadelphia: Westminster, 1977.

Driver, S.R. *An Introduction to the Literature of the Old Testament*. 6th edition. Edinburgh: T. & T. Clark, 1897.

—*Notes on the Hebrew Text and the Topography of the Books of Samuel*. 2nd edition. Oxford: Clarendon, 1913.

Duhm, H. *Das Buch Jeremia*. KHCAT, 11. Tübingen: J.C.B. Mohr, 1901.

Eissfeldt, Otto. Die Composition der Samuelis Bücher. Leipzig: J.C. Hindrichs, 1965.

—*The Old Testament: An Introduction*. Translated by Peter R. Ackroyd. New York: Harper & Row, 1965.

Engnell, I. *A Rigid Scrutiny*. Translated by J.T. Willis. Nashville: Vanderbilt University, 1969.

Eslinger, Lyle M. *Kingship of God in Crisis: A Close Reading of 1 Samuel 1-12*. Sheffield: Almond, 1985.

Ewald, H. 'The Rise and Splendour of the Hebrew Monarchy'. Vol. III of *The History of Israel*. London: Longmans, Green, 1871.

Fichtner, Johannes. *Das erste Buch von den Königen*. Stuttgart: Calwer, 1964.

Finegan, Jack. *Handbook of Biblical Chronology: Principles of Time Reckoning in the Ancient World and Problems of Chronology in the Bible*. Princeton: Princeton University, 1964.

Flanagan, James W. 'Court History or Succession Document? A Study of 2 Samuel 9-20 and 1 Kings 1-2'. *JBL* 91 (1972): 172-191.

—'Judah in All Israel'. In *No Famine in the Land. Studies in Honor of John L. McKenzie*, pp. 101-116. Edited by J.W. Flanagan and A. W. Robinson. Missoula, MT: Scholars, 101-116.

—'The Relocation of the Davidic Capital'. *JAAR* 47 (1979): 223-244.

Fohrer, Georg. *Introduction to the Old Testament*. Initiated by Ernst Sellin. Translated by David E. Green. Nashville: Abingdon, 1968.

Fokkelman, L.P. *King David (II Sam 9-20 & I Kings 1-2)*. Vol. 1. *Narrative Art and Poetry in the Books of Samuel*. Translated by G. van Drien, R. Vreeland, & J. Frishman. Assen: Van Gorcum, 1981.

Fontaine, C. 'The Bearing of Wisdom on the Shape of 2 Samuel 11-12 and 1 Kings 3'. *JSOT* 34 (1986): 61-77.

Forresti, F. *The Rejection of Saul in the Perspective of the Deuteronomistic School: A Study of 1 Samuel 15 and Related Texts*. STT. Rome: Edizione del Teresianum, 1984.

Frankfort, Henri. *Kingship and the Gods: A Study of Ancient Near Eastern Religion as the Integration of Society and Nature*. Chicago: The University of Chicago, 1978.

Freedman, D.N. 'The Age of David and Solomon'. In *The World History of the Jewish People*, Edited by Abraham Malamat and Israel Eph'al. Jerusalem: Massada, 1979, IV: 101-125.

—'Pentateuch'. In *IDB*, III: 714-727. 4 vols. Edited by G.A. Buttrick. Nashville: Abingdon, 1962.

Fretheim, T. *Deuteronomic History*. Nashville: Abingdon, 1983.

Frick, F.S. *The City in Ancient Israel*. SBLDS 36. Missoula, MT: Scholars, 1977.

Fricke, Klaus D. *Das zweite Buch von den Königen*. Stuttgart: Calwer, 1972.

Friedman, R.E. *The Exile and Biblical Narrative: The Formation of the Deuteronomistic and Priestly Works*. Chico, CA: Scholars, 1981.

Fuchs, Esther. 'The Rhetoric of Rape in the Bible'. Unpublished paper at the SBL Anaheim, CA November 24, 1985.

Gehrke, R.D. *1 and 2 Samuel*. St. Louis: Concordia, 1968.

Gerleman, T. 'Der Wurzel *šlm*'. *ZAW* 85 (1973): 13.

Gold, V.R. 'Giloh'. *IDB*, II: 39.

Gottwald, N.K. *The Tribes of Yahweh: A Sociology of the Religon of Liberated Israel, 1250-1050 BCE*. Maryknoll, NY: Orbis, 1979.

Goudoever, J. van. *Biblical Calendars*. Leiden: E.J. Brill, 1959.

Graetz, H. *Volkstümliche Geschichte der Juden*. 3 vols. Leipzig: Ostar Leiner, 1888.

Gray, John. *I and II Kings*. 2nd edition OTL. Philadelphia: Westminster, 1970.

—*Joshua Judges, and Ruth*. NCB. Grand Rapids: Eerdmans, 1986.

Green, A.R. 'Regnal Formulas in the Hebrew and Greek Texts of the Books of Kings'. *JNES* 42 (1983): 167-180.

Gressmann, H. *Die Älteste Geschichtsschreibung und Prophetie Israels von Samuel bis Amos und Hosea*. Göttingen: Vandenhoeck & Ruprecht, 1910.

—'Stories of David and his Sons'. Translated by D.E. Orton. In *Narrative and Novelle in Samuel. Studies by Hugo Gressmann and Other Scholars 1906-1923*. Edited by

D. Gunn. Sheffield: Almond (forthcoming).

Grønbaek, J.H. *Die Geschichte vom Aufstieg Davids (1. Sam. 15–2 Sam. 5: Tradition und Komposition*. Copenhagen: Munksgaard, 1971.

Gunn, David M. 'David and the Gift of the Kingdom (2 Sam 9–20, 1 Kg 1–2)'. *Semeia* 3 (1975): 14–45.

—*The Fate of King Saul*. Sheffield: JSOT, 1980.

—'From Jerusalem to the Jordan and Back: Symmetry in 2 Samuel XV–XX'. *VT* 30 (1980): 109–113.

—*The Story of King David: Genre and Interpretation*. JSOTS, 6. Sheffield: JSOT, 1982.

Gutbrod, Karl. *Das zweite Buch Samuel*. BDAT. Stuttgart: Calwer, 1958.

Guthrie, H.H. *God and History in the Old Testament*. Greenwich, CT: Seabury, 1960.

Habel, N. *Literary Criticism of the Old Testament*. Philadelphia: Fortress, 1971.

Hagan, Harry. 'Deception as Motif and Theme in 2 Sam 9–20; 1 Kings 1–2'. *Bib* 60 (1979): 301-326.

Halo, William W. and William K. Simpson. *The Ancient Near East: A History*. San Diego: Harcourt, Brace, Jovanovich, 1971.

Halpern, B. 'Sectionalism and the Schism'. *JBL* 93 (1974): 519-532.

Harrison, R.K. 'The Matriarchate and Hebrew Regal Succession'. *Evangelical Quarterly* 29 (1957): 29-34.

Harvey, J. *Le Plaidoyer prophétique contre Israel après la rupture de l'Alliance*. Studia: Travaux de Recherche, 22. Bruges: Descalée, 1967.

Hauser, A.S. 'His Father's Son: Amnon's Rape of his Sister Tamar', unpublished paper presented at the International Meeting of the SBL, Copenhagen, August 1989.

Hayes, John H. *An Introduction to Old Testament Study*. Nashville: Abingdon, 1979.

Heaton, E.W. *The Hebrew Kingdoms*. The New Clarendon Bible, 3. London: Oxford University, 1968.

Hempel, J. *Das Ethos des Alten Testaments*. BZAW 67. Berlin: Töpelmann, 1938.

Herion, Gray A. 'The Role of Historical Narrative in Biblical Thought: The Tendencies Underlying Old Testament Historiography'. *JSOT* 21 (1981): 25-57.

Hermann, Siegfried. *A History of Israel in Old Testament Times*. 2nd edition. Translated by John Bowden. Philadelphia: Fortress, 1981.

Hertzberg, Hans Wilhelm. *I and II Samuel*. Translated by J.S. Bowden. OTL. Philadelphia: Westminster, 1976.

Hoffmann, Hans-Detlef. *Reform und Reformen: Untersuchungen zu einen Grundthema der deuteronomistischen Geschichtsschreibung*. Abhandlungen zur Theologie des Alten und Neuen Testaments, 66. Zürich: Theologischer Verlag, 1980.

Hoftijzer, J. 'David and the Tekoite Woman'. *VT* 20 (1970): 419-444.

Hölscher, G. 'Das Buch der Könige, seine Quellen und seine Redaktion'. *Eucharisterion*. Festschrift H. Gunkel. FRLANT, 36. Göttingen: Vandenhoeck & Ruprecht, 1923, 158-213.

—*Geschichtsschreibung in Israel: Untersuchungen zum Yahwisten und Elohisten*. Lund: C.W.K. Gleerup, 1952.

Hong, C. *Israel in Ancient Near Eastern Setting*. Ann Arbor: University Microfilms International, 1980.

Horn, S.H. 'The Crown of the King of the Ammonites'. *BASOR* 193 (1969): 170-180.

Ishida, Tomoo. *The Royal Dynasties in Ancient Israel: A Study on the Formation and*

Development of Royal Dynastic Ideology. BZAW 142. Berlin: Walter de Gruyter, 1977.

—'Solomon's Succession to the Throne of David-A Political Analysis'. In *Studies in the Period of David and Solomon and Other Essays*. Winona Lake, IN: Eisenbrauns, 1982, 175-87.

Jackson, J.J. 'David's Throne: Patterns in the Succession Story'. *CJT* 11 (1965): 183-195.

Jacobs, E. 'L'Ancient Testament et la vision de l'histoire'. *Revue de théologie et de philosophie* 7 (1957): 254-265.

—'Histoire et historiens dans l'Ancien Testament'. *Revue de théologie et de philosophie* 35 (1955): 26-35.

Jagersma, Henk. *A History of Israel in the Old Testament Period*. Philadelphia: Fortress, 1983.

Janssen, E. *Juda in der Exilszeit: Ein Beitrag zur Frage der Entstehung des Judentums*. FRLANT 69. Göttingen: Vandenhoeck & Ruprecht, 1956.

Jepsen, A. *Die Quellen der Königsbücher*. 2nd edition. Halle: Niemeyer, 1956.

—and R. Hunhart. *Untersuchungen zur israelitisch-jüdischen Chronologie*. BZAW 88. Berlin: Alfred Töpelmann, 1964.

Johnson, M.D. *The Purpose of Biblical Genealogies*. Cambridge: Cambridge University, 1969.

Jones, G.H. *1 and 2 Kings*. NCBC. Grand Rapids: Eerdmans, 1984.

Josephus. *Antiquities of the Jews*. Translated by William Whiston. Grand Rapids: Kregel, 1978.

Kaiser, O. *Introduction to the Old Testament: A Presentation of its Results and Problems*. Translated by J. Sturdy. Minneapolis: Augsburg, 1977.

Keil, C.F. *Die Bücher Samuelis*. BCAT II/2. 2nd edition. Leipzig: Dörffling & Franke, 1875.

Kent, C.F. *A History of the Hebrew People*. 2 vols. New York: Charles Scribner's Sons, 1919.

—*Israel's Historical and Biographical Narratives: From the Establishment of the Hebrew Kingdom to the End of the Maccabean Struggle*. New York: Charles Scribner's Sons, 1905.

Kenyon, K.M. *Archaeology in the Holy Land*. 4th edition. New York: W.W. Norton, 1979.

—*Digging Up Jericho: The Results of the Jericho Excavations 1952-1956*. New York: F.A. Praeger, 1957.

King, J. 'The Role of Solomon in the Deuteronomic History'. Ph. D. dissertation, The Southern Baptist Theological Seminary, 1978.

Kittel, R. *A History of the Hebrews*. Vol. II. *Sources of Information and History of the Period Down to the Babylonian Exile*. London: Williams & Norgate, 1909.

—*Geschichte des Volkes Israel*. Vol. I. 5th/6th edition. Stuttgart: Friedrich Andreas, 1923.

Klein, R.W. *1 Samuel*. WBC. Waco, TX: Word Books, 1983.

—*Israel in Exile: A Theological Interpretation*. Philadelphia: Fortress Press, 1979.

Klostermann, A. *Die Bucher Samuelis und der Könige*. Kurzgefasster Kommentar zu den heiligen Schriften Alten und Neuen Testaments, 3. Nordlingen: C.H. Beck, 1887.

Koch, K. *The Prophets: The Assyrian Period*. Translated by M. Kohl. Philadelphia: Fortress, 1984.

Kohler, L. *Hebrew Man*. Nashville: Abingdon, 1956.

Kosmala, H. '*gbr*'. *TDOT*. Edited by G. Botterweck & H. Ringgren. Grand Rapids:

Eerdmans, 1975, II: 376-382.

Landes, G.M. 'Ammon'. *IDB*. 4 vols. Nashville: Abingdon, 1962, 108-114.

Langlamet, F. 'Absolom et les Concubines de son Père: Recherches sur II Sam 16:21-22'. *RevBib* 84 (1977): 161-209.

—'Affinités sacerdotales, deutéronomiques, élohistes dans l'Histoire de la succession (2 S 9-20; 1 R 1-2)'. *AOAT* 212 (1981): 233-246.

—'Pour ou contre Salomon: La rédaction prosalomonienne de I Rois, I-II'. *RevBib* 83 (1976): 481-528.

Leach, E. 'The Legitimacy of Solomon—Some Structural Aspects of Old Testament History'. *Archives Européennes de Sociologie* 7 (1966): 58-101.

Levenson, J.D. 'The Davidic Covenant and its Modern Interpreters'. *CBQ* 41 (1979): 205-219.

—'1 Samuel 25 as Literature and as History'. *CBQ* 40 (1978): 11-28.

—and Baruch Halpern. 'The Political Import of David's Marriages'. *JBL* 99 (1980): 507-518.

Liddel, H.G. and R. Scott. *A Greek-English Lexicon*. Revised edition. 2 vols. Oxford: Clarendon, 1948.

Lods, A. *Histoire de la littérature hébraïque et juive*. Paris: Payot, 1950.

Lohr, M. and O. Thenius. *Die Bücher Samuelis*. 3rd edition. Leipzig: Vandenhoeck & Ruprecht, 1898.

Long, B.O. *1 Kings With an Introduction to Historical Literature*. FOTL 9. Grand Rapids: Eerdmans, 1984.

—*The Problem of the Etiological Narrative in the Old Testament*. Berlin: Alfred Töpelmann, 1968.

Louis, K.R.R.G. 'The Difficulty of Ruling Well: King David of Israel'. *Semeia* 8 (1977): 15-33.

Luther, B. 'Die Novelle von Juda und Tamar und andere israelitische Novellen'. In *Die Israeliten und ihre Nachbarstämme*, pp. 177-206. Edited by E. Meyer. Halle: M. Niemeyer, 1906.

Macholz, G. 'Die Stellung des Königs in der israelitischen Gerichtsverfassung'. *ZAW* 84 (1972): 157-182.

McCarter, P.K., Jr. 'The Historical David'. *Interp* 40 (1986): 117-129.

—*I Samuel*. AB. Garden City: Doubleday, 1980.

—*II Samuel*. AB. Garden City: Doubleday, 1984.

—'"Plots, True or False": The Succession Narrative as Court Apologetic'. *Interp* 35 (181): 355-67.

McCarthy, D.J. 'The Inauguration of Monarchy in Israel'. *Interp* 27 (1973): 401-412.

McKane, W. *Prophets and Wise Men*. Studies in Biblical Theology, 44. Naperville, IL: Alec R. Allenson, 1965.

Maisler, B. 'Ancient Israelite Historiography'. *IEJ* 2 (1952): 82-88.

Malamat, A. 'Aspects of the Foreign Policies of David and Solomon'. *JNES* 22 (1963): 1-17.

—'Comments on E. Leach: The Legitimacy of Solomon—Some Structural Aspects of Old Testament History'. *Archives Européennes de Sociologie* 8 (1967): 165-167.

—'Doctrines of Causality in Hittite and Biblical Historiography: A Parallel'. *VT* 5 (1955): 1-12.

—'The Last Years of the Kingdom of Judah'. In *The World History of the Jewish People*. IV: 205-221. Edited by A. Malamat and I. Eph'al. Jerusalem: Massada, 1979.

—'Origins of Statecraft in the Israelite Monarchy'. *BAR* 3 (1970): 163-198.

Maly, E.H. *The World of David and Solomon*. Englewood Cliffs: Prentice-Hall, 1966.

Mauchline, J. 'Implicit Sign of a Persistent Belief in the Davidic Empire'. *VT* 20 (1970): 287-303.

—*1 and 2 Samuel*. NCBC. London: Oliphants, 1971.

Mayes, A.D.H. *Deuteronomy*. NEB. Greenwood, SC: Attic, 1979.

—*The Story of Israel between Settlement and Exile: A Redactional Study of the Deuteronomistic History*. London: SCM, 1983.

Mazar, B. 'Geshur and Maacah'. *JBL* 80 (1961): 16-28.

Meadows, J.N. 'A Traditio-Historical Study of II Samuel 9-20, I Kings 1, 2'. Ph.D. dissertation, Southern Baptist Theological Seminary, 1975.

Mettinger, T.N.D. *King and Messiah: The Civil and Sacral Legitimation of the Israelite Monarchy*. Coniectanea Biblica Old Testament Series, 8. Lund: Gleerup, 1976.

—*Solomonic State Officials: A Study of the Civil Government Officials of the Israelite Monarchy*. Coniectanea Biblica Old Testament Series, 5. Lund: Gleerup, 1971.

Meyer, E. *Geschichte des Altertums*. 3rd edition. Stuttgart: Schwarg, 1953.

Meyers, C.L. 'Roots of Restriction: Women in Early Israel'. In *The Bible and Liberation: Political and Social Hermeneutics*. Edited by Norman K. Gottwald. Maryknoll, New York: Orbis, 1983, 289-306.

Miller, J.M. 'Another Look at the Chronology of the Early Divided Monarchy'. *JBL* 86 (1967): 276-288.

—*The Old Testament and the Historian*. Philadelphia: Fortress, 1976.

—'The Omride Dynasty in the Light of Recent Literary and Archaeological Research'. Ph.D. dissertation, Emory University, 1964.

—and John H. Hayes. *A History of Ancient Israel and Judah*. Philadelphia: Westminster, 1986.

Miller, P.D. and Roberts, J. J. M. *The Hand of the Lord: A Reassessment of the 'Ark Narrative' of I Samuel*. Baltimore: Johns Hopkins University, 1977.

Milman, H.H. *The History of the Jews From the Earliest Period Down to Modern Times*. 3 vols. New York: W.J. Widdleton, 1874.

Molin, G. 'Die Stellung der Gebirah im Staate Juda'. *Theologische Zeitschrift* 10 (1954): 161-175.

Montgomery, J.A. 'Archival Data in the Book of Kings'. *JBL* 53 (1934), 46-52.

—*The Books of Kings*. ICC. Edinburgh: T. & T. Clark, 1951.

Mowinckel, S. 'Israelite Historiography'. *ASTI* 2 (1963): 4-26.

—*The Psalms in Israel's Worship*. Translated by D.R. Ap-Thomas. Nashville: Abingdon, 1962.

—'Der Ursprung der Bileamsage'. *ZAW* 48 (1930): 233-71.

—'Die vorderasiatischen Königs- und Fürsteninschriften. Eine stilistische Studie'. In *Eucharisterion: Festschrift Hermann Gunkel* FRLANT, 19. Göttingen: Vandenhoeck & Ruprecht, 1923, I, 278-322.

Myers, J.M. *I Chronicles*. AB. Garden City: Doubleday, 1965.

—*II Chronicles*. AB. Garden City: Doubleday, 1965.

Napier, B.D. *From Faith to Faith: Essays on Old Testament Literature*. New York: Harper & Brothers, 1955.

Neff, R.W. 'The Announcement in Old Testament Birth Stories'. Ph.D. Dissertation, Yale University, 1969.

Neher, A. and Neher, R. *Histoire Biblique du Peuple d'Israël*. Paris: Andrien-Maisonneuve, 1962.

Nelson, R.D. *The Double Redaction of the Deuteronomistic History*. Sheffield: JSOT, 1981.

Newsome, J.D. Jr. *By the Waters of Babylon: An Introduction to the History and Theology of the Exile*. Atlanta: John Knox, 1979.

Nicholson, E.W. *Deuteronomy and Tradition*. Philadelphia: Fortress, 1967.

—*Preaching to the Exiles: A Study of the Prose Tradition in the Book of Jeremiah*. Oxford: Blackwell, 1970.

Noth, M. *The Deuteronomistic History*. Translated by M.D. Rutter. Sheffield: JSOT, 1981.

—'For All Who Rely On Works of the Law Are Under a Curse'. In *The Laws in the Pentateuch and Other Studies*. London: SCM, 1984.

—*The History of Israel*. Revised edition. Translated by P.R. Ackroyd. New York: Harper & Row, 1960.

—*History of Pentateuchal Traditions*. Chico, CA: Scholars, 1977.

—*Die israelitischen Personennamen im Rahmen der gemeinsemitischen Namengebung*. BWANT 3.10. Stuttgart: W. Kohlhammer, 1928.

—*Könige*. Biblischer Kommentar zum Alten Testament. Neukirchen-Vluyn: Neukirchener Erziehungsverein, 1968.

Nowack, W. *Deuteronomium und Regnum*. BZAW 41. Marti Festschrift. (1925), 221-231.

—*Richter, Ruth und Bücher Samuelis übersetzt und erklärt*. HKAT I/4. Göttingen: Vandenhoeck & Ruprecht, 1902.

Oettli, D.S. *Geschichte Israels bis auf Alexander den Grossen*. Stuttgart: Vereinsbuchhandlung, 1905.

Otwell, J.H. *And Sarah Laughed: The Status of Woman in the Old Testament*. Philadelphia: Westminster, 1977.

Pace, J.H. 'The Caleb Traditions and the Role of the Calebites in the History of Israel'. Ph.D. dissertation, Emory University, 1976.

Peckham, B. *The Composition of the Deuteronomistic History*. Harvard Semitic Monographs, 35. Atlanta: Scholars, 1985.

Perdue, L.G. '"Is There Anyone Left of the House of Saul .. .?" Ambiguity and the Characterization of David in the Succession Narrative'. *JSOT* 30 (1984): 67-84.

Peritz, I.J. *Old Testament History*. New York: Abingdon, 1915.

Perry, M. and M. Sternberger. 'The King through Ironic Eyes'. *Ha-Sifrut* 1 (1968): 263-292.

Petersen, D.L. 'Portraits of David: Canonical and Otherwise'. *Interp* 40 (1986): 130-142.

Pfeiffer, R.H. 'Facts and Faith in Biblical History'. *JBL* 70 (1951): 1-14.

—*Introduction to the Old Testament*. New York: Harper & Brothers, 1941.

—and W.G. Pollard. *The Hebrew Iliad: The History of the Rise of Israel under Saul and David*. New York: Harper & Brothers, 1957.

Pitard, W.T. *Ancient Damascus: A Historical Study of the Syrian City-State from Earliest Times until its Fall to the Assyrians in 732 B.C.E.* Winona Lake, IN: Eisenbrauns, 1986.

Porter, J.R. 'Old Testament Historiography'. In *Tradition and Interpretation*, pp. 125-162. Edited by G. W. Anderson. Oxford: Clarendon, 1979.

Prag, K. 'The Intermediate Early Bronze—Middle Bronze Age Sequences at Jericho and Tell Iktanu Reviewed'. *BASOR* 264 (1986): 61-72.

Pruyser, P.W. 'Nathan and David: A Psychological Footnote'. *PP* 12 (1962): 14-18.

Rad, G. von. 'The Beginnings of Historical Writing in Ancient Israel'. In *The Problem of the Hexateuch and Other Essays*, pp. 166-205. New York: McGraw-Hill, 1965.

—'The Deuteronomistic Theology of History in the Books of Kings'. In *Studies in Deuteronomy*, pp. 74-91. London: SCM, 1953.

—*Deuteronomy*. OTL. Philadelphia: Westminster 1966.

—'Deuteronomy and the Holy War'. In *Studies in Deuteronomy*, pp. 45-59. London: SCM, 1953.

—*Genesis*. Philadelphia: Westminster, 1972.

—*Old Testament Theology*. 2 vols. New York: Harper & Row, 1965.

—'The Royal Ritual in Judah'. In *The Problem of the Hexateuch and Other Essays*, pp. 222-231. New York: McGraw-Hill, 1965.

—*Wisdom in Israel*. Nashville: Abingdon, 1972.

Radjawane, A.N. 'Das deuteronomistische Geschichtswerk: ein Forschungsbericht'. *Theologische Rundschau* 38 (1974): 177-216.

Rast, W. *Tradition History and the Old Testament*. Philadelphia: Fortress Press, 1972.

Rehm, M. *Das erste Buch der Könige*. Frankische: Echter Verlag, 1979.

—*Das zweite Buch der Könige*. Frankische: Echter Verlag, 1982.

Rendsburg, G.A. 'David and His Circle in Genesis XXXVIII'. *VT* 36 (1986): 438-446.

Ricciotti, G. 'From the Beginning to the Exile'. Vol. I of *The History of Israel*. Milwaukee: Bruce, 1958.

Richter, W. *Die Bearbeitungen des 'Retterbuches' in der deuteronomischen Epoche*. BBB, 21. Bonn: Peter Hanstein, 1964.

—*Traditionsgeschichtliche Untersuchungen zum Richterbuch*. BBB. Bonn: Peter Hanstein, 1966.

Ridout, G.P. 'Prose Composition Techniques in the Succession Narrative (2 Sam. 7, 9-10; 1 Kings 1-2)'. Ph.D. dissertation. Graduate Theological Union, 1971.

Roche, M. de. 'Yahweh's *rîb* against Israel: A Reassessment of the So-Called 'Prophetic Lawsuit' in the Preexilic Prophets'. *JBL* 102 (1983): 563-574.

Rofé, A. 'The Strata of the Law about Centralization of Worship in Deuteronomy and the History of the Deuteronomic Movement'. *SVT* 22 (1972): 221-226.

Rost, L. *The Succession to the Throne of David*. HTIBS, 1. Sheffield: Almond, 1982.

Roth, W.M.W. 'The Wooing of Rebecca'. *CBQ* 34 (1972): 177-187.

—'"You are the Man". Structural Interaction in 2 Sam 10-12'. *Semeia* 8 (1977): 1-12.

Rowley, H.H. *The Growth of the Old Testament*. London: Hutchinson, 1958.

Sacon, K.K. 'A Study of the Literary Structure of 'The Succession Narrative'. In *Studies in the Period of David and Solomon and Other Essays*. Edited by T. Ishida, 27-54. Winona Lake, IN: 1982.

Sakenfeld, K.D. *Faithfulness in Action: Loyalty in Biblical Perspective* Philadelphia: Fortress, 1985.

—'Old Testament Perspectives: Methodological Issues'. *JSOT* 22 (1982): 13-20.

—*The Meaning of Hesed In the Hebrew Bible: A New Inquiry*. Harvard Semitic Monographs 17. Missoula, MT: Scholars, 1978.

Schmidt, H. *Die Geschichtsschreibung im Alten Testament*. Religionsgeschichtliche Volksbücher. 2nd series, 16. Tübingen: J.C.B. Mohr, 1911.

Schmidt, L. 'König und Charisma im Alten Testament: Beobachtungen zur Struktur des Königtums im alten Israel'. *Kirche und Dogma* 28 (1982): 73-87.

Schulman, A.R. 'Diplomatic Marriage in the Egyptian New Kingdom'. *JNES* 38 (1979): 177-193.

Schulte, H. *Die Entstehung der Geschichtsschreibung im Alten Israel*. BZAW 128. Berlin: Walter de Gruyter, 1972.

Scott, R.B.Y. 'The Study of the Wisdom Literature'. *Interp* 24 (1970): 20-45.

—*The Way of Wisdom in the Old Testament*. New York: Macmillan, 1971.

Seebass, H. 'Nathan und David in II Samuel 12'. *ZAW* 86 (1974): 203-211.

Segal, M.H. 'The Composition of the Books of Samuel'. In *The Pentateuch: Its Composition and its Authorship and Other Biblical Studies*. Jerusalem: Magnes, 1967.

Sellin, E. *Introduction to the Old Testament*. New York: Doran, 1923.

Shenkel, J.D. *Chronology and Recensional Development in the Greek Text of Kings*. Cambridge, MA: Harvard University Press, 1968.

Simon, U. 'The Poor Man's Ewe Lamb: An Example of Juridical Parable (2 Sam 12,1-15)'. *Bib* 48 (1967): 207-242.

Simpson, C.A. *Composition of the Book of Judges*. Oxford: Blackwell, 1957.

—*The Early Traditions of Israel*. Oxford: Blackwell, 1948.

Smend, R., 'Das Gesetz und die Völker: Ein Beitrag zur deuteronomischen Redaktionsgeschichte'. In *Probleme Biblischer Theologie. Festschrift von Rad*, pp. 494-509. Edited by H.W. Wolff. Munich: Kaiser, 1971.

Smend, R., Sr. 'JE in den geschichtlichen Büchern des AT'. *ZAW* 39 (1921): 181-217.

—'Beiträge zur Geschichte und Topographie des Ortjordanlandes'. *ZAW* 22 (1902): 129-158.

Smith, H.P. *Old Testament History*. New York: Charles Scribner's Sons, 1903.

—*Samuel*. ICC. Edinburgh: T. & T. Clark, 1977.

Smith, M. 'The So-Called "Biography of David" in the Books of Samuel and Kings'. *HTR* 44 (1951): 167-169.

Smith, W.R. *Kingship and Marriage in Early Arabia*. London: A. & C. Black, 1903. Reprinted Boston: Beacon Press [n.d.].

Soggin, J.A. 'The Davidic-Solomonic Kingdom'. In *Israelite and Judean History*, pp. 332-380. Edited by J.H. Hays and J.M. Miller. OTL. Philadelphia: Westminster, 1977.

—'Der Entstehungsort des deuteronomistischen Geschichtswerkes'. *Theologische Literaturzeitung* 100 (1975): cols. 3-8.

—*A History of Ancient Israel from the Beginnings to the Bar Kochba Revolt, A.D. 135*. Philadelphia: Westminster, 1984.

—*Introduction to the Old Testament: From its Origins to the Closing of the Alexandrian Canon*. Revised edition. OTL. Philadelphia: Westminster, 1980.

—*Joshua*. OTL. Philadelphia: Westminster, 1972.

—*Judges*. OTL. Philadelphia: Westminster, 1981.

—*Das Königtum in Israel*. BZAW 104. Berlin: Alfred Töpelmann, 1967.

Speiser, E.A. 'The Biblical Idea of History in its Common Near Eastern Setting'. *IEJ* (1957): 201-216.

Stamm, J.J. 'Der Name des Königs Salomo'. *ThZ* 16 (1960): 283-97.

Sternberg, Meir. *The Poetics of Biblical Narrative: Ideological Literature and the Drama of Reading*. Bloomington: Indiana University, 1985.

Steuernagel, C. *Lehrbuch der Einleitung in das Alte Testament*. Tübingen: J.C.B. Mohr, 1912.

Stoebe, H.J. 'David and Uriah: Reflections about the Tradition of 2 Sam 11'. *Bib* 66 (1986): 388-396.

Swanston, H. *The Kings and the Covenant*. London: Burns & Oates, 1968.

Szikszai, S. 'King, Kingship'. *IDB* III (1962): 11-17.

Tadmor, H. '"The People" and the Kingship in Ancient Israel: The Role of Political Institutions in the Biblical Period'. *JWH* 11 (1968): 34-50.

Thieberger, F. *King Solomon*. London: East and West Library, 1947.

Thomas, D.W. 'The Lachish Letters'. *JTS* 40 (1939) 1-15.

Thompson, M.E.W. *Situation and Theology: Old Testament Interpretations of the Syro-Ephraimite War*. Prophets and Historians Series, 1. Sheffield: Almond, 1982.

Thornton, T.C.G. 'Charismatic Kingship in Israel and Judah'. *JTS* 14 (1963): 1-11.

—'Solomonic Apologetic in Samuel and Kings'. *ChQR* 149 (1968): 159-166.

Tidwell, N.L. 'The Philistine Incursions into the Valley of Rephaim'. In *Studies in the Historical Books of the Old Testament*. Edited by J.A. Emerton. SVT. Leiden: E. J. Brill, 1979, 190-212.

Trible, P. 'Depatriarchalizing in Biblical Interpretation'. *JAAR* 41 (1973): 30-48.

—*God and the Rhetoric of Sexuality*. OBT. Philadelphia: Fortress, 1978.

—'Tamar: The Royal Rape of Wisdom'. In *Texts of Terror: Literary-Feminist Readings of Biblical Narratives*. OBT. Philadelphia: Fortress, 1984, 37-63.

Trompf, G.W. 'Notions of Historical Recurrence in Classic Hebrew Historiography'. *VT* 30 (1979): 219-224.

Tsevat, M. 'Marriage and Monarchical Legitimacy in Ugarit and Israel'. *JSS* 3 (1958): 237-243.

Tucker, G.M. *Form Criticism of the Old Testament*. Philadelphia: Fortress, 1971.

—'The Rehab Saga (Joshua 2): Some Form Critical and Traditio-Historical Observations'. In *The Use of the Old Testament in the New and Other Essays*. Edited by J.M. Efird. Durham, NC: Duke University Press, 1972, 66-86.

Van Seters, J. 'Problems in the Literary Analysis of the Court History of David'. *JSOT* 1 (1976): 22-29.

—*In Search of History*. New Haven: Yale University Press, 1983.

Vatwer, Bruce. *On Genesis: A New Reading*. Garden City: Doubleday, 1977.

Vaux, R. de. *Ancient Israel*. 2 vols. New York: McGraw-Hill, 1961.

—*The Early History of Israel*. Philadelphia: Westminster, 1978.

Veijola, T. *Die ewige Dynastie David und die Entstehung seiner Dynastie nach der deuteronomischen Darstellung*. AASF. Helsinki: Suomalainen Tiedeakatemia, 1975.

—*Das Königtum in der Beurteilung der deuteronomischen Historiographie: Eine redaktionsgeschichtliche Untersuchung*. AASF. Helsinki: Suomalainen Tiedeakatemia, 1977.

—'Salomo—der Erstgeborene Bathsebas'. *VT* 30 (1979) 230-50.

—*Verheissung in der Krise. Studien zur Literatur und Theologie der Exilszeit anhand des 89 Psalms*. AASF, 220. Helsinki: Suomalainen Tiedeakatemia, 1982.

Vries, S.J. de. 'Chronology of the OT'. In *IDB* II: 580-599. 4 vols. Nashville: Abingdon, 1962.

—'Chronology of the OT'. In *IDBS* V: 161-166. Nashville: Abingdon, 1976.

Vriezen, T.C. *The Religion of Ancient Israel*. Philadelphia: Westminster, 1967.

Wagner, S. 'darash'. *TDOT* III (1978): 293-307.

Wakeman, M.K. 'Sacred Marriage: Appendices of Sumerian Biblical Developments and Deities'. *JSOT* 22 (1982): 21-31.

Ward, R.L. 'The Story of David's Rise: A Traditio-Historical Study of I Samuel xvi 14–II Samuel V'. Ph.D. dissertation, Vanderbilt University, 1967.

Weavers, J.W. 'Hebrew Variants in the Books of Kings'. Th.D. dissertation. Princeton Theological Seminary, 1945.

Weber, G. *Das Volk Israel in der alttestamentlichen Zeit*. Leipzig: Wilhelm Engelmann, 1867.

Weinfeld, M. *Deuteronomy and the Deuteronomic School*. Oxford: Clarendon, 1972.

—'Literary Creativity'. In *The Age of the Monarchies: Culture and Society*. vol. 4.2 of *The World History of the Jewish People*. Jerusalem: Massada, 1979, 27-70.

Weingreen, J. 'The Rebellion of Absalom'. *VT* 19 (1969): 263-266.

Weippert, H. 'Die "deuteronomistischen" Beurteilungen der Könige von Israel und Juda und das Problem der Redaktion der Königsbücher'. *Bib* 53 (1972): 301-339.

Weiser, A. *The Old Testament: Its Formation and Development*. New York: Association, 1961.

—*Samuel. Seine geschichtliche Aufgabe und religiöse Bedeutung*. FRLANT 81. Göttingen: Vandenhoeck & Ruprecht, 1962.

Welch, A.C. *The Work of the Chronicler: Its Purpose and its Date*. London: Oxford University, 1939.

Wellhausen, J. *Einleitung in das Alte Testament*. 4th revised edition. Berlin: Georg Reimer, 1878.

—*Prolegomena to the History of Ancient Israel*. Translated by J.S. Black and A. Menzies. With a reprint of the article 'Israel' from the *Encyclopedia Britannica*. New York: Meridian, 1957.

—*Sketch of the History of Israel and Judah*. 3rd edition. London: A & C Black, 1891.

Westermann, C. 'Zum Geschichtsverständnis des Alten Testaments'. In *Probleme biblischer Theologie*. Edited by H.W. Wolff. Munich: Kaiser, 1971, 611-19.

Wevers, J.W. 'The Hebrew Variants in the Books of Kings and their Relationship to the Old Greek and the Greek Recensions'. Th.D. dissertation, Princeton Theological Seminary, 1945.

Wharton, J.A. 'A Plausible Tale: Story and Theology in II Samuel 9–20, I Kings 1–2'. *Interp* 35 (1981): 341-354.

Whitelam, K. *The Just King: Monarchical Judicial Authority in Ancient Israel*, JSOTS 12. Sheffield: JSOT, 1979.

Whybray, R.N. *The Succession Narrative: A Study of II Sam. 9–20 and I Kings 1 and 2*. Studies in Biblical Theology. 2nd series, 9. London: SCM, 1968.

Wiener, H.M. *The Composition of Judges 11 11 to I Kings 11 46*. Leipzig: J.C. Hinrichs, 1929.

Williams, J.G. *Women Recounted: Narrative Thinking and the God of Israel*. BLS. Sheffield: Almond, 1982.

Williamson, H.G.M. *I and II Chronicles*. NCBC. Grand Rapids: Eerdmans, 1982.

Wilson, E.B. 'Rîb in Israel's Historical and Legal Traditions: A Study of the Israelite Setting of the Rîb-Form'. Ph.D. dissertation: Drew University, 1970.

Wilson, R.R. *Genealogy and History in the Biblical World*. New Haven: Yale University Press, 1977.

—*Prophecy and Society in Ancient Israel*. Philadelphia: Fortress, 1980.

Winckler, H. *Geschichte Israels in Einzeldarstellungen*. Völker und Staaten des alten Orients, 2-3. Leipzig: Pfeiffer, 1892-1900.

Wolff, H.W. *Amos the Prophet: The Man and his Background*. Philadelphia: Fortress, 1973.

—*Joel and Amos*. Hermeneia. Philadelphia: Fortress, 1977.

—'The Kerygma of the Deuteronomic Historical Work'. In *The Vitality of Old Testament Traditions*, pp. 83-100. 2nd edition. Edited by W. Brueggemann and H.W. Wolff. Atlanta: John Knox, 1982.

Wood, L. *A Survey of Israel's History*. Grand Rapids: Zondervan, 1970.

Würthwein, E. *Die Bücher der Könige 1. Könige 1-16*. ATD. Göttingen: Vandenhoeck & Ruprecht, 1977.

—*Die Erzählung von der Thronfolge Davids—theologische oder politische Geschichts-schreibung?* Zürich: Theologischer Verlag, 1974.

Yadin, Y. 'Some Aspects of the Strategy of Ahab and David'. *Bib* 36 (1955): 332-51.

Yee, G.A. 'Literary Ambiguity and 2 Sam 11: The David and Bathsheba Story'. SBL Annual Meeting, Anaheim, CA: November 245, 1985. ['"Fraught with Background": Literary Ambiguity in II Samuel 12'. *Interp* 42 (1988), 240-53.

INDEXES

INDEX OF BIBLICAL PASSAGES

ITEM CHARGED

P.Barcode:

Due Date: 2/16/2017 10:30 PM

Title: David in love and war : the pursuit
of power in 2 Samuel 10-12 /
Randall C. Bailey

Author: Bailey, Randall C., 1947-

CallNo.: BS1325.2 .B340 1990

Enum.:

Chron.:

Copy: 1

I.Barcode:

INDEX OF AUTHORS

JOURNAL FOR THE STUDY OF THE OLD TESTAMENT

Supplement Series

 * (Out of Print)